STOCK CAR
MODEL KIT
ncyclopedia and Price Guide

BILL
COULTER

Published by

**krause
publications**

700 E. State Street • Iola, WI 54990-0001
Telephone: 715/445-2214

Please, call or write us for our free catalog of antiques and collectibles publications. To place an
order or receive our free catalog, call 800-258-0929. For editorial comment and further information,
use our regular business telephone at (715) 445-2214

Library of Congress Catalog Number: 99-61254
ISBN: 0-87341-732-1

Printed in the United States of America

On the front cover

'32 Ford by Bill Burtnett
'56 Ford by Tom Dill
'96 Pontiac by Drew Hierwarter
'87 T-Bird by Wayne Doebling

On the back cover

'65 Chevy by Dave Bauer
'72 Dodge Dart by Bill Coulter
'65 Ford by Wayne Moyer
'57 Ford by Tom Dill
Wing Modified by Bill Coulter
'87 Monte Carlo by Bill Coulter

Acknowledgments

In the production of this book, I'd like to thank many, many people for their support and encouragement. Without every last one of these folks it would not have happened. Let's hope I haven't forgotten anyone!

They include: Wayne Moyer, Leonard Carsner, Bill Burtnett, Joel Naprstek, Daryl Huhtala, Drew Hierwarter, Mike Madlinger, Tom Dill, Roy Vaughn, Dave Bauer, Dave Dodge, William Brigman, Glen Marek, Doug Whyte, Karl Stark, Randy Derr, Tom Anderson, Pat Covert, Pat Mulligan, Terry Jessee, Laverne Zachery, Robert Pizio, Fred Bradley, Ronnie Setzer, Trevor Bladon, Jeff Quedenfeld, Bob Johnson, Mike Sells, Buford Wilburn...

and my "long-suffering" wife of 35 years, Gail Ann...

and the One who guides my every step.

Thank you! Thank you! Thank you!
Bill Coulter, 1999

Table of Contents

Chapter 4

Chapter 5

Chapter 6

Chapter 7

Chapter 8

Chapter 9

Chapter 10

Introduction

Historical Perspective

Major League American stock car racing celebrated its 50th birthday in 1998. Reflecting on just how far the sport has come in such a short time staggers the imagination. NASCAR-style (National Association for Stock Car Auto Racing) competition originated on the back country roads of the southeast with those legendary skirmishes between rumrunners in their hot-rods trying to outrun the Feds. Those rough and tumble halcyon days have given way to today's 3,500-pound billboards promoting corporate America while circling the nations speedways at nearly 200 mph!

When you add to this the hundreds of stock car events contested in ARCA (Automobile Racing Club of America), ASA (American Speed Association) and the activities of other sanctioning bodies, special events and series seen all across North America on quarter-mile dirt tracks to 3/8th mile paved ovals, you can get a more accurate view of just how vast the interest in stock car racing is today.

In NASCAR's many touring series alone, hundreds of thousands of fans pay to watch a high-tech, high-speed ballet, in person, dozens of times a year. Many millions more watch Winston Cup, the Busch Grand National series or the Craftsman trucks in action on TV coast-to-coast and around the world via satellite. Fans read about stock car racing in hundreds of newspapers and magazines or listen to the action on a national radio network. The huge interest in American stock car racing has resulted in hundreds of millions of dollars being spent each year for souvenirs and collectibles, ranging from videos and books to jackets, hats, T-shirts, diecast cars and plastic model kits.

Building and collecting scale model stock cars has become a mega-business from rather simple and humble beginnings just a few short years ago. For example, Revell-Monogram's 1/24th scale series of stock car kits, introduced in 1983, has become the best selling plastic model kit series of all time. Young or old, male or female, today's builders and kit collectors come in all shapes, sizes and ages. Building and collecting stock car model kits is one of the most active market segments of the modeling hobby.

Ever wonder if your favorite drivers' race cars were made into model kits? How many different kits were made? What scale? Which manufacturer made it? Is it still available? If not, where can I find one? What will it cost me? Or maybe you've hung on to a few stock car model kits over the years. What are they worth today? Whatever scale you're interested in—1/43rd, 1/32nd, 1/25th, 1/24th or even larger—the answers are contained in this book.

After a short time browsing through this book, you'll answer many of these questions and become a more confident and skilled builder by following just a few of the simple modeling tips and techniques contained within. You'll increase your knowledge on the fine points of kit collecting, swapping and trading. Above all, you're bound to know a lot more about your favorite hobby. And who knows…some day people might even consider you an expert!

Building Tips and Techniques

Beyond listing what model kits have been produced in what scales up to the time of publication, this book covers a lot more ground than you might ever have expected when you first picked it up. Stock car model builders put a high value on essential things such as what tools or materials are needed to build a contest quality replica. What are the best glues to use? How can I learn to use automotive finishes on styrene plastics? Who makes detailing accessories to help me correctly and accurately wire up my current stock car model building project car?

Maybe you've always wanted to build a model of Fred Lorenzen's Daytona 500 winning Ford Galaxie from 1965. What kit or kits are available to start this project and in what scales? What are the sources for finding the correct paint colors? Where do I find decals for this race car? Does anyone make period-correct stock car wheels and tires? Are there any reference materials (magazines, books, etc.) that will help me build an accurate model?

Beyond the mere existence of plastic kits and their individual values, you will be overwhelmed with the vast inventory of items available from the after-market. This is a fairly recent phenomenon. Not too many years ago, stock car model builders were pretty much on their own. There were few if any resin parts or after-market kits, specific decals, uniquely accurate and authentic paint colors and detailing items.

Over the last 35 years, the stock car model kit segment of the model building hobby has grown from a few street-stock annual kits with generic racing parts and fictional decals to hundreds of dedicated race version-only stock car kits. Getting to the point we are today has often been slow in happening, and many times we've suffered through brief product interruptions (such as 1976 to 1983, from MPC's last stock car replica release to Revell-Monogram's introduction its first 1/24th scale stock car kits).

Getting More Specific

The hobby has seen the phenomenal interest and growth of building 1/43rd stock car kits which came on like gangbusters at first. That market segment has been buffeted by licensing difficulties and the unbelievable growth in the collecting of diecast stock car models in a multitude of scales. Who could foresee that in a few short years we would be looking at 1/43rd stock car kits from an historical perspective?

Wayne Moyer, known as one of the most knowledgeable 1/43rd-scale builders and collectors, was invited on board to compile the considerable material on 1/43rd-scale models. Currently there is no other source on this subject that is this thorough and complete.

Another area covered is the puzzling lack of domestic interest in 1/32nd scale, which probably explains the short list of product in this size. Leonard Carsner has built an excellent replica using a modern 1/32nd-scale stock car kit, along with after-market paint and decals.

The chapter covering 1/25th scale reveals the diversity of different types of stock cars, from vintage Grand National to Eastern Modifieds. We thoroughly enjoyed reviewing these kits and exploring the building options and techniques in this scale.

The 1/24th chapter presents the nearly overwhelming number of stock car kits in this scale. You will notice there are a few Revell-Monogram items with the same product number. It was explained to me that retail shelf space at leading department and discount stores necessitates this situation. Retaining the same numbers for successive kits allows them to maintain a lock on extremely valuable shelf space. Changing product numbers requires both manufacturer and distributor to start back at square-one with the retail buyer and vie for shelf space all over again.

The 1/24th-scale Kroger/Pepsi '87 Chevrolet Monte Carlo Aero Coupe I built for this chapter represents the classic Laughlin front-steer chassis design used almost exclusively in the Winston Cup and Busch series today. The Revell-Monogram tool responsible for this kit has turned out between 2.5 to 3 million impressions.

The chapter on large scale stock car kits may be light on product listings, but the two models built for this chapter are eye poppers! Fred Bradley got a rare opportunity to build the kit that many feel is the high-water mark in stock car kit technology. The 1/8th-scale '32 Ford jalopy with Corvette V-8 power by Bill Burnett is a true piece of automotive artwork.

Enjoy Yourself!

Collecting and building stock car model kits continues as a robust market segment. Even though frequently challenging, this hobby can be rewarding and educational. But whatever your personal choices may be, always keep things in proper perspective and, above all, enjoy your hobby!

FYI

Included in this book is building and collecting information for stock car models in the most popular scales. This handy chart is included here for your reference:

Scale	1 inch	1 millimeter
1/8	4 in.	125 mm
1/16	16 in.	62.5 mm
1/24	24 in.	41.7 mm
1/25	25 in.	40.0 mm
1/32	32 in.	31.25 mm
1/43	43 in.	23.25 mm

Collecting Stock Car Model Kits

If you are new to the subject of collecting stock car model kits, I hope you're willing to settle for currently available model kit releases or that you have a bundle of money in reserve! As you might have concluded by now, early stock car kit releases from AMT, MPC, Jo-Han and even the more recent kits from Revell-Monogram have risen rapidly in value over the years. If you've been around this hobby for many years (and collected some of these kits), at today's estimated values, you may be sitting on a small fortune!

Most of the MPC stock car kits from the early 1970s currently are ranging in price between $150 to $250 each. AMT stock cars from the period do not bring as much money—$100 to $125—but are still rare and highly sought after. The Revell-Monogram early releases (1983-1985) can bring between $75 and $100. Even more recent releases, especially those limited production items, are rising in value due to short supply and increased demand. Keep in mind these prices are based on an original sealed unassembled kit. The universal rule of thumb is that once the seal is broken and the contents compromised in any fashion, the value plummets quickly.

In the late 1990s, interest in plastic model stock car kits is strong and still growing. Even remnants are in demand. Some stock car model builders relentlessly scavenge for the remains of vintage kits, including whole and partially built models, broken pieces, any odd part or assembly that can be disassembled, cleaned up, salvaged, reconditioned and combined to form a complete model. Not surprisingly, even these relics are not cheap today. Some after-market manufacturers offer resin copies of chassis components or whole body shells, while some after-market decal makers reproduce excellent copies of original kit water-slide markings.

You may have a few of these highly desirable items and desire to increase your collection. Maybe this is all new information and you are profoundly overwhelmed and don't know quite where to turn at this point. Practical advice from an experienced source is in order here, especially because of the large amount of money needed to buy vintage stock car kits at today's prices.

Unless the ultimate price is not important, good advice is to be a patient and careful shopper. Often our natural instinct is to buy the first thing we find. Knowing *when* to buy as well as *what* to buy will become part of the learning experience. Already deciding what you might hope to accomplish by either starting, increasing your present collection or grooming it is important. In other words, adopt a game plan!

Decisions, Decisions, Decisions!

Important, too, is determining if your kit collection is to be sealed and unopened or if you are trying to find kits to build for display. Kit builders can be kit collectors and vice versa, but this is not always the case. Many stock car modelers find it very difficult to open a sealed $150 kit and build it, especially realizing the market value will drop like a rock. The value of these vintage kits will continue to increase and more old factory-sealed kits will forever become part of collections never to be built.

It might be possible to collect one of every stock car model kit ever made, but it might be better to establish some sort of theme to your collection. Today it will be much easier (and less expensive) to start a collection of Jeff Gordon stock car kits, than Dale Earnhardt or Richard Petty. Gordon has only been in the big leagues for a short time. Earnhardt has been at it since the late 1970s. Petty enjoyed a 33-year career that started in 1958, and he continues to field cars as an owner. Making a decision early on as to what and how to collect will save you time and money.

You could wait for the time when Revell-Monogram, Ertl-AMT, MPC and so on, reissue some of these old highly-prized kits. Manufacturers, of course, frequently do that sort of thing with a few of their older race car kits! The AMT AMC Matador from the mid-1970s is a good example. This scenario is possible for many of the dozens of NASCAR stock car kits that Revell-Monogram has produced; but, even if it happens, it could take years. While a reissued kit from the 1960s, 1970s or even the 1980s may be highly desirable for you, other collectors and builders new to the hobby may not share your particular interests.

Many older stock car kits from Ertl/AMT, MPC or Jo-Han are not likely to return to store shelves anytime soon . A couple of years ago, Ertl announced the reissue of Richard Petty's 1972 pre-STP Plymouth, only to find everything but the body shell was missing from the tooling. Ertl had no way of reissuing this or any of the other dozen-plus original 1970s MPC NASCAR stockers without spending thousands of dollars on new tooling to replace what was missing.

At Jo-Han, the story isn't much better. After being acquired by Detroit-area plastic injection molding company Seville, it was discovered in the waning days the company had struggled to stay afloat, and many of the critical parts of the tooling were missing. Apparently, disgruntled employees had removed and sold these pieces to precious metal dealers.

Again, first determine what direction you want to take for your collection. Then check out the classified ads in model car, racing collectible and toy magazines, such as *Toy Cars and Vehicles, Toy Shop* or *Scale Auto Enthusiast*. Contact mail-order companies such as Hobby Heaven or Model Empire, which offer catalogs full of highly desirable old model kits. Try running classified ads with your wants. Frequenting local and large regional model car swap meets can often turn up a bargain. Check the listings of upcoming events in special interest car magazines and model and hobby publications. When you find a bargain, buy it even if it doesn't fit your kit collection guidelines. Such items make great trading stock.

Licensing

One of the major factors governing the stock car model kit business today is licensing fees. Licensing (the legal authorization to use the name or likeness of a driver or make of automobile) is the mother's milk making it possible for manufacturers to be allowed to legally produce specific stock car model kits. A few years ago, manufacturers could contact a race team and request permission to produce a replica of its race car. In exchange for a few cases of kits, permission was usually granted. In those days, a driver, corporate sponsor or race team saw the benefits of using the packaged model

kit as a promotional device and would quickly okay the deal.

Currently, many new stock car model kits retail from $15-$25. And that price will continue to go ever higher. If you wonder why the price is so high, add royalties of 8% to 15% percent of the retail price or more to the development and production costs of $100,000 to $150,000, and you can now see why new kits are getting increasingly more costly.

Today, drivers and corporate sponsors change affiliations more often than they change their socks. Even when there has been a long-term relationship today, it can be very difficult to get all parties involved to put their names on the dotted line.

Sources

Having made decisions about collecting stock car model kits, you may be asking where to find those special items. There are many sources, including garage and yard sales, swap meets big and small, classified magazine ads and retail and mail-order sources that specialize in out-of-production kits. Two establishments I've dealt with and can recommend are Model Empire in West Allis, Wisconsin, and Hobby Haven in Grand Rapids, Michigan.

Hobby Heaven

Tom Carter is a life-long model car builder. From an early age, Carter was always buying, swapping

Tom Carter, with two Hobby Heaven employees, is ready for customers at a recent Toledo Toy Fair.

and trading stuff with other collectors and builders. It was only natural that an activity like this could grow into a regular business. In 1981, Carter decided it was time to get serious about things. He registered the name Hobby Heaven and ran the mail order-only business from his residence (he said it took up more than just the garage or basement). All the time, he was still working his regular job at the U.S. Post Office, while trying to manage a steadily-growing enterprise.

In 1988, Hobby Heaven had finally outgrown all expectations and had just about managed to crowd the Carter family out into the street. A new 10,000 square-foot facility was constructed while the eight HH employees never miss-a-beat filling the steady flow of mail orders during the transition to the new location. Today, Hobby Heaven continues to specialize in plastic model car kits. Carter is a race fan (as well as modeler) at heart, so HH has some of the most extensive lines of old, as well as the latest stock car model kits and supplies.

Hobby Heaven ships product to 45 different countries and sets up at the Spring and Fall Toledo Toy Fair at the Lucas County Recreation Center, Maumee, Ohio, each year. A Hobby Heaven web site is being developed and will be on-line sometime in 1999.

Model Empire

Alex Geiger is the second-generation proprietor of the combination retail and mail-order business called Model Empire. The business was originally started by his parents in 1968, when Gerald and Laverne Geiger set up at weekend flea markets selling close-out kits. What began as a small retail business has grown into a highly respected hobby shop and widely used mail-order model building and collecting source.

The retail business has been serving hobbyists worldwide from its present location in West Allis, Wisconsin (near Milwaukee) since the early 1970s. Model Empire features virtually any item imaginable from vintage kits to tools to paints and decals for stock car modelers.

Over the years, Gerald Geiger put together an extensive collection of model kits in a special area on premises known as the Model Car Museum. The company publishes an extensive catalog annually and stocks a considerable list of out-of-production stock car models.

If you don't live near Milwaukee, check with them to see what their show schedule is. Then you can look for the Model Empire banner atop a mountain of kits and supplies at a shows from Milwaukee to Chicago to New Jersey.

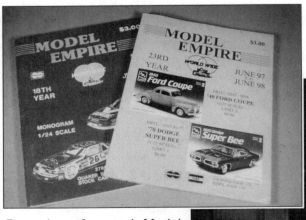

Examples of annual Model Empire mail-order catalogs.

Model Empire's Alex Geiger, with the help of his young son, make last-minute preparations for the onslaught of eager customers at a typical model car swap meet.

Glossary

Common Modeling and Racing Terms

Americans are unique in many ways. Certainly we put our own spin on everything from food to music to cars to our language. It's referred to as "syntax" in technical terms. In school it's said we're learning to read and write English. It might be more accurate if we just admitted that we speak American on these shores! If you'd like definite confirmation of my premise, just try hanging around with a bunch of serious American stock car racing fans. You want opinions? You want partisanship? You want vibrato? You want to know what they're all talking about?

You could say there are a few stock car racing fans who are not model builders, and you'd be correct most of the time. But I doubt you'll find even one in of a group of stock car modelers that isn't a dedicated, dyed-in-the-wool, card-carrying, high-volume race fan. If you were to eavesdrop on their conversations, you'd be hard pressed to know where the stock car chatter ends and the model car building lingo begins.

For this reason, the following glossary is composed of both racing and modeling terms. And, by the way, you can figure a modeler is talking racing if he doesn't have an X-Acto knife or a tube of putty in hand!

A

Aerodynamics: Technology of the forces of resistance and pressures that result from the flow of air rapidly moving around, over and under a 3-D object.

Acrylic: Recently developed decorative paint which is water-based and can be thinned with Naphtha. There is no chemical reaction with polystyrene plastics.

After-market: Cottage industries responsible for non-kit items such as decals, resin parts and photo-etch to enhance model stock car building and detailing projects.

Air Dam: Material located directly below the front bumper used to control the flow of air around, under and over the front of a race car.

Anodizing: Applying a decorative or protective finish via electrolytic or vacuum-plating.

Apron: Paved area of the track separating the racing surface from the infield.

ARCA: Automobile Racing Club of America

Articulate: Constructing an assembly with functional or moveable parts.

ASA: American Speed Association

B

Banjo: The late Banjo Matthews made a name for himself as a driver in the early years of NASCAR. He became legendary as one of the first independent stock car chassis builders. An excellent replica of his front-steer chassis can be found under the original 1983 Monogram T-Bird kit which uses the suspension geometry of the Holman-Moody 1965 Galaxie.

Banking: Sloped portion of the race track particularly through the corners.

Bear Grease: Slang term used to describe any sealer, traction-enhancing or patching materials used on the track surface.

Bezel: Trim enclosure surrounding the head light or tail light on a race car.

Bite: The turning of or making an adjustment to a race car's weight-jacking screws. Describe as a "round of bite."

Block Sanding: Placing an adhesive material like automotive sandpaper over a solid object to form a rigid finishing tool and using it to achieve a uniformly smooth surface.

Blown Engine: When some part(s) of an internal combustion racing engine breaks, causing it to cease functioning.

Blue Oval: Slang term derived from Ford Motor Company's blue oval emblem or logo and used to describe the cars of that specific manufacturer.

Bow Tie: Slang term referring to the Chevrolet logo or emblem used to describe this brand of car.

Buffing: To repeatedly rub a material like Metalizer paints or foil with a soft cloth to enhance the final appearance.

Bumping: When the number of starting positions has been reached while other race cars remain to qualify. Any of the remaining cars running faster take their place on the starting grid or "bump" them from the starting field.

Burnishing: Rubbing a material with a tool or soft cloth to increase its adhesion.

C

Came apart: When a connecting rod comes loose, knocking a hole in the block, causing pieces of metal and motor oil to be strewn over the racing surface.

Charger: Go fast or blow-up style driver; he runs flat-out all the time.

Chief Mechanic: Person responsible for a race car's performance including engine horsepower output and chassis setup.

Chrome Horn: When one driver gets his race car close enough to the one ahead of him and bumps against the other car just to remind the other driver he's back there.

Cool suit: Special space-age style uniform worn by race car drivers with liquid cooling tubes sewn into the lining. Cold water from a small reservoir is pumped through the tubes helping to keep the head and upper body cool and the driver more alert under high temperature conditions.

Compound: Manufacturing formula that determines the composition of racing tires. Left side tires are much softer compound than right sides.

Conversion: Making a different version of a race car, combining kit parts with hand-made pieces, etc.

Cottage Industry: Same as after-market. Usually home-based, small businesses that manufacture specialized products for model builders.

Cowl Flap: Small rectangular panels (two) located on the horizontal surface between the rear of the hood and base of the windshield, designed to be forced open by air pressure in the event a stock car goes out of control.

Crew Chief: Team leader in charge of virtually all aspects of managing the efforts of the crew.

Curbside: Model building style where panels are not open and when judged in a contest are neither picked up or examined underneath.

D

Decal: Usually a multi-color printed image silk-screened or offset printed onto paper with a water-soluble backing separating the two.

Dirt-Tracking: Controlled power slide through the corners of a race track.

Downforce: Air pressure applied over various surface areas of race car at speed.

Drafting: A method used on a super speedway in which two or more race cars line up single-file, bumper-to-bumper. The air flowing over the multi-car "train" is smoother and allows them to move easier through the air. They experience less wind resistance running together.

Drag: Object's or (car's) resistance to passage through the air at speed. The smoother and more rounded the car's surface, the lower the resistance.

Dyno: Short for dynamometer. A machine used to measure power characteristics and overall performance of racing engines.

Dump pipe: Large-diameter ducting connected to the exhaust manifold on a race car exiting under the rocker panel.

E

Enamel: Type of paint for decorative application containing a resin carrier and requiring a particular reducer for diluting. Requires a protective primer coat for use on polystyrene plastics.

Endo: When a race car flips end-over-end.

Epoxy: Adhesive composed of two-parts. When a resin-based material is combined with a catalyst, it causes a chemical reaction resulting in rapid hardening of the material into a bonding agent.

Equalize: Racing tires have an inner liner or a tire within a tire. When the inner liner springs a leak the air rushes into the outside causing the air pressure to become equal in both.

F

Factory Team: When a racing team receives a significant amount of its financial backing from a major automobile manufacturer (i.e., General Motors, Ford Motor Co., etc.).

Fish-eyes: Small, circular and concave depressions in a paint finish. Usually this is the result of a chemical reaction to an oily coating on the surface. More prevalent with resin material release agents.

Flat out: When the driver runs the race car at its maximum limit or as fast as it will go.

Foil: Thin metallic material with an adhesive backing applied over trim details on a model car to depict a chrome finish, etc.

Front-Steer: When the steering components on a race car are located ahead of the front spindles.

Fuel Cell: Large rectangular metal box equipped with a foam bladder and baffling inside that serves as a race car's gas tank.

G

Garage: Work area in which race cars are housed in preparation for competition.

Grand National: Official term used to designate the top division of NASCAR stock car racing from 1949 until the series adopted the name Winston Cup in 1983. Currently the term is used for the Busch series, as in Busch Grand National Series (BGN).

Groove: Best and quickest route around the race track.

Gum Ball: A qualifying or soft-compound racing tire featuring superior grip but with a short life under racing conditions.

H

Handling: When the race car's chassis and suspension have been adjusted to a point where the driver can drive the car to its optimum limit.

Header: Exhaust system composed of individual tubes running from each exhaust port and culminating into a common tube called the collector.

Holman-Moody: Ford Motor Company's factory race shop located in Charlotte, North Carolina The two principles of the company were businessman John Holman and former stock car driver Ralph Moody.

Honking: When the race car is performing extremely well.

Hood Pin: Two-part device used to secure the hood or rear deck lid on a race car. Composed of a vertical pin with an open eyelet into which is inserted a Cotter-type or retainer clip.

Hutcherson-Pagan: Former driver Dick Hutcherson joined forces a few years ago with former crew chief and fabricator Eddie Pagan to establish one of the popular chassis and race car construction shops serving the stock car industry.

I

IMCA: International Motor Contest Association.

Independent: Driver or team without corporate sponsorship or financial backing.

Instant glue: Type of adhesive composed of a chemical compound containing cyanacrylate ester; it is an eye irritant which can join rapidly most materials, especially human skin.

J

Jerrico: Special type of four-speed, heavy-duty racing transmission with straight-cut gear teeth, allowing seamless shifting at speed without engaging the clutch.

K

Kitbash: Parts from two or more commercially-produced kits are used together to build a unique model.

L

Lacquer: A type of paint for decorative application containing an acrylic resin carrier and a hot solvent resulting in a very short drying time. Has a very hard surface finish but requires a protective primer coat when used with polystyrene plastics.

Late Model Sportsman: The journeyman division under Winston Cup and renamed Grand National starting with the 1983 season.

Laughlin: Mike Laughlin is one of a select group of stock car chassis constructors gaining prominence in recent years. He is most noted for the development of the front-steer chassis utilizing Chevrolet Camaro derived geometry.

Loose: Sometimes referred to as "over-steer," where the rear of the race car tends to break traction and drift toward the outside wall.

M

Marbles: The chunks of tire tread and general track debris which collects between the racing groove and the retaining walls.

Micro Balloons: A fine-granule ceramic product that, when combined with epoxy or instant glues, quickly produces a chemical reaction. The resulting composite make a hard and durable filler.

Mold Line: The raised seam, usually found along the individual horizontal surfaces which are formed by the dividing line between the die work sections during the injection molding process.

Mopar: Automobiles of trucks manufactured by Chrysler Corporation, including nameplates such as Plymouth, Dodge or Chrysler.

More Bite: Increased or heavier wedging

N

NASCAR: National Association for Stock Car Auto Racing.

Notch Back: Stock car body with a decidedly upright and squared-off rear roof line.

O

Orange Peel: When a visual texture results in a painted finish caused by the wet paint drying too quickly.

Overhead Valve: Exhaust and intake valve assembly located into the engine cylinder head.

P

Pack: When several cars run close together on a race track.

Pacing: Predetermined speed, as to conserve driver stamina and racing equipment until near the finish in a race.

Parts Tree: (See Sprue)

Photo Etch: Small, delicate parts are formed from thin-sheet brass when placed over a photographic negative and are then exposed to an intense light source.

Pits: The line of specially marked stalls, adjacent the racing surface, where race car are taken for service.

Pit Board: Hand-held placard on which information is written to communicate with the driver.

Pit Crew: Group of people who service the race car at the track.

Pole Position: The No. 1 starting place in a race.

Polystyrene: Type of easily worked plastic derived from petroleum distillation used in injection molding of model hobby kits.

Primer: Protective and preparation coat applied to a surface to be painted.

Push: Sometimes referred to as "under-steer," in which the front of the car tends to move toward the outside wall through the corners.

Q

Qualifying: Timed speed trials to determine each starting position in a race.

R

Ragged Edge: When the driver pushes a race car up to and sometime beyond its capabilities.

Rear Steer: When the steering components of a race car are located behind the front axles.

Restrictor Plate: Aluminum plate containing four identical holes inserted between the four-barrel carburetor and port on the intake manifold to reduce the fuel and air mixture, thereby reducing the engine's horsepower and slowing the race car down.

Resin: Substance derived from a plant and vegetable base used in varnishes, paints, plastics and adhesives.

Rookie: Newcomer to racing or first time driver at a race track.

Rookie Strip: Piece of yellow tape displayed on the rear bumper of a rookie's race car.

Roof Flap: Small rectangular panel (two) located on either side of the center line of the top of a stock car, designed to be forced open by air pressure. They are employed only in the event the race car gets sideways or turned around as the result of a spin.

Roof Rail: Strip of sheet metal (two) located on either side of the center line of the top of a stock car and parallel to that line. Designed to effect the air flow over a spinning race car and keeping it from becoming airborne.

Rubber: A disk-shaped piece of hard black rubber occasionally inserted between the coils on a race car suspension spring to change the travel rate.

Rubbing Out: Using a polishing kit containing various fine grades of sandpaper along with special polish on a soft cloth to enhance the final appearance of a painted surface.

S

Sandbagging: When it is suspected a driver does not push a race car to its full potential during practice, qualifying or competition.

Scratch: Slang term used for the final position in a starting field of stock cars (i.e., starting scratch on the field).

Scratch Building: When a variety of raw materials (wood, plastic and metal) are used to hand-build a three-dimensional object.

Scuffs: Race teams run a set of tires a few laps, roughing up the tread surface, to better prepare them for racing conditions.

Shotgun: Slang term for the final position in a starting field of stock cars (i.e., starting shotgun on the field).

Short Track: Any race track with a measured distance around it of 1 mile or less.

Side Skirt: Valance attached to the lower part of both sides of the body on a stock car designed to manage the airflow under and around the sides of the race car.

Skid Lid: Slang term for a driver's racing helmet.

Slicks: Slang term for racing tires with a smooth, treadless surface.

Sling-Shot: To quickly pull out and pass the race car directly ahead of you due to the vacuum created behind that race car as the result of drafting.

Spindle: Pivoting horizontal metal rod located between the top and bottom control arms. The front axles are attached to this piece allowing the front wheels to steer.

Spoiler: Usually flat, straight piece of sheet metal bolted to the rear edge of the deck lid on a stock car which interrupts the smooth flow of air over the rear of the car. Primarily used to manage airflow, downforce and drag.

Sponsor: The commercial enterprise providing direct financial support for a race team in exchange for advertising, marketing and sales benefits.

Stabilizer: Solid metal bar mounted to the suspension and frame to dampen rapid movement.

Stagger: The difference in circumference between the tires used on the left and right side of the race car. Most prevalent in bias-ply tires.

Stand On It: Slamming the accelerator to the floor and leaving it there.

Stickers: Brand-new unused racing tire with manufacturer's label on the tread surface.

Stroker: Driver who keeps a steady pace to ensure a good finish.

Strut Rod: The metal bars attached to a race cars' frame and lower control arms that help to maintain location and stability.

Super Speedway: Large high-banked race track of at least two miles in length, such as Daytona and Talladega.

T

Taxi: Slang term used to describe a stock production-based race car a few years ago.

Tight: When the front of the car tends to drift high through a corner at speed.

Tri-Oval: A race track with a kink in the front straightaway providing an additional corner beyond the customary four.

Two-Hundred MPH Tape: Adhesive tape, similar to that used in the heating and AC industry, with such stickiness that it can withstand extreme pressures.

U

USAC: United States Auto Club.

V

Vacuum Form: A molding process using the rapid removal of air from the underside of a (usually heated) pliable sheet of material drawn down quickly over a convex object to form a copy in relief.

Valance: The current term used to describe the adjustable extreme bottom edge of the front spoiler on a stock car.

W

Wedge: (See Bite)

Wet Sanding: Automotive sand paper is soaked in tap water which enhances its ability to be self-cleaning, thereby improving the ability to produce a smooth surface.

Wing: Usually a lateral surface mounted to a race car for the sole purpose of applying large amounts of down force at speed.

Chapter 1

How Plastic Model Stock Car Kits are Made

Since the late-1940s, scale model kit manufacturers have been using polystyrene plastic and injection molding. Since then, this material and manufacturing process has opened up a true treasure trove, resulting in literally millions of hobby kits having been produced. It's really not a complicated process when you begin to understand how it's done, but it's time consuming and expensive.

There is hardly a week that goes by that someone doesn't ask me, "I've always wondered why XYZ company never made such-and-such a stock car kit." I used to ponder that thought many times myself until I learned about everything that's involved in moving an idea through the process into that neatly wrapped kit box on your local hobby shop shelf.

All plastic model kits begin with a concept or idea that a group or individual feels confident will be a good selling retail product. These things are never pursued on a notion or an emotionally driven whim. The last 50-plus years is littered with items that at first blush seemed like a sure thing. But for whatever reason, the stock car model kit(s) did not sell well enough to either be profitable or deemed a success. And remember that these were all items finely sifted, closely scrutinized and thoroughly evaluated. In spite of the known risks, after considerable deliberation, test-market research and a final "best-guess" as to how this item might be received, the decision is made to move forward to the next level.

Occasionally, blue-prints or actual engineering drawings are made available to the kit manufacturer by an automobile company, fabrication shop or race team. This is by far the desired starting point for such a process. Today's computerized high-tech environment may even make it possible for the kit manufacturer to start from data captured in electronic files.

If these basic building blocks are not available, engineers, technicians and designers will resort to locating an example of the full-size race car to be reduced to miniature. Literally hundreds of photographs are then taken from every possible angle. No surface, interior or exterior panel or hidden crevasse is overlooked. Every nook and cranny is explored, often with a measuring tape affixed to some surfaces and intricate details so the final pictures will not only indicate the unique shape and contour, but the actual dimensions of these features.

From this mountain of information, designers (working on CAD or drawing board), prepare a series of highly detailed and precise engineering drawings. These drawings contain not only images of the overall shapes, top, bottom, side and so on, but horizontal and diagonal cross sections at specifically predetermined increments.

A Revell-Monogram designer is working on the model kit control drawings. This is the top view of the subject and he is adding dimensions to the drawings along with critical tolerances that are calculated to one thousandth of an inch (.001 in.). Also note the designer references photographs and measurements that were originally taken during the research phase of the project subject.

A Revell-Monogram product planner discusses the attributes of a future stock car kit release. A 1/10th resin test shot of the body shell is shown on the cabinet top.

Along with all of this general information, there is also a complete series of drawings of the smallest parts, literally down to every screw, washer and bolt head. This plethora of technical materials is next given to a team of highly-skilled craftsmen who then generate a series of 3-D mock-ups in wood at 1/10th scale. Each of the wood pieces faithfully represents each part of the full-size subject and will be used as a guide to engrave the die-work for each part of the plastic kit. Understandably, the more effort given to making these wood patterns as exact as possible results in a highly accurate model.

Today, these wooden pieces are reproduced using a simple molding process. The resin replicas of each pattern piece is then passed on to the team of craftsmen given the task of making the steel tooling. An age-old piece of equipment called a Pantograph is employed to reduce the size of each component to the proper scale. Convex and concave cavities are precision-cut into case-hardened steel blocks which form the two-piece molds.

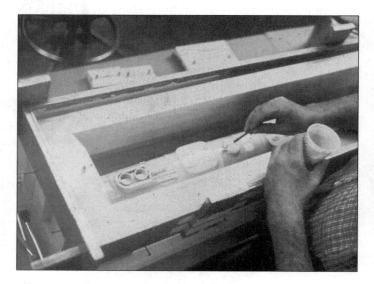

The technician works on the "bowl," the positive half of the mold or convex pattern that the impressions will be taken from to create a concave mold cavity. He is applying a parting or release agent, a polymer with a high Teflon content, so that the eventual two compatible parts can be separated.

Shown here is the business end of a Pantograph machine. The instrument on the left is the cutter which is the device that actually cuts impressions in the block of steel. On the right is the actual master pattern. Pantographing is very old technology but it is reliable and still in general use.

A technician traces the pattern with a stylus. He is making final adjustment to the Pantograph as it cuts impressions in the steel block.

Another view of the core side of the tool laying down and the cavity side standing up.

In this shot, the core side of the mold is on the left, the part that is laying horizontal, while the cavity side of the mold is standing vertical in the middle of the photo. Note the ejector plate on the right hanging from the crane hook which is an essential part of the tool and responsible for accurately lining up the two mold halves during production.

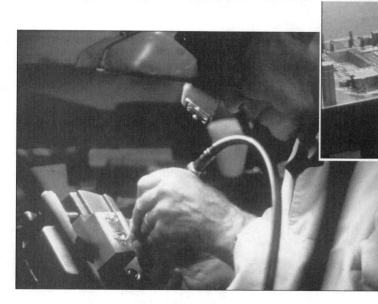

The technician is "maintenancing" the tool. He is carefully performing a final clean-up and using the Dremel tool to remove excess materials, sharpen edges or reestablish critical surfaces.

Once the initial steel dies have been produced, the die-work is refined by a precision craftsman who cleans up each mold and adds all the final surface details that may include badging, scripts, panel textures, bolt heads and other hardware details. At this point, the dies are inserted into an injection molding machine which is capable of forcing liquid styrene into the mold at extremely high pressures. This initial run of the kit components is referred to as the "test shots." There may be as many as four phases of test shots. The goal is to refine the die-work to ensure accuracy, finish, alignment and fit. As a final step, the engraver cleans up the molds and polishes each part's surface to a mirror-like sheen. Then production begins.

Keeping stride with the engineers, technicians, pattern makers and engravers are the efforts to develop the instruction sheet(s), the decals and the box art. Artists, photographers and printers produce all of these accessory items in preparation for packaging the final model kit contents.

Actually, the styrene portion of each model kit begins as a drum of tiny granules. There are clear granules for transparent parts like the window glass. Granules for the other components can vary from pure white to a vast array of colors depending on the kit requirements. The various granules are blended together and heated to a fluid state in preparation for injection into the molds at extreme pressure. After each cycle of the injection molding machine, water is distributed over the tooling to rapidly cool it and allow the newly formed parts to solidify. The parts are then ejected from the die-work and the process starts over again.

Those parts that are to be plated are then separated from the rest. The bright chrome-like finish for some model kit parts is accomplished by a process called "vacuum plating." The parts are attached to a rotary-style rack, sprayed with a clear lacquer and then inserted into a vacuum chamber. Next, all the air is pumped from the chamber, and electrical current is used to evaporate pieces of aluminum which literally

The plastic blenders, located between the silos outside the plant and injection molding machines inside, take the granules from the silos and blend them into the colors or shades of plastic specified for the next product run prior to being introduced into the molding machinery. In the foreground is a big container box on a pallet of white plastic granules.

This is the backside of an injection molding machine. Here the blended granules are heated, melted and drawn into a cylinder by an auger where the liquid mixture is forced into the steel tooling inside the machine where it is injected into the tool cavity under pressure to form various plastic kit parts.

These are granular plastic silos outside Revell-Monogram's Illinois manufacturing facility. In side of each silo is a large volume of different types of plastic pellets, particles or granules in various colors including gray, white, red, clear, etc. This finely ground-up plastic is vacuumed from large delivery trucks into each silo. These silos are constantly filled to maintain capacity for the constant injection molding production schedule requirements.

explode in all directions covering the surface of anything that happens to be present inside the chamber.

The final step brings all the contents of each kit together along an assembly line where the instruction sheet, decals, tires, chrome parts and clear parts join the remainder of the kit's plastic parts. The loaded kit box is shrink-wrapped and sent to the warehouse. From here, cases of kits are sent to distributors, wholesalers and ultimately to resellers for sale to the public.

You can quickly see that this is an involved process, time consuming and one in which mistakes and delays are critical and costly. Today, the cost of a set of die-work to produce a scale model stock car kit can run between $150,000 to $250,000. The normal time required to develop the concept, engineer the tooling and produce the kit contents may take from nine to 12 months.

This is currently the way all injection-molded model stock car kits are produced. You will see that not all stock car kits are done in this fashion, however. This is particularly true for 1/43rd scale kits. In Chapter 3, Wayne Moyer will explain in great detail the process in general practice for manufacturing this type of stock car kit.

The ejector pin block contains the actual ejector pins and springs and the large diameter locator pins arranged in precise order on the tray. These individual elements work together to ensure that all critical edges and surfaces line up in the molding machine time-after-time and make it possible that the two tool halves separate properly allowing the molded parts to be removed safely. If you study most plastic parts you'll notice many little round shallow depressions on some surfaces created by these ejector pins.

The core mold is resting in a prone position. Note the six ejector springs that control side action in the assembled tool. These are smaller tools that are located inside the big tool. These devices allow the tool to produce undercuts. Also note the large cylinders in the foreground that are primary locator pins.

Shown here is a 100-ton press that is a key element in the injection molding process. In the foreground are the parts that were just removed from this machine. In the background, the two sides of the mold are vertical, facing each other behind a glass door in the open position. The loops of black hose shown here are actually cooling tubes that carry glycanol liquid (like automotive antifreeze) that is used to cool the mold to aid removal of the plastic kit parts.

Company Histories

AMT (Aluminum Model Toy)

The acronym "AMT" came from the original company name Aluminum Model Toy. The new company began producing metal promotional models in 1947, but quickly switched to injection-molded plastic. AMT is credited with establishing the widely accepted 1/25th scale in the United States when its first 3-in-1 annual kits were introduced in 1958. The unusual scale was arrived at when 1/10th-scale auto factory-supplied blueprints were reduced 2.5 times, producing a size of model that would fit into a standard size promo box.

AMT was always known for its extensive line of injection-molded plastic car kits which permitted early stock car model builders to replicate in miniature that which was competing on the nation's race tracks for the first time.

AMT remained a leader worldwide and a major influence in automotive model kits until Matchbox/Lesney of Great Britain purchased the company lock, stock and molding machine in 1978. From that point on, the kit box logo reflected the new acquisition with the use of the AMT/Matchbox icon. When Lesney went bankrupt in the early-1982, The Ertl Company of Iowa, came to the rescue and acquired all the steel tools, injection molding machines and rights to the high visibility product line name.

IMC (Industro-Motive Corporation)

This company produced its first plastic car kits in 1965 in both 1/32nd and 1/25th scale. The company continued to produce plastic kits for the hobby market until 1977 when Testors (the hobby paint manufacturer) acquired the complete operation. Eventually, IMC, Lindberg and Testors products lines were absorbed by the RPM corporation.

The first 1/32nd-scale stock car kits released in 1965 were offered exclusively as slot car body shells originally. Later, these same items were fitted with a generic chassis and reissued as unassembled kits.

Jo-Han

The Jo-Han Company was started by John Haenle in the mid-1950s (the company name being a contraction of the first few letters of his name). The first 1/25th scale plastic kits were released in 1959. Jo-Han continued to produce street-stock and racing car kits until Haenle's steadily declining health stopped production in the early-1980s. There have been no new kit releases since that time. During the period the

company assets were acquired by Seville Enterprises a plastic-injection automotive-parts manufacturer in the Detroit area.

Virtually none of the original tooling has survived the ravages of time. None of the most popular stock car kits—'64 Petty Plymouth, Petty Superbird and '72 Ford Torino stock car kits—are likely ever to be seen on store shelves again.

Lindberg

Lindberg is the oldest plastic kit manufacturer still producing product in the United States. The company was founded by Paul Lindberg (and a partner whose last name was Olsen) under the name O-Lin Models in 1933 and soon became one of the forerunners in the model kit hobby industry. In the early years, O-Lin (Lindberg) mostly concentrated its efforts on balsa wood ship and airplane model kits.

O-Lin produced its first plastic kits in the late-1940s, changing the company name officially to "Lindberg Models" in 1950. The company introduced its first automotive kits in the early-1960s, but also continued manufacturing its extensive line of plastic airplane and ship model kits, as the company does currently. With the assistance of George Toteff, Lindberg was purchased by Craft House from Jim Perkins in 1989. Since that time, the company has moved to become a major contender in the automotive model kit business.

To date, Lindberg's lone stock-car kit release is the excellent Richard Petty 1964 Plymouth Beleverde, as raced to victory in that year's Daytona 500. The Lindberg product line also contains other street-stock car kits that readily lend themselves to conversion to racing application.

MPC (Model Products Corporation)

MPC was started by George Toteff and partners in the early-1960s in Mt. Clemens, Michigan, after he had left AMT. Toteff started his career as an AMT pattern-maker. While there, Toteff was credited with inventing the slide mechanism which allows for the injection molding of one-piece body shells. George eventually moved into the marketing department and is the person to thank for the idea of offering unassembled promotional models, cast in styrene plastic as the first Craftsman kits.

Toteff led the new company into first producing model kit tooling for well-established companies like

AMT. MPC released the first 1/25th scale plastic kit under its own name in 1964, which was the new Corvette coupe. MPC continued as an independent manufacturer until the late 1970s when consumer-product giant General Mills bought the company. Under the new parent company, MPC continued to produce model car kits until The Ertl Company purchased the GM subsidiary in 1985. The MPC logo and product line continued under the new ownership until Ertl folded it into the AMT line and dropped the familiar MPC designation in the early-1990s.

MPC grew into a major player in the plastic kit business producing both street-driven annual car kits and a wide variety of motorsports subjects.

Monogram

This company was the brainchild of Bob Reder and Jack Besser in late 1945 near Chicago. The partners began by manufacturing balsa wood kits of World War II warships. After manufacturing wooden kits for a period, the company quickly switched to injection-molded plastic by the early 1950s. In 1954, Monogram introduced its first all-plastic model car kit, number P-1, the Midget Racer. It wasn't long before the demand for similar kits led Reder and Besser to produce nothing but injection-molded plastic model kits.

The whole plastic hobby kit business virtually exploded at this point, and Monogram was riding the crest of the wave. What followed was a veritable history of contemporary American civilization, as reflected in the automotive kit subject material. Monogram has always been noted for high quality and diverse product mix. Today, a company spokesman is quick to confess that model car subjects now comprise more than 60 percent of the company's business.

In 1968, Monogram was purchased by Mattel, Inc., the world's largest toy manufacturer. Mattel eventually took control of all product development, marketing and sales for the Monogram plastic kit line. Some observers believe that the parent company tried to turn Monogram Models into a toy company. When this new approach didn't work (i.e., a sharp decline in sales), Mattel returned product development, marketing and sales back to the Monogram staff in 1972.

The entire domestic hobby business suffered a shakeup when hand-held and parlor electronic games were introduced. Of course, add to that a mild recession in the United States. Mattel experienced cash-flow problems as its type of hand-held, battery-operated video games were not selling. For Monogram, funding for new tooling was drastically cut, forcing them to concentrate on revising and converting older tooling into new products.

Economic conditions began improving by 1983. Bob Johnson, Monogram's risk-taking product manager, proposed development of a totally new line of NASCAR-style stock car model kits. The first four releases in the series included two Ford Thunderbirds and two Buick Regals. Johnson, who has since left Monogram to start his own hobby kit company said, "Those four releases put Monogram on the map as a serious manufacturer of stock car model kits for all time."

Since their introduction in 1983, dozens of different superspeedway race cars have been produced in the line, including Fords, Chevrolets, Buicks, Oldsmobiles and Pontiacs. "You're probably looking today at a model kit series that has produced more than three to four million pieces," added Johnson with a smile. Reliable sources confirm that the stock car line has become a mainstay to Monogram's bottom line each year since their introduction.

In 1984, Tom Gannon (former MMI president) and a group of investors successfully purchased Monogram from Mattel. The company continued to grow and expand its product line; by mid-1986, Odyssey Partners (and investment group) purchased Monogram. Shortly after that acquisition, Odyssey also acquired the assets of Revell, Inc., which surveys had shown was still the most recognized name in the hobby business.

Recently, Revell-Monogram (R-M) was purchased by Binney and Smith owners of Hallmark greeting cards and Crayola crayons. R-M is comfortably positioned into the leisure-time consumer products division with these other highly-visible product groups.

In 1998, R-M again moved forward into uncharted waters by expanding once more its stock car kit line. The first four of an ongoing series of new Snaptite 1/24th scale NASCAR stock car kits were released. This kit range proved once again that being innovative (at least for this company) was nothing new.

Revell

Lew Glaser started Revell in California just prior to World War II. Eventually, Revell would become the largest manufacturer of plastic kits in the world. The Revell logo proved to be the recognizable in the hobby business. Revell's first all-plastic model car kit was a 1/16th scale 1910 Maxwell released in 1951. Revell didn't produce any stock car model kits until the acquisition by Monogram. The ASA stock cars were Revell's first and only venture into the oval track racer market.

Revell remained a wholly owned American company until 1979 when French toy producer Compagnie Generale Du Jouet acquired the company assets. In 1986, Odyssey Partners, owners of Monogram Models, Inc., bought Revell. All physical assets were phased out in Venice, California, and moved to Des Plaines, Illinois, a short distance from the long-standing Monogram facilities in nearby Morton Grove.

Chapter 2

The Essentials

Workplace, Tools, Supplies, Tips & Techniques for Stock Car Model Building

Building a good model of your favorite stock car is not an impossible task. Whether you're a novice modeler or even an experienced builder, there are a few basic tips, tools, techniques and straight forward words of advice that can go a long way to help you build a better stock car replica.

The Workplace

You need a place to work...someplace where you're not constantly in other people's way. It's always nice if you can set aside a dedicated area to work. It could be a garage workshop, your den, an extra bedroom or maybe a small table in a clean corner of the basement. If these are not options, some model builders work well just setting-up-shop at the kitchen table or temporarily on a folding or card table. Start out by sitting on a comfortable chair and working under the concentrated illumination of a Tensor-type light.

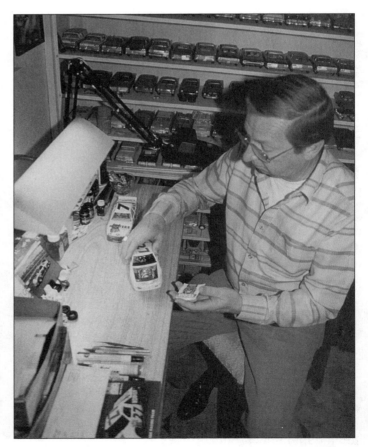

Tom Dill works at this wooden desk which is large enough to afford ample working surface. Note the bright light on a swing arm which is readily adjusted to shine right where you need it most.

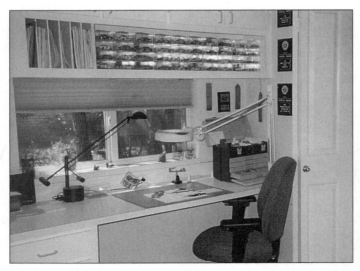

The work/storage/display area incorporated into Roy Vaughn's modeling work area is just about perfect. The close proximity of works surface to enclosed spray booth and the artificial and natural lighting makes this a comfortable and enjoyable place to build models.

Tom Dill does his model building seated at an old wooden desk in a spare bedroom with plenty of drawers for storage and ample work surface on top to stretch out a bit. By contrast, Roy Vaughn was fortunate enough to include in the building plans for his new residence in Florida a dedicated model building, storage, display and spray painting area. Note that Roy also has an excellent location for plenty of natural light. And everything is close at hand, reducing the steps between various operations. Even the spray booth is enclosed behind a folding door.

Tools and Supplies

Having selected the model you want to build, buy tools and supplies to work with. Those first investments should include a No. 11 X-Acto hobby knife. This is the one tool you will likely have in your hand most often during the building process. A word of caution here. I selected a brand similar to X-Acto which comes with a protective cover. Hobby knife blades are extremely sharp and must be handled with great care to avoid painful cuts.

To the tool list, add a jewelers file, emery board, tweezers, sprue cutters and at least two grades of automotive-type wet/dry sand paper (like a medium 320 and a fine grade 600). Also, buy two or three types of glue, a small tube of automotive-type body filler and masking tape.

Recommended choices for types of glues require some discussion. There is a wide variety and types of glues that are frequently used in stock car model building. The most basic of these is a tube of styrene cement. This type is good for the novice, but it dries very slowly and gets stringy with age.

Liquid glues (often in a clear bottle with a brush applicator included) are excellent for attaching styrene parts. However, styrene cements or liquid glues of this type make it nearly impossible to bond other types of materials to plastic or vice versa.

By contrast, super glues are fast drying and will bond virtually any type materials together. They can be a bit tricky to use as they do not always form a strong bond and can become ineffective quickly due to their short shelf life once opened. Be forewarned that since super glue bonds virtually any materials, it's easy to stick your fingers together (or to your model parts) if you're not careful. Also remember that super glues should never be used around clear or plated parts as the fumes will leave a haze or fog on such parts.

A couple of good quality tweezers with fine pointed tips are essential tools for the serious modeler.

Basic modeling tools might include an X-Acto knife with cover, small sewing scissors and needle-nose pliers.

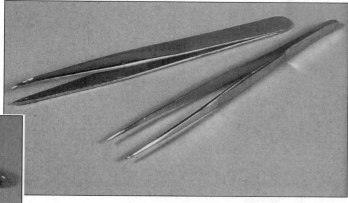

A sprue cutter will make it much easier to trim those delicate parts from the tree as shown here.

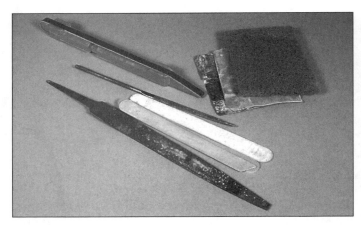

Sanding sticks, emery boards, files of various types, scotch bright and various grades of automotive wet/dry sand paper will aid you in performing body work or removing ejector pin marks or mold separation lines.

A choice of different types of glue is important. White glue for clear and plated parts, two-part epoxy for permanent bonding, super glue and a kicker for quick assembly and styrene glue for general usage.

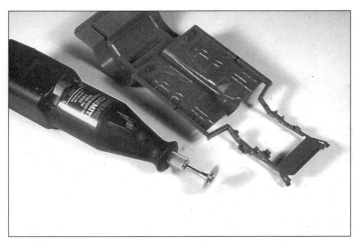

For unhampered cutting, drilling and grinding, Dremel's Mini-Mite, a battery-powered motor tool, has become an essential part of my model building tool arsenal.

For working in restricted or cramped area where finishing is very difficult, I use this Nick-Sander found at an auto supply store.

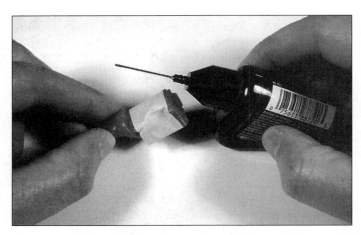

Styrene glue is okay for the novice builder and for a solid bond when drying time is not important.

Using a tire sanding tool makes the simulated wear on this stock car tire a quick and painless job.

This miter box, when used with a razor saw will allow you to make clean precise cuts on plastic rod and tubing like that used when making exhaust dumps.

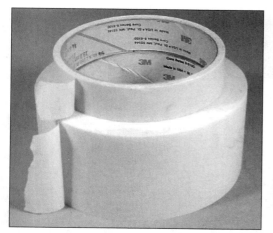

If you need to use body putty, I recommend using Dr. Microtools which is compatible with plastic and does not experience severe shrinkage.

You'll need a couple of different widths of masking tape for holding parts in place for painting or masking off for two-tone paint jobs.

For best results when removing parts from the kit sprue trees, use a sprue cutter. This is especially good advice when removing plated and clear parts. If the part is removed improperly, a nick in the edge of a plated bumper or section of window glass, it will be nearly impossible to repair.

For clearing away excess flashing or remnants of the little tags where parts were attached to the sprue use a jewelers file, emery board or sand paper. When using body putty apply sparingly in layers, building up thin coats. This is especially important when large areas or deep recesses are to be filled. Quite often, applying fillers in any other fashion will result in shrinkage and unwanted surface cracks in the putty.

Bottle Paints and Brushes

When hand-painting small parts with bottle paints, use a good quality artist's brush, such as those offered by Testors. In most cases, a number 1, 0 and 000 brush will cover all applications. Avoid brush-painting large flat areas that are in plain view as unevenness caused by individual brush stroke marks will likely be quite noticeable.

Use curls of masking tape to attach small parts and assemblies to a piece of cardboard to be primed. Then you can also save a lot of time and effort by rearranging these primed parts into groups that are to all be eventually painted the same color. In some instances, you may need to reposition a few parts to get complete paint coverage.

Assemblies like the engine, front and rear suspension and even the wheels that may require separate detail-painting, can still be group-painted when the application of a basic color is required. An example would be the typical race car engine and transmission: You could paint this assembly with a gun-metal color first. Once it's thoroughly dry, mask-off the engine from the transmission, then spray paint the transmission with aluminum. This could be done with a brush, but it will look so much better when spray painted.

Testors has one of the most complete lines of enamel paints designed specifically for styrene plastic models. There is a variety of colors and shades in spray cans and bottles.

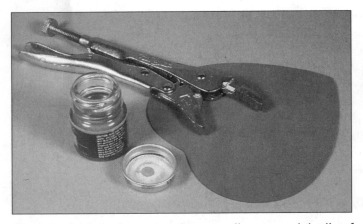

Keep the lid free of excess paint, as well as around the lip of the bottle. Dried paint forms an excellent bond and may often require using something like small vice grips for opening.

Testors Metallizer paints, which include various shades of metallic finishes, are ideal for bringing out the details in a stock car model.

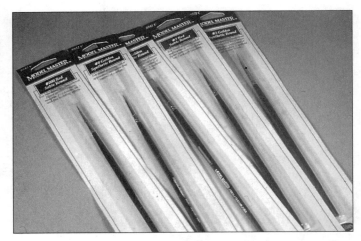

Do not scrimp when buying paint brushes. I've found the Testors line to be an excellent choice. When properly cleaned and maintained, they will do a good job for a long time.

Spray Painting

When spray painting, seek out a well-ventilated work area. Some builders use their heated garages. If the weather conditions are good (warm temperatures, no high winds etc.) spray painting models outdoors is possible. Quite often, spraying primers and paints indoors is a necessity. Just be sure to stay away from high-heat sources (especially any device with an open flame) or appliances like gas clothes dryers or a forced-air furnace.

Try to select an area where a window can be opened for ventilation. I strongly recommend that you wear some type of protective gear like a spray mask which covers your nose and mouth so you don't breathe in all those fumes and paint particles. The ideal situation is a commercial model spray paint booth. When properly set up and ventilated, this unit will give years of trouble-free operation, not to mention all those great paint jobs.

Whatever stock car model you've selected, there are a number of excellent brands of paint that can be used for the job. Testors has been making model paint for about as long as I can remember. But it's only been recently that the company addressed the needs of the stock car model builder. Testors Racing Colors are available in convenient spray cans, and many of the top NASCAR team's colors are in the line. Other Testors colors found in its regular line of hobby enamels will all be compatible with the new paints.

When painting parts like a body shell, attach them to either a paint stand like the Shabo unit or make a fixture fashioned from a metal coat hanger. Shake each paint can thoroughly before spraying. Practice your spraying technique on some scrap plastic pieces to get the feel of the paint flow and the pattern of coverage before you start on your model. When spraying your model, move in a continuous motion from end-to-end and side-to-side to assure an even and thorough coat. Keep the can about 8-10 inches from the model surface.

Especially when using model enamels, be sure to allow the final color coats time to dry thoroughly. A good rule of thumb for this type of paint is 7-10 days. Store the painted model body, for example, in a warm, dry and dust-free environment for the duration.

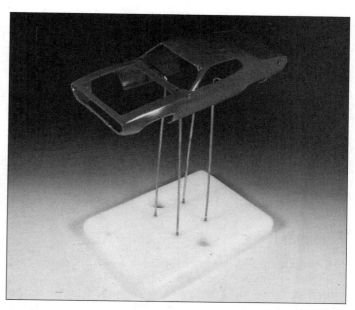

This Shabo spray paint stand is ideal for securely holding your model body shell at all angles.

Use curls of masking tape to attach small parts to a strip of cardboard for spray painting.

The ideal set up for spray painting is a commercial booth like this one from Badger. When properly configured, spray painting is convenient, clean and safe.

A good quality air brush is the next logical choice for spray painting your models. You can use a compressor or canned propellant. Always use a spray mask to be safe and remember to clean the air brush frequently using thinner and a pipe cleaner.

Applying Decals

When applying water-slide decals on your painted model, be patient and take your time. I use a small pair of sharp sewing scissors, fine pointed tweezers and plenty of clean dry facial tissues. Using the scissors, carefully trim out each decal to be applied to the models surface. Run a small amount of tap water into a flat tray-type container (which is difficult to tip over in your work area). Place the trimmed decal into the tray of water. Allow the decal to float in the water for a minute or so, checking occasionally to see if the decal film will slide around freely on the backing paper.

Apply a bit of water to the area on the model where the decal is to go. Remove the decal from the tray keeping the decal film on the backing paper. Then slowly slide the film off the paper onto the surface of the model. Once in place, carefully press the decal with a damp (but not wet) tissue to remove the excess moisture. Allow the decal a few minutes to completely dry. At this point, proceeding cautiously, use a dry tissue to lightly buff the decal to get out any air bubbles and remove water marks and finger prints.

Shown here is a full range of decal positioning and softening liquids. Also, on the far right is Micro Superfilm. When lightly brushed over old decals, it heals the ravages of aging so they can be used successfully.

Finishing

Once the paint is dry, the decals are in place and final assembly is taking place, it's time to bring up the ultimate shine and removing the last vestiges of the building process. A clean, soft cloth can be used to apply a generous coating of Pledge furniture wax. I've found this final step is an opportunity to clean away any remaining finger prints, water streaks or smudges and coax out that last bit of high luster to the paint and markings that may well set your stock car model apart from all the others on the display table.

Inexpensive reading glasses can be quite helpful when working with those mighty small parts and pieces. I found these make-up brushes in a close-out store. They have no equal for cleaning dust and lint from the surface of your finished models.

These three household cleaning and polishing agents will work wonders on your finished models. The Fantastik and rubbing alcohol can be used to clean away finger prints and smudges due to handling. I use Pledge furniture polish on every one of my models before it goes in the display case.

This low-priced plastic food storage container is great for housing all the stuff from your modeling project or for safely transporting them to contests and shows.

Sources

The 1999 Model Car Buyer's Guide, compiled and published by Scale Sports in Sterling, Virginia, is a complete reference library for the model car hobby. It list many sources for hobby items targeted to the stock car model builder. Look for it at your local hobby shop.

Chapter 3

By Wayne Moyer

Stock Cars in 1/43 Scale

Why 1/43 Scale?

The very first 1/43-scale models were stock cars; not NASCAR stock cars, but the cars found on the streets and roads of Europe. Although the first diecast metal models were made in 1914 by the Dowst Manufacturing Company of Chicago, no attempt to produce a series of accurate models in a consistent scale seems to have been made until 1935 when Dinky introduced a series of accurate, nicely detailed miniature automobiles as accessories for European O-Gauge model railway sets. European O-Gauge scale is a compromise between the metric system used on the Continent and the English system: 7 millimeters = 1 foot. That works out to 1/42.5, or as we know it, 1/43 scale.

The success of these new Dinky Toys proved that accurate models were more popular with both adults and children than the generic vehicles previously made, and that their relatively small size did not hurt their play value. Before the war ended production, 1/43-scale Dinky models were being made in Britain and France, and Marklin was making some very nice 1/45 scale diecasts in Germany. The pre-war models that survived suddenly became collector's items after the war, and, as Europe slowly returned to normal, the production of 1/43-scale models as both children's toys and as miniature vehicles for collectors entered a boom era.

Today, the 1/43-scale kit industry offers its customers the greatest selection of subjects in the model car world. No other scale even comes close; each year nearly 1,000 new 1/43-scale kits are released; one shop, Grand Prix Models of England, has more than 6,000 1/43-scale kits and models in its inventory at any time, and that does not include the many new 1/43-scale diecast models that are produced each year.

Dinky Toys began making 1/43-scale diecast models before World War II. Dinky added models of American sedans like this Hudson to its line in the 1950s. Compare this model, with no chrome, glass, or interior, to the Revell Quality Care Thunderbird to see how much diecast models have improved. (photo by Moyer)

Diecast, White-Metal, Resin & Multi-Medium Models

Diecast models

Although the term *diecast* is often used to refer to any metal 1/43-scale model, it actually is correct only for models that are made by injecting a molten alloy of zinc, aluminum, copper, and magnesium (called Zamac) in even harder steel molds or dies. Matchbox, Dinky, Corgi, Road Champs and similar toys are all diecast models, as are the higher-quality models like Minichamps, Vitesse, Solido, Detail Cars and virtually all the larger scale metal models. Zamac melts at high temperatures and is forced into the mold (called the die) under high pressure to make it flow into all parts of the mold before it starts to cool. Dies must be machined from hard tool steel to withstand the temperature and pressure and cost thousands of dollars to create, so the manufacturer must count on selling many thousands of copies of a diecast model to pay for the investment in a new tool. Zamac castings are thin and have very good surface detail but the metal is hard and will break instead of bending. It's relatively hard to work with, and, although some 1/43-scale diecast kits have been made (usually unpainted, unassembled versions of a production diecast with some extra plastic pieces and/or new decals), there are *no* 1/43-scale diecast kits of NASCAR cars, to my knowledge.

White-metal models

The term *white-metal* is applied to a soft, easily bent tin-lead alloy that melts at low temperatures. Older kits had high lead contents, but safety issues have caused many current manufacturers to now use low-lead alloys, despite the higher cost of the metal and harder castings. White-metal kits are produced by first sandwiching all the separate parts for a model (the master model) between two disks of raw rubber. The rubber is then vulcanized (hardened) under high pressure and high temperature, and flows completely around the master parts during the process. Once cured, the rubber disks are split, the master parts are removed and channels are cut from the center of the mold to each cavity. The molds are placed in the centrifugal (spin casting) machine and spun at fairly high speed while molten metal is poured in at the center. Centrifugal force (hence the name) causes the liquid metal to flow out into the cavities where it cools to form the parts of the model. The rubber molds can be made for only a couple of hundred dollars (while steel dies cost thousands) and the master can be made from almost any material that will not melt during the vulcanizing process; brass, plaster and even wood were popular in the early days. Rubber molds last for only a few dozen castings, though, so several molds are required for a typical production run of 300-500 kits. The low costs of the molds make it possible for a small cottage industry to profitably produce only a couple of hundred kits of any given model. Although the first 1/43-scale NASCAR stock car kits were made in white-metal, there are none being made today. The superb multi-media kits by Renaissance have many white-metal components, including a full roll cage.

Resin models

Early resin castings were made by mixing two liquids together and pouring the mixture into a mold at room temperature and pressure. By eliminating the requirement for vulcanized rubber molds and molten metal, resin casting made it possible for individuals all over the world to become kit manufacturers. The epoxy resin used in early kits was very brittle, didn't pick up surface details, and often had large bubble holes in the castings, so resin kits did not gain an immediate acceptance in the hobby. However, polyurethane resin, which is easy to work with and can produce incredibly detailed castings, was introduced in the mid-1980s and revolutionized the 1/43-scale kit industry. Most resin kit manufacturers now use dense

John Day's model of A.J. Foyt's Chevelle was accurate and included a roll cage, but its decals were crude. Starter's easy-to-build resin kits, like this model of Labonte's 1984 Championship Monte Carlo, made 1/43-scale stock car models popular in both Europe and the United States. The multi-medium kits Renaissance makes are the best yet in 1/43 scale. (photo by Moyer)

but flexible RTV (Room Temperature Vulcanizing) rubber molds and pressurize the molds after the resin has been poured to produce exceptionally smooth, highly detailed castings that are virtually free from bubble holes. All the NASCAR kits produced since 1984 have been either resin or multi-medium kits with resin bodies and baseplates.

Multi-medium models

Multi-medium kits were introduced in the mid-1990s, with resin, white-metal, machined metal and photo-etched parts all used to their best advantage. These kits will usually have resin body shells, interiors and baseplates, though sometimes white-metal baseplates are used to give added heft to a model. The resin castings can be highly detailed: engines cast in place with coolant lines and spark plug wires are not uncommon. Resin castings require much less clean-up and preparation than those done in white-metal. White-metal castings are used for small parts that must have some strength or need to be polished or chrome-plated; roll cages and interior bars, steering wheels, gearshifts, axle housings and other small, thin parts, for example. Wheels and hubs are often machined from aluminum and/or brass; hood pins may be machined or photo-etched; and thin, detailed parts like window nets, spoilers, windshield braces, roof-top trip strips and side skirts are almost always photo-etched. A well engineered multi-medium kit can be a joy to build and rival its larger 1/25 scale cousins in the amount of visible detail.

Development of 1/43-Scale Kits

In the Beginning

The development of 1/43-scale kits began in England as a cottage industry and spread to the Continent before reaching the United States. It's no surprise that almost all of the early model cars were European. The few American cars (Cunninghams and Nash-Healeys) had competed in the major European races. Most of the early manufacturers were racing enthusiasts, not businessmen, so the majority of early 1/43-scale kits were of racing, sports-racing and sports cars like Ferraris, Aston Martins and Jaguars. The first 1/43-scale white-metal kits were the Ferrari GTO and Porsche 904 made by Marc Europa, but production seems to have been limited to a literal handful of kits and built-up models. British Army Chaplain A.P. "Paddy" Stanley began producing larger numbers of white-metal kits of pre-WW II Grand Prix cars in the early 1970s.

But the industry as we know it was virtually created by yet another Englishman, John Day. Altogether, Day made more than 300 white-metal kits under several names. While Day's kits were instrumental in the development of 1/43-scale modeling (as opposed to collecting), only three of them were kits of NASCAR stock cars. The only other white-metal NASCAR kit in 1/43-scale is the fine 1952 Hudson Hornet made by the pioneering American company, Precision Miniatures.

The Golden Years: Resin Kits by Starter

A small French company, Starter, made a major contribution to the 1/43-scale hobby in the early 1980s when it introduced polyurethane resin kits. This resin would pick up the finest detail, could be sanded easily and would not shatter if a piece was dropped. Starter also developed very soft rubber molds that allowed complex, highly detailed castings to be made; part of the roll cage was cast in the *inside* of its body shells and the baseplate included the firewall, dashboard, seat, transverse roll-hoop and rear shelf. Starter also used pressure casting techniques to reduce the number and size of the bubble holes that had plagued resin castings up to this point. Starter proved that resin kits could not only produce much more highly detailed

Starter intended to model every NASCAR Championship car. Among the 26 kits of Championship cars were Richard Petty's 1964 and 1965 Plymouths, Bobby Isaac's 1970 Dodge, Cale Yarborough's 1978 Oldsmobile, Waltrip's Buicks from 1981 and 1982, Earnhardt's 1986 and 1987 Wrangler Chevrolet, Elliot's 1988 Thunderbird, Rusty Wallace's 1989 Pontiac, Earnhardt's 1990 and 1991 Lumina and Alan Kulwicki's 1992 Thunderbird. (photo by Moyer)

Develotech's kit (left) of Jeff Gordon's 1994 Brickyard 400 winner was the first highly detailed multi-medium 1/43-scale stock car kit, but its Thunderbird had serious flaws. The Monte Carlo (right) and Grand Prix kits from Renaissance are simply superb. (photo by Moyer)

models than their white-metal counterparts, but ones that were easier to build and cheaper. A number of factors influenced the rapid rise in the popularity of Starter's resin NASCAR kits and their even more rapid decline. Starter's effect on the hobby can be gauged from the fact that between November 1984 and June 1997, it produced 185 different 1/43-scale resin kits of NASCAR race cars. Two other French companies, Turbo and Provence Moulage, made a couple of resin kits of cars that competed in the short-lived NASCAR Le Mans class of the late 1970s and early-1980s; these kits are also included with this resin kit listing.

Multi-Medium Kits: Develotech and Renaissance

An American company, Develotech, was the first to produce a highly detailed multi-medium 1/43-scale kit of a NASCAR racer. Their kits had nicely cast resin bodies and baseplates, white-metal castings for the roll cage, interior, air ducts, chassis and frame components and a host of photo-etched parts that included the window net, skirts and trip strips. Develotech produced only five kits before disappearing from the 1/43-scale scene.

The French company, Renaissance, is the only 1/43-scale manufacturer currently making 1/43-scale kits of NASCAR cars. Their kits are the best NASCAR kits ever made in 1/43 scale, with excellent resin and white-metal castings, the best roll cage in the 1/43-scale industry and photo-etched wheel centers that have been stamped to the correct shape. Renaissance kits are superb. At this writing, however, only four kits have been released with three more to be announced. Brian Harvey, proprietor of Grand Prix Models, one of the world's largest 1/43-scale hobby shops and editor of the British magazine *Four Small Wheels*, said: "Renaissance production is very slow because the company is virtually a one-man band. Etienne Dhont does everything and so his production will always be slow." Based on the first releases, Renaissance NASCAR kits will definitely be worth the wait.

1/43-Scale Stock Car Kits: Collector's Items?

Given the flourishing collector's market for out-of-production plastic kits of stock cars and the VERY limited production runs of 1/43-scale kits, it would be reasonable to expect old kits to command premium prices. That's not the case, however. Only a few kits have appreciated and many can now be found at model swap meets or in publications like *Trader's Horn* for less than their original price. The same holds true of most 1/43-scale kits. Brian Harvey said: "Very few older kits have any value. There are few *collectors* for them and there seems to be no marque or label loyalty except for AMR kits. A few old kits of special-interest cars—for example, the Disney Band Porsche 962—command higher prices, but very few ever do."

In the latter part of the 1980s the American market for these kits was strong because Starter made kits of cars that plastic kit manufacturers could not afford to produce. Some of the Starter kits, especially the early Bill Elliot cars with full Coors graphics and early Dale Earnhardt cars, reached three-figure values. However, by the end of the decade the after-market decal industry made it possible to model an even wider range of NASCAR racers in the more familiar (to American modelers) 1/25 scale and at about half the cost. The introduction of American-made resin 1/25-scale bodies that had never been available in plastic also hurt the demand for 1/43-scale kits. Today, values of even those desirable Starter NASCAR kits have fallen to about half of their peak value. Values quoted should be taken as a general guide. Condition of the kit and how badly the buyer wants it establish the true value.

Stock Car Kits in 1/43 Scale

Develotech

This American company deserves credit for introducing the first multi-medium 1/43-scale NASCAR kits. The firm's kit of Jeff Gordon's 1994 DuPont Lumina included a complete white-metal roll cage, accurate driver seat, electronics boxes and fire bottle, cooling ducts from window scoops to mechanical components and all the new aerodynamic devices, including the roof flaps. Among the many photo-etched parts were the window net, hood pins, skirts and trip strips, window braces, straps and retaining clips. Those with a critical eye noted that the windshield and roof weren't quite right and the body was just a bit too wide, but, all in all, Develotech's Lumina was well received. But Develotech's next kit, the 1994 Thunderbird, was a disaster. Its body just didn't look right from any angle and many of the photo-etched parts simply didn't fit. News of the kit's flaws circulated quickly among the small close-knit fraternity of American 1/43-scale modelers and dealers found they couldn't give the kits away. Aside from decal variations of these two kits, no further kits have been released by Develotech.

Develotech 1/43-scale Stock Car Kits

Year	Make/Model	Sponsor	#	Driver	Release Date	Value
1994	Chevrolet Lumina	DuPont	24	Jeff Gordon	1996	$20.00
1994	Ford Thunderbird	Miller	2	Rusty Wallace	1996	$20.00
1994	Ford Thunderbird	Budweiser	11	Bill Elliot	1996	$20.00
1994	Ford Thunderbird	Valvoline	6	Mark Martin	1996	$20.00
1995	Ford Thunderbird	McDonald's	94	Bill Elliot	1996	$20.00

John Day

John Day successfully adapted the centrifugal casting techniques of the custom jewelry industry to produce a model car with a detailed one-piece, rounded body shell and then made large numbers (as many as 2,000 of some kits, according to a 1996 interview with Day) of each kit. John Day kits are relatively crude by today's standards and the scale fidelity of some are questionable, but every 1/43-scale kit made today can trace its ancestry straight back to John Day's first white-metal kits. Although the vast majority of 1/43-scale model builders in the 1970s wanted sports cars and Formula One models, John Day created a fairly extensive line of Indianapolis 500 winners and tried his hand at models of NASCAR stock cars as well. John Day's kits of David Pearson's #21 Ford Torino, Richard Petty's 1976 #43 Dodge Charger and A.J. Foyt's 1976 #28 Chevelle were the first 1/43-scale NASCAR kits produced. Like many John Day kits, the stock cars suffered most from rather crude decals with some of the major graphics drawn freehand. Replacing the kit decals with more modern art-work can make a good-looking model from an old John Day kit.

John Day's stock car kits were simple and easy to build, but the graphics, like those on Foyt's Chevelle, were often crude. Using modern decals and Bare-Metal® Foil, as was done on this John Day kit of Petty's 1975 Charger, results in a very pleasing model. (photo by Moyer)

John Day 1/43-scale Stock Car Kits

Year	Make/Model	Sponsor	#	Driver	Release Date	Value
1976?	Ford Torino	Purolator	21	David Pearson	1977	$20.00
1976	Dodge Charger	STP	43	Richard Petty	1977	$20.00
1976	Chevrolet Chevelle	Gilmore	28	A.J. Foyt	1977	$40.00

Precision Miniatures

Precision Miniatures' Hudson Hornet was the first really well-made 1/43-scale kit of a NASCAR stock car. "The Hudson almost drove Lloyd Asbury nuts," said Gene Parrill, Asbury's partner in this California company. "It took almost two years to develop the casting techniques and to find the right alloy to let him cast such a large body to our standards." Those standards were high; this 20-year old kit will hold its own with current models. Precision Miniatures didn't start out to produce a NASCAR model; Parrill had learned to drive in a 1952 Hudson Hornet and wanted a model of his car. Once the street model had finally been made, the NASCAR Fabulous Hudson Hornet kit was produced to get more return from the investment in this model. Fine castings, excellent detail and great decals make it possible to build a very good model from this kit. With the almost total lack of early NASCAR models, this kit should be in much greater demand than it seems to be.

Precision Miniatures' 1952 Hudson Hornet was far ahead of its time in terms of casting quality and is still a fine kit by today's standards. (photo by Moyer)

Precision Miniatures 1/43-scale Stock Car Kits

Year	Make/Model	Sponsor	#	Driver	Release Date	Value
* 1952	Hudson Hornet	Hudson	6, 92	2 drivers	1982	$45.00

* Decals for two cars; drivers are Marshall Teague/Herb Thomas

Provence Moulage

Provence Moulage is the *other* French resin kit manufacturer. Although the company competed ferociously with Starter for home market sales, Provence Moulage made very few kits aimed primarily at foreign markets. Provence Moulage has concentrated heavily on models of Le Mans cars and did make kits of two Camaros that ran in the Le Mans NASCAR class. These resin kits are easy to build and produce fine models of some of the first cars to carry the NASCAR banner outside the United States. Provence Moulage also made a fine kit of the 1963 Ford Galaxie (more accurate than the Starter version) that simply overwhelmed the competition in British Saloon Car Championship racing. The company also made a beautiful kit of the NASCAR-ized Oldsmobile 88 that Herschel McGriff drove to win the Large Sedan class in the very first Mexican Road Race. That kit was marketed under the Tron label.

Provence Moulage made these two kits of Camaros that ran in the NASCAR class in the 1982 Le Mans 24-Hours. (photo by Coulter)

Provence Moulage 1/43-scale Stock Car Kits

Year	Make/Model	Sponsor	#	Driver	Release Date	Value
1950	Oldsmobile 88 *	Seattle	52	Herschel McGriff		$50.00
1963	Ford Galaxie **	None	84	Dan Gurney		$50.00
1982	Chevrolet Camaro***	Sea-Air	80	Hagan/Felton	1988	$30.00
1982	Chevrolet Camaro***	Sea-Air	81	Brooks/McGriff	1988	$30.00

* Mexican Road Race, sold under Tron name

** British Saloon Racing Series

*** Le Mans NASCAR Class

Renaissance

The multi-medium Renaissance kits are not just the only NASCAR kits currently being made in 1/43 scale, but they are by any standards simply the best NASCAR kits ever made in this scale. Their resin body shells and baseplates are beautifully detailed and require very little cleanup and the white-metal castings are equally good. Somehow Renaissance manages to cast the roll cage as one 3-D metal piece—one that is already formed to shape and has the correct bulge in the side rails. Many tiny pieces, like the hood pins, are machined to shape; tiny photo-etched locks

and cables fit over the machined pins. Each windshield brace is made from two photo-etched pieces. The list goes on. In spite of their complexity, Renaissance kits are not difficult to build because everything fits well. All this makes them expensive; a collector can buy a couple of the Revell Collection diecast models for the price of a single Renaissance kit. However, a well-built Renaissance kit is simply the best stock car model seen yet in 1/43 scale, outside of a few one-off masterpieces created by master craftsmen like Derek Brown and Peter Doebeli.

Renaissance 1/43-scale Stock Car Kits

Year	Make/Model	Sponsor	#	Driver	Release Date	Value
1995	Chevrolet Monte Carlo	Kodak	3	Sterling Marlin	1995	$75.00
1995	Chevrolet Monte Carlo	DuPont	24	Jeff Gordon	1996	$60.00
1996	Pontiac Grand Prix	STP 25th Annvrs.	43	Bobby Hamilton	1997	*
1996	Pontiac Grand Prix	STP	43	Bobby Hamilton	1998	*
1996	Pontiac Grand Prix	Pennzoil	30	Johnny Benson	**	
1996	Pontiac Grand Prix	Hooters	1	Rick Mast	**	
1996	Pontiac Grand Prix	Coors	42	Kyle Petty	**	

Still available

** *Announced but not available yet*

Starter

They're like peanuts—you can't have just one. The golden era of 1/43-scale stock car models began in November 1984 when a French company, Starter, released a polyurethane resin kit of Dale Earnhardt's 1983 Wrangler Thunderbird. There were a couple of factors in the sudden interest in Starter's NASCAR models. "TV coverage of every round of the Winston Cup Championship via satellite helped to create Euro-

pean interest in NASCAR racing," said Brian Harvey. At that point in time Formula One racing had degenerated into a parade in which the driver on the pole either won the race or broke down. A typical NASCAR race might have more on-track passes for the lead than would be seen in an entire F.1 season. Suddenly, Continental racing fans were seeing events in which the lead might be exchanged several times on a single

Starter's list of NASCAR kits includes models like Tiny Lund's 1963 Daytona 500 winner, the winged Dodges, almost all of Richard Petty's cars, Bill Elliot's Million Dollar Thunderbird and more. (photo by Moyer)

These Starter models trace Alan Kulwicki's career from his first Quincy's car to the Zerex T-Bird with which he won his first race (and initiated the Polish Victory Lap) to the Hooters T-Bird he drove to win the 1992 Championship. The models also illustrate the development of the Thunderbird. (photo by Moyer)

lap and as many as 20 to 30 times during the course of a race. The second factor was American interest. A review of Starter's Wrangler Thunderbird appeared in the July/August 1985 issue of *FineScale Modeler* and a feature story on Starter's second kit, Bill Elliot's Million Dollar 1985 Coors Thunderbird was in the Sept/Oct issue of *Scale Auto Enthusiast*.

American modelers took to these small but very nicely detailed, colorful and easy-to-build miniatures in sufficient numbers that Starter, which typically released 10 to 12 new kits every *month*, sometimes offered as many as four new stock car kits a month from 1986-1996. Starter's kits at first were those of current NASCAR competitors, but in the early 1990s they began a program to model all the NASCAR Championship cars as well as all the Daytona 500 winners. Their line eventually encompassed 185 kits ranging from the 1959 Chevrolet of Junior Johnson to the 1997 Thunderbird of Rusty Wallace and included all the NASCAR Champions from 1964 through 1996 with the exception of David Pearson's 1966 and 1969 Fords.

Many of these were simply decal variations; to the eyes of the French craftsmen who made the master models for Starter, one NASCAR Thunderbird looked just like another. The minor differences between cars of different teams were ignored and it took American enthusiasts quite a while to make Starter aware of the differences between short track and superspeedway bodies used by the same team.

Philippe Roche, Starter's marketing manager, quickly developed a rapport with many American NASCAR enthusiasts. Modelers would shoot photographs of the latest NASCAR cars and new color schemes with an eye towards the requirements of kit production and send them to France. In return, when a new kit was produced, those who had provided data to Starter would find a couple of kits in their mailbox. After making a couple of serious errors (Mario Andretti's 1967 Fairlane stretched to the overall length of a '65 Galaxy and Junior Johnson's Daytona-winning *Impala*—Johnson really drove a Biscayne), Roche began asking selected American modelers for assistance. He received photos, dimensional data and, in some cases, detailed drawings from Americans and used this information to

make more accurate models. European interest in NASCAR racing diminished, according to Harvey, "Because of sporadic TV coverage in subsequent seasons and boredom." Without the week-to-week drama of the Winston Cup chase, European enthusiasts lost interest in watching brightly colored cars, none of which they recognized, go round in circles—somewhat the same reaction many Americans expressed about F.1 races of that period.

The increasing numbers of more traditional (and less expensive!) 1/25 scale plastic kits from American manufacturers and, more importantly, a burgeoning industry producing after-market alternative decals for these kits, cut into the American market for Starter kits, as well. When Roche passed away in June 1994, his successor at Starter made little attempt to continue the working relationship with American enthusiasts. Errors resulted; roll cages were not updated, important sponsor graphics were omitted if there was a hint of licensing problems (Roche had, with one exception, treated the growing licensing problem with typical Gaelic indifference) and body shells weren't brought up to current standards. Starter achieved a new low by simply putting Monte Carlo front and rear clips on their Lumina body, ignoring the fact that the windshield, rear quarter windows and rear window were all quite different from the Lumina. Starter's 1996-1997 Chevrolet kits were the most inaccurate models the company ever made, and they ignored comments to that effect from American customers. Starter produced only four NASCAR kits in 1997, ending the NASCAR's golden years for 1/43-scale modelers.

In passing, it needs to be noted that licensing problems did drive Starter to offer some kits, most notably those of Bill Elliot's 1987 and 1988 Championship Motorcraft Thunderbird and Harry Gant's Bandit (Starter's names for these models), without the primary sponsor decals. Although they were never widely publicized, Starter did offer a set of three decal sheets. Scattered through these were bits and pieces, a "C" on one, "oo" on another and "rs" on yet another sheet. When pieced together, these *random scraps* fitted perfectly and provided the missing graphics.

Starter never officially produced Bill Elliot's 1988 Coors Thunderbird. The 1988 Champion kit had no Coors decals or driver's name, but these could be found on a set of Starter after-market decals. (photo by Moyer)

Box Colors: Starter's Color Codes

Most Starter kits are found in red and white boxes, which denote standard production models. That, for Starter, was usually about 400-500 copies of a kit; ironically, this was governed by the production of decal sheets. The economics of decal printing make about 500 sheets the minimum number to produce, so Starter would make enough kits to use up one batch of decals, reserving some for spares, of course. If the kit sold out quickly, Starter might produce a second run of 300-400 kits, but this rarely (if ever) happened with their stock car models. Blue and white Starter boxes denote a limited production kit; Brian Harvey said, "But no one—not even the shops—were ever told how many of any limited production kits were ever made." Finally, larger green and white boxes were used for double kits, one box with two complete kits, like Bobby Allison's Miller Buicks. Some double kits included unique accessories like the motorized pit carts used by the Jaguar teams at Le Mans, but there is no record of similar accessories being included with NASCAR models.

The Scarcest Starter Stock Car

Starter made just a few stock car models in factory-built form only and among these was Fireball Roberts' 1963 Ford Galaxie. These factory-built models did not sell well at all and the model was quickly dropped from their line. Roche sent a few decal sheets for this model to American builders who'd helped with the research, and it turned out to also contain the decals for Roberts' 1964 Ford, a model that Starter never released in either kit or factory-built form. The decals, of course, do fit any of its 1964 Ford kits and produce the perfect companion to the factory-built 1963 model. Probably less than a half-dozen copies of this decal sheet found their way to the United States; at this writing, only two 1/43-scale models of Fireball's '64 Galaxie are known to exist.

As noted, Starter usually printed more decal sheets than what were used in a typical production run of a kit. These surplus decals were sometimes offered to retailers, who made them available to their customers. Bill Coulter used a set of decals from Starter's 1989 Pontiac Kodiak Grand Prix on one of its '86 Grand Prix 2+2 kits to create a unique model of Rusty's 1987 Kodiak car. Similarly, the decals from the 1970 Petty Ford Talladaga could be used, with some Letraset letters, on the body shell from the Pearson straight Torino to model the car Petty drove to win the 1970 Riverside race, his first victory in a Ford. Because of the small number of 1/43-scale kits made, there are virtually no after-market 1/43-scale NASCAR decal sets except for a sheet of 1990s sponsor decal.

Starter only made "Fireball" Roberts 1963 Galaxie as a factory-built model. They printed decals to make the 1964 car (right) as well, but never produced it. A VERY small number of decal sheets were released and this is one of two models of Roberts' '64 Galaxie known to exist. (photo by Moyer)

Simple decal swaps make it possible to make accurate 1/43-scale models that Starter never produced. The decals for Rusty Wallace's 1989 Pontiac Grand Prix (left) were applied to one of its '86 Grand Prix 2+2 kits to make this unique model of Rusty's 1987 Kodiak-sponsored car. (photo by Coulter)

Starter 1/43-scale Stock Car Kits

Year/Make/Model	Sponsor	#	Driver	Rel. Date	Value
1979 Chevrolet Monte Carlo	Hawaiian Tropic	1	Donnie Allison	4/94	$30.00
1996 Pontiac Grand Prix	Hooters	1	Rick Mast	3/97	$30.00
1980 Chevrolet Monte Carlo	Curb Records	2	Dale Earnhardt	5/ 93	$35.00
1992 Pontiac Grand Prix	Miller Genuine Draft	2	Rusty Wallace	12/92	$30.00
1994 Ford Thunderbird	Miller Genuine Draft	2	Rusty Wallace	1/95	$30.00
1996 Ford thunderbird	Miller	2	Rusty Wallace	7/96	$35.00
1997 Ford Thunderbird	Miller Lite	2	Rusty Wallace	6/97	$35.00
1987 Chevrolet Monte Carlo Aero Coupe	Wrangler	3	Dale Earnhardt	11/87	$40.00
1988 Chevrolet Monte Carlo Aero Coupe	Goodwrench	3	Dale Earnhardt	9/88	$30.00
1990 Chevrolet Lumina	Goodwrench	3	Dale Earnhardt	11/90	$35.00
1991 Chevrolet Lumina	Goodwrench	3	Dale Earnhardt	2/92	$30.00
1992 Oldsmobile Cutlass	Team USA	3	Kerry Teague	11/92	$20.00
1993 Chevrolet Lumina	Goodwrench	3	Dale Earnhardt	3/94	$30.00
1994 Chevrolet Lumina	Goodwrench	3	Dale Earnhardt	12/94	$35.00
1989 Oldsmobile Cutlass	Kodak	4	Rick Wilson	4/90	$25.00
1991 Chevrolet Lumina	Kodak	4	Ernie Irvan	1/92	$30.00
1994 Chevrolet Lumina	Kodak	4	Sterling Marlin	4/94	$35.00
1995 Chevrolet Monte Carlo	Kodak	4	Sterling Marlin	6/95	$35.00
1986 Chevrolet Monte Carlo Aero Coupe	Levi Garrett	5	Geoff Bodine	7/86	$30.00
1994 Chevrolet Lumina	Kellogg's	5	Terry Labonte	7/94	$30.00
1996 Chevrolet Monte Carlo	Kellogg's	5	Terry Labonte	4/97	$20.00
1969 Dodge Charger Daytona	Dodge	6	Buddy Baker	1/93	$30.00
1990 Ford Thunderbird	Folgers	6	Mark Martin	12/90	$30.00
1992 Ford Thunderbird	Valvoline	6	Mark Martin	7/92	$30.00
1995 Ford Thunderbird	Valvoline	6	Mark Martin	12/95	$35.00
1988 Ford Thunderbird	Zerex	7	Alan Kulwicki	3/87	$45.00
1991 Ford Thunderbird	Hooters	7	Alan Kulwicki	6/92	$50.00
1991 Ford Thunderbird	U.S. Army	7	Alan Kulwicki	5/91	$40.00
1992 Ford Thunderbird	Zerex	7	Alan Kulwicki	3/93	$50.00
1994 Ford Thunderbird	Exide	7	Geoff Bodine	12/94	$25.00
1996 Ford Thunderbird	QVC	7	Geoff Bodine	12/96	$30.00
1988 Buick Regal	Miller High Life	8	Bobby Hillin Jr.	10/88	$30.00
1991 Buick Regal	Snickers	8	Rick Wilson	5/92	$25.00
1972 Plymouth GTX	Housby Racing	9	Pete Hamilton	3/93	$25.00
1985 Ford Thunderbird	Coors	9	Bill Elliot	2/85	$100.00
1987 Ford Thunderbird	Motorcraft	9	Bill Elliot	6/94	$30.00
1988 Ford Thunderbird	Motorcraft	9	Bill Elliot	4/94	$45.00
1992 Ford Thunderbird	Mayflower	9	Chad Little	1/95	$30.00
1990 Chevrolet Lumina	Purolator	10	Derrike Cope	7/90	$40.00
1994 Ford Thunderbird	Tide	10	Ricky Rudd	11/94	$30.00
1965 Ford Galaxie	Richmond Ford	11	Ned Jarrett	7/94	$35.00
1967 Ford Fairlane	Bonnell	11	Mario Andretti	4/92	$25.00
1968 Ford Galaxie	Bonnell	11	Mario Andretti	7/92	$30.00
1969 Ford Talladega	Don Wagner Ford	11	A.J. Foyt	11/92	$35.00
1971 Dodge Charger	Dodge by Petty	11	Buddy Baker	1/94	$30.00
1972 Dodge Charger	STP	11	Buddy Baker	2/93	$30.00
1973 Chevrolet Laguna	Kar-Kare	11	Cale Yarborough	5/94	$25.00
1976 Chevrolet Laguna S-3	Holly Farms	11	Cale Yarborough	8/93	$35.00
1977 Oldsmobile Cutlass 4-4-2	First National City	11	Cale Yarborough	6/93	$35.00
1977 Chevrolet Laguna	Holly Farms	11	Cale Yarborough	10/93	$30.00
1981 Buick Regal	Mountain Dew	11	Darrell Waltrip	5/92	$30.00
1985 Chevrolet Monte Carlo	Budweiser	11	Darrell Waltrip	1/86	$35.00
1973 Chevrolet Laguna	Coca-Cola	12	Bobby Allison	1/94	$30.00
1985 Chevrolet Monte Carlo	Budweiser	12	Neil Bonnett	1/86	$35.00
1988 Buick Regal	Miller High Life	12	Bobby Allison	12/93	$30.00

Year/Make/Model	Sponsor	#	Driver	Rel. Date	Value
1991 Buick Regal	Raybestos	12	Hut Stricklin	12/91	$25.00
1993 Chevrolet Lumina	Kellogg's	14	Terry Labonte	10/93	$30.00
1978 Ford Thunderbird	Norris	15	Bobby Allison	5/93	$35.00
1984 Ford Thunderbird	Wrangler	15	Dale Earnhardt	11/84	$75.00
1987 Ford Thunderbird	Motorcraft	15	Ricky Rudd	1/88	$30.00
1990 Ford Thunderbird	Motorcraft	15	Morgan Shepherd	3/91	$30.00
1992 Ford Thunderbird	Motorcraft	15	Geoff Bodine	7/93	$25.00
1989 Buick Regal	Chattanooga Chew	16	Larry Pearson	4/91	$25.00
1992 Ford Thunderbird	Keystone	16	Wally Dallenbach Jr	10/92	$30.00
1994 Ford Thunderbird	The Family Channel	16	Ted Musgrave	6/94	$30.00
1968 Ford Torino	East Tennessee	17	David Pearson	9/91	$35.00
1987 Chevrolet Monte Carlo Aero Coupe	Tide	17	Darrell Waltrip	12/87	$30.00
1991 Chevrolet Lumina	Western Auto	17	Darrell Waltrip	10/91	$30.00
1996 Chevrolet Monte Carlo	Parts America	17	Darrell Waltrip	9/96	$25.00
1974 Dodge Charger	Boraxo	18	Joe Frasson	12/93	$25.00
1991 Chevrolet Lumina	Navy	18	Greg Sacks	5/91	$30.00
1992 Chevrolet Lumina	Interstate Batteries	18	Dale Jarrett	6/92	$35.00
1993 Chevrolet Lumina	Interstate Batteries	18	Dale Jarrett	8/93	$30.00
1995 Chevrolet Monte Carlo	Interstate Batteries	18	Bobby Labonte	10/95	$20.00
1993 Ford Thunderbird	Fina Lube	20	Joe Ruttman	11/93	$25.00
1963 Ford Galaxie	English Motors	21	Tiny Lund	2/94	$45.00
1968 Mercury Cyclone	60 Minute Cleaners	21	Cale Yarborough	3/92	$30.00
1972 Mercury Cyclone	Purolator	21	A.J. Foyt	4/91	$35.00
1972 Mercury Cyclone	Purolator	21	David Pearson	5/92	$30.00
1976 Mercury Montego	Purolator	21	David Pearson	8/93	$40.00
1984 Ford Thunderbird	Valvoline	21	Buddy Baker	5/85	$40.00
1987 Ford Thunderbird	Citgo	21	Kyle Petty	11/88	$30.00
1993 Ford Thunderbird	Citgo	21	Morgan Shepherd	3/94	$25.00
1996 Ford Thunderbird	Citgo	21	Michael Waltrip	11/96	$35.00
1969 Dodge Charger Daytona	Joe Britt	22	Bobby Allison	3/92	$30.00
1983 Buick Regal	Miller High Life	22	Bobby Allison	7/93	$35.00
1985 Buick Regal	Miller American	22	Bobby Allison	2/86	$30.00
1991 Ford Thunderbird	Maxwell House	22	Sterling Marlin	4/92	$30.00
1994 Pontiac Grand Prix	Maxwell House	22	Bobby Labonte	2/94	$30.00
1995 Pontiac Grand Prix	MBNA	22	Randy LaJoie	3/96	$25.00
1994 Ford Thunderbird	Smokin' Joe's	23	Hut Stricklin	3/95	$35.00
1991 Pontiac Grand Prix	U.S. Air Force	24	Mickey Gibbs	12/91	$25.00
1993 Chevrolet Lumina	DuPont	24	Jeff Gordon	4/93	$45.00
1995 Chevrolet Monte Carlo	DuPont	24	Jeff Gordon	9/95	$25.00
1964 Plymouth Belvedere	Plymouth	25	Paul Goldsmith	6/93	$30.00
1986 Chevrolet Monte Carlo Aero Coupe	Folgers	25	Tim Richmond	12/86	$45.00
1995 Chevrolet Monte Carlo	GMAC	25	Ken Schrader	1/96	$30.00
1964 Ford Galaxie	Ed Martin Ford	26	Curtis Turner	10/94	$45.00
1989 Buick Regal	Quaker State	26	Ricky Rudd	6/90	$30.00
1994 Ford Thunderbird	Quaker State	26	Brett Bodine	7/94	$30.00
1959 Chevrolet Impala	Daytona Kennel Club	27	Junior Johnson	10/92	$25.00
1969 Ford Talladega	Sunny King Ford	27	Donnie Allison	11/92	$30.00
1986 Pontiac Grand Prix 2+2	Alugard	27	Rusty Wallace	11/86	$30.00
1989 Pontiac Grand Prix	Kodiak	27	Rusty Wallace	10/89	$30.00
1993 Ford Thunderbird	McDonald's	27	Hut Stricklin	5/93	$30.00
1995 Ford Thunderbird	Little Caesar's	27	Elton Sawyer	2/96	$30.00
1963 Ford Galaxie (2 sets of Decals)	LaFayette Ford	28	Lorenzen/Gurney	6/94	$40.00
1965 Ford Galaxie	LaFayette Ford	28	Fred Lorenzen	9/94	$30.00
1977 Oldsmobile Cutlass 4-4-2	Napa	28	Buddy Baker	3/93	$30.00
1983 Pontiac Le Mans	Hardee's	28	Cale Yarborough	3/94	$30.00
1984 Chevrolet Monte Carlo	Hardee's	28	Cale Yarborough	1/93	$30.00
1985 Ford Thunderbird	Hardee's	28	Cale Yarborough	9/85	$40.00

Year/Make/Model	Sponsor	#	Driver	Rel. Date	Value
1987 Ford Thunderbird	Havoline	28	Davey Allison	6/88	$60.00
1991 Ford Thunderbird	Havoline	28	Davey Allison	9/91	$35.00
1995 Ford Thunderbird	Havoline	28	Ernie Irvan	11/95	$35.00
1964 Ford Galaxie	Ron's Ford Sales	29	Larry Frank	11/94	$30.00
1968 Ford Torino	Long-Lewis	29	Bobby Allison	11/93	$30.00
1969 Dodge Charger Daytona	Winter Park	30	Dave Marcis	6/92	$25.00
1989 Pontiac Grand Prix	Country Time/Post	30	Michael Waltrip	1/89	$25.00
1991 Pontiac Grand Prix	Pennzoil	30	Michael Waltrip	12/91	$30.00
1995 Pontiac Grand Prix	Pennzoil	30	Michael Waltrip	7/95	$30.00
1985 Chevrolet Monte Carlo	Skoal Bandit	33	Harry Gant	7/85	$45.00
1995 Chevrolet Monte Carlo	Skoal	33	Robert Pressley	4/96	$20.00
1986 Ford Thunderbird	Quincy's Steak House	35	Alan Kulwicki	3/93	$40.00
1970 Plymouth Superbird	7-UP	40	Pete Hamilton	6/91	$30.00
1993 Pontiac Grand Prix	Dirt Devil	40	Kenny Wallace	10/93	$25.00
1996 Chevrolet Monte Carlo	Kodiak	41	Ricky Craven	1/97	$20.00
1960 Plymouth Belvedere	Plymouth	42	Lee Petty	5/94	$35.00
1981 Buick Regal	STP	42	Kyle Petty	10/93	$30.00
1990 Pontiac Grand Prix	Peak	42	Kyle Petty	9/90	$30.00
1991 Pontiac Grand Prix	Mello-Yello	42	Kyle Petty	6/91	$30.00
1995 Pontiac Grand Prix	Coors Silver Bullet	42	Kyle Petty	9/95	$30.00
1974 Dodge Charger (2 sets of Decals)	STP	43	Richard Petty	8/75	$35.00
1964 Plymouth Belvedere	Patterson	43	Richard Petty	2/93	$35.00
1966 Plymouth Satellite	Plymouth	43	Richard Petty	10/93	$35.00
1969 Ford Talladega	East Tennessee	43	Richard Petty	10/91	$35.00
1970 Plymouth Superbird	Plymouth	43	Richard Petty	2/91	$40.00
1971 Plymouth GTX	Southern Chry/Plym	43	Richard Petty	4/92	$30.00
1972 Plymouth GTX	STP	43	Richard Petty	12/72	$35.00
1977 Oldsmobile Cutlass 4-4-2	STP	43	Richard Petty	12/92	$30.00
1978 Dodge Magnum	STP	43	Richard Petty	12/94	$35.00
1979 Chevrolet Monte Carlo	STP	43	Richard Petty	1/93	$35.00
1981 Buick Regal	STP	43	Richard Petty	11/92	$30.00
1985 Pontiac Grand Prix	STP	43	Richard Petty	12/85	$45.00
1986 Pontiac Grand Prix 2+2	STP	43	Richard Petty	3/87	$35.00
1989 Pontiac Grand Prix	STP	43	Richard Petty	11/89	$30.00
1994 Pontiac Grand Prix	STP	43	Bobby Hamilton	2/95	$30.00
1996 Pontiac Grand Prix	STP 25th Anniversary	43	Bobby Hamilton	6/96	$35.00
1984 Chevrolet Monte Carlo	Piedmont	44	Terry Labonte	3/85	$45.00
1993 Pontiac Grand Prix	STP	44	Rick Wilson	1/94	$30.00
1993 Chevrolet Lumina	Valvoline	46	Al Unser Jr.	11/93	$30.00
1985 Buick Regal	Valvoline	47	Ron Bouchard	5/86	$30.00
1992 Chevrolet Lumina	Ameritron	49	Stanley Smith	2/93	$20.00
1994 Chevrolet Lumina	Country Time	51	N. Bonnett/J. Purvis	1/95	$25.00
1990 Pontiac Grand Prix	Alka-Seltzer	52	Jimmy Means	6/93	$30.00
1993 Ford Thunderbird	NAPA	52	Jimmy Means	2/94	$30.00
1993 Ford Thunderbird	Jasper/U S Air	55	Ted Musgrave	1/94	$30.00
1992 Ford Thunderbird	Trop-Artic	66	Jimmy Hensley	3/93	$25.00
1959 Chevrolet Impala	Rigers Esso	67	David Pearson	2/93	$20.00
1970 Dodge Charger Daytona	K & K Insurance	71	Bobby Isaac	11/91	$45.00
1991 Chevrolet Lumina	Coast Guard	71	Dave Marcis	7/91	$25.00
1971 Mercury Cyclone	Pop Kola	72	Benny Parsons	1/92	$25.00
1973 Chevrolet Laguna	Union 76	72	Benny Parsons	4/93	$35.00
1975 Chevrolet Laguna S-3	Kings Row Fireplace	72	Benny Parsons	7/93	$30.00
1977 Oldsmobile Cutlass 4-4-2	First National City	72	Benny Parsons	2/94	$30.00
1989 Pontiac Grand Prix	Valvoline	75	Morgan Shepherd	12/89	$30.00
1991 Oldsmobile Cutlass	Dinner Bell/Food Lion	75	Joe Ruttman	12/92	$25.00
1994 Ford Thunderbird	Factory Stores	75	Todd Bodine	4/95	$25.00

Year/Make/Model	Sponsor	#	Driver	Rel. Date	Value
1988 Buick Regal	Miller High Life	84	Dick Trickle	12/93	$30.00
1959 Chevrolet Impala	Thor	87	Buck Baker	2/93	$20.00
1975 Chevrolet Laguna S-3	Gatorade	88	Darrell Waltrip	12/93	$30.00
1981 Buick Regal	Gatorade	88	Darrell Waltrip	4/93	$30.00
1982 Buick Regal	Gatorade	88	Bobby Allison	4/93	$30.00
1991 Pontiac Grand Prix	Marines	88	Buddy Baker	11/91	$25.00
1996 Ford Thunderbird	Ford Quality Care	88	Dale Jarrett	5/96	$40.00
1976 Ford Torino	Truxmore	90	*	3/94	$25.00
1992 Ford Thunderbird	Hellig-Meyers	90	Bobby Hillin Jr.	6/93	$25.00
1990 Oldsmobile Cutlass	Sunoco	94	Sterling Marlin	1/91	$25.00
1991 Chevrolet Lumina	Ferrari of Los Gatos	96	Phil Parsons	12/91	$30.00
1996 Pontiac Grand Prix	Sterling Cowboy	97	Chad little	10/96	$30.00
1969 Mercury Cyclone	Jim Robbins Spl.	98	L.R. Yarborough	2/92	$30.00
1969 Ford Talladega	Jim Robbins Spl.	98	L.R. Yarborough	6/92	$30.00
1993 Ford Thunderbird	Bojangles	98	Derrike Cope	12/93	$25.00
1966 Plymouth Satellite	Plymouth	99	Paul Goldsmith	2/94	$25.00
1968 Ford Torino	Ron's Ford	121	Dan Gurney	3/91	$35.00

Le Mans NASCAR Category

Turbo

This small French company made only a few 1/43-scale kits, but one was the big Dodge Charger that Herschel McGriff drove in the NASCAR class at the 1978 Le Mans 24-Hours. While not officially a Grand National car, it does make a very interesting companion to the Provence Moulage/Tron kit of McGriff's 1950 Mexican Road Race Oldsmobile, which was for all intents a NASCAR-ized Olds.

Turbo 1/43-scale Stock Car Kits

Year	Make/Model	Sponsor	#	Driver	Release Date	Value
1976	* Dodge Charger	Olympia Beer	4	Herschel McGriff		$35.00

Le Mans NASCAR Category

Building a 1/43-scale Stock Car Kit—The Basics

Since there were so few white-metal stock car kits and even fewer after-market decals available to transform diecast models into NASCAR racers, we'll concentrate on the basics of building resin and multi-medium 1/43-scale kits. Actually, the skills and techniques required to build one of these kits are no different than for conventional plastic kits, though some of the tools (especially the glues) are a little different.

We'll show the basics for one of Starter's simple stock car models and then expand on them during construction of a multi-medium Renaissance kit.

Tools and Materials

Unlike modern plastic kits, 1/43-scale models will almost always require some clean-up and preparation of the parts before the actual construction can begin. The

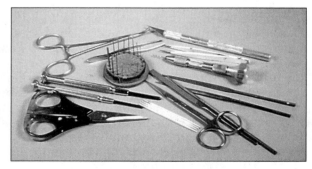

The basic tools required to build a 1/43-scale model are simple and in-expensive; a hobby knife, small scissors, some tweezers and holding tools, miniature screwdrivers, files and emery boards and a pin vise with a set of miniature drill bits. (photo by Moyer)

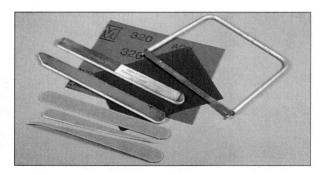

Much of the preparation of a resin kit consists of sanding mold lines and feed tags. Wet-or-dry sandpaper and emery boards are readily available, while better hobby and mail-order shops carry both multi-grit sanding sticks and Flex-I-File sets. (photo by Moyer)

relatively soft rubber molds used to make resin and white-metal parts will almost always leave some mold parting lines on body shells and small pieces and possibly some thin flash (resin or metal that's been forced out between the mold faces) in the windows, roll hoop or around the fender openings and around both sides of smaller pieces. Older kits will have larger mold lines, more flash and possibly some bubble holes that need to be filled, while newer kits from major manufacturers often have flawless surfaces with the molds designed so that all parting lines fall on edges of the castings.

The tools needed for 1/43-scale models are really very simple. A modeling knife (X-Acto type) will be needed to do rough trimming or cut parts from their trees and will work on both resin and white-metal. I save old blades that are too dull for plastic kits to use when working with white-metal parts. I do almost all the rough sanding on resin pieces with ordinary emery boards. These can be cut to a point with scissors to get into tiny openings. Small, fine-tooth modeler's files in flat, knife, half-round and round shapes will be required for metal parts and will work on resin, too. Wet-or-dry sandpaper (320-, 400- and 600-grit) should be used to smooth out file and emery board marks. Other necessities include tweezers (a couple of styles/sizes), small scissors, some holding tools like clothespins or forceps, toothpicks, paintbrushes and the usual miscellaneous modeling tools. One tool I've found to be very useful is a Flex-I-File set; the coarse grit strip will work on both metal and resin.

Resin/metal kits differ from plastic kits in two important areas. First, regular plastic model cement will not work on these kits; you'll need to use either alpha cyanacrylate (ACC or a super glue) or epoxy to hold major components together and a clear water-based adhesive like Micro Kristal Klear for windows and tiny trim pieces. Second, it will be necessary to prime the parts before painting them. Finally, putty may be needed to fill larger bubble holes or surface blemishes; I recommend a two-part epoxy putty (A + B in the U.S., Milliput in Europe) or a catalyzed spot putty like Euro-soft since lacquer-based auto putties will continue to shrink for months—epoxies and cata-

lyzed putties cure instead of drying with attendant shrinkage that will show up long after your model is completed.

Preparation

Always examine a kit as soon as you get it to make sure you have all the parts. Remember, only a few hundred of these kits were made and the manufacturer doesn't have space to keep spare parts for hundreds of kits on hand for years. Most of the major kit makers are very good about supplying missing pieces—and possibly even one you've fouled up beyond all recall—but only in the months right after release of a kit. When you're ready to build, read the instructions, even if they consist of only a drawing and words in a language you can't read (not uncommon with 1/43-scale kits) and be sure you know where everything fits.

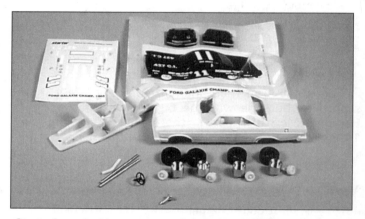

Starter's resin kits are very simple but include a surprising amount of very well done detail. Add accurate lines and excellent decals and it's easy to see why they became so popular. (photo by Moyer)

A Starter kit is pretty simple with just a body shell (part of the roll cage may be cast on the inside), baseplate with dash, seat, rear shelf and the transverse roll hoop, metal wheels with resin inserts to make the correct style spider, rubber tires and maybe a few smaller pieces. These make good-looking models right out of the box and provide plenty of room for those who like adding details to the roll cage, seat belts, windshield braces and other visible areas.

Remove the mold lines from the body (inside and out, if necessary) with emery boards or files, then sand the filed areas with #320 and #400 sandpaper. Thicker flash can be cut away with a razor knife and the Flex-I-File comes in very handy for smoothing rounded castings like the roll cage bars. Thin flash and rough edges like those in wheel arch openings can be simply sanded smooth with #320 sandpaper wrapped around a finger.

Build up as much of the model as possible before putting on the first primer coat. I like to attach spoilers (*if* they are to be painted the same color as the body), additional roll cage details and similar pieces before priming because glue bonds to resin more strongly than to primer. A small drill (about #60) should be used in a pin vise to make a pilot hole for the screws

Resin and white-metal kits require either epoxy or super glues. Two-part quick curing putty will speed up the building process and give better results. Finally, both resin and metal kits should be primed before color coats are sprayed on. (photo by Moyer)

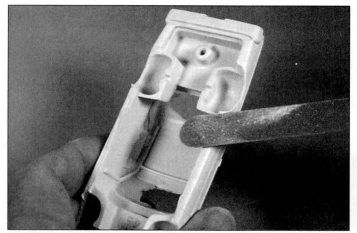

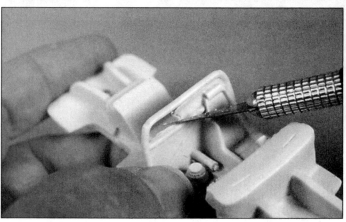

Thin flash in windows and the thicker flash usually found in the roll hoop of Starter models should be carefully cut away with a sharp hobby knife. (photo by Moyer)

Small mold lines and feed tags (the end on the runner through which the resin was poured) can be quickly and easily sanded off with an emery board. (photo by Moyer)

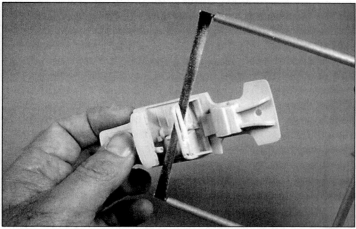

The rough edges left when flash is cut out must be sanded smooth. Emery boards can be cut down to fit into tight corners, but the Flex-I-File is ideal for sanding both sides of the roll hoop tubes. (photo by Moyer)

that attach the baseplate to the body—the cast-in holes are never deep enough. Don't use a power tool—it's too easy to get carried away and drill right through the body shell. The final step in preparation is washing the pieces to remove both the mold release agent and oils from your fingers. I first soak the pieces in warm water and dish-washing detergent for a half-hour (or more) and then scrub them thoroughly with an old toothbrush before rinsing in hot water.

Priming, Filling and Painting

White-metal castings must be primed before being painted. Although it's possible to paint resin parts without first priming them, the primer coat makes it easy to see (and fix) those minor surface blemishes that are almost impossible to spot in the bare casting. Primer should be sprayed on—I prefer using an airbrush but aerosol cans will work; be very careful to apply thin coats to avoid filling all that delicate surface detail. Be sure that the primer and paints you select will be compatible—don't use an enamel primer if you plan to use lacquer paint. I recommend primers formulated specifically for models—the pigment grains are ground finer, which means that less sanding will be required to get a good smooth primer surface.

The first primer coat will often show surface blemishes—bubble holes and nicks you didn't see and even file marks that weren't sanded smooth. Small holes can be filled with a drop or two of thick, partially dried primer; larger holes need to be filled with putty. An artist's palette knife works very well for applying

A pallet knife works well for applying putty to large flat areas, but a toothpick will work very nicely when filling small spots of tiny bubble holes. (photo by Moyer)

putty to large spots and a toothpick cut to a chisel edge is perfect for working putty into small spots. Very tiny blemishes, surface ripples and file marks can be eliminated by simply sanding the surrounding area down to bare resin, leaving primer as a filler in the blemish. Once any rough spots are filled and sanded smooth, either spot-prime or completely re-prime the model as needed. If no blemishes are visible, sand the primer surface smooth and the model is ready for the color coats. I use the 2400- and 3200-grit cloths from one of the model car polishing kits for this task.

There have been several good magazine articles on painting. Pat Covert's excellent book, *The Modeler's Guide to Scale Automotive Finishes*, covers the subject in detail, so I'll just say that a smooth primer surface and five or six thin coats of paint, rather than a single heavy one, are the secrets to a good paint job. Another handy trick is to use different kinds of paint (i.e., acrylic, enamel and lacquer) where overpainting and touch-up are required. Water-based acrylics can be applied over both lacquer and enamel (and vice versa) without eating into the paint under it, and excess paint can be removed with a toothpick.

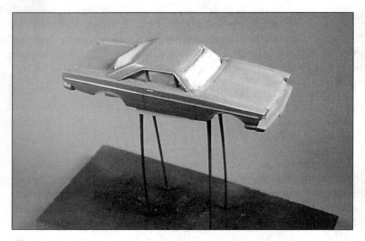

The interior has been painted and masked and the model is mounted on a spray stand for the color coats. (photo by Moyer)

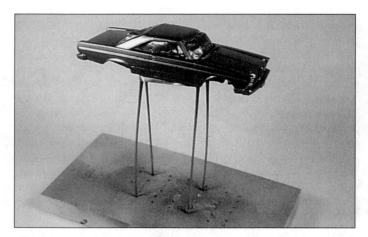

The spray stand is used while applying color coats, too. The spring action of the legs makes it easy to take the body shell off to sand between coats of paint. (photo by Moyer)

The interior of this model is a good example; the inner body panels appear to be unpolished aluminum, the floor and roll cage are light gray, and the seat, dash and rear shelf are flat black. I began by spraying the inside of the body with Tamiya acrylic Flat Aluminum and the baseplate/interior casting with Model Car World Dove Gray. When that was dry I masked off the interior and mounted the body on a simple spray stand so it could be turned and twisted while the model was sprayed. After the first couple of coats of Ford Guardsman Blue MCW lacquer were applied with my airbrush, the surface was lightly sanded with 3200- and 4000-grit sanding cloth before each following coat was applied.

In spite of masking, there was some overspray inside the body shell. The acrylic aluminum paint can be brushed on over the blue lacquer with no problems. If some gets on the outer edges or the windows it can be polished away with no damage. (photo by Moyer)

The internal roll bars can be painted by hand, then touched up as necessary. (photo by Moyer)

After the final body coat was dry the masking tape was removed. It wasn't possible to mask the interior perfectly where roll cage bars were close to the windows, so there was some overspray. More Flat Aluminum acrylic was brushed over the dark blue overspray and when that was dry the integral roll cage bars were painted with the Dove Gray lacquer. My hand-painting is far from perfect, but using different kinds of paint makes touchup very quick and easy. If I'd used lacquers for both the aluminum and gray, each coat would have eaten into the one below it, producing a muddy silver-gray wherever any touch-up was done. Plan ahead before you start to paint!

Those Little Extras

Starter's models have enough detail to make very nice display models when built right out of the box, but there is a variety of after-market photo-etched pieces, decals and ordinary items that can be used to make them even more realistic. We'll look at some simple but effective additions to a model of Ned Jarrett's 1965 NASCAR championship Ford. One of the easiest and most effective things you can do is to use different shades of the same correct color in the interior. I used Model Master Flat Black on the firewall, dashboard and rear shelf, a semi-gloss black for electrical boxes and the rubber gearshift boot and Pactra Scale Black (a noticeably more gray shade), for the upholstered seat and steering wheel rim. The instrument panel portion of the dash was painted with the Tamiya acrylic Flat Aluminum, which did not affect the black enamel under it; individual decal gauge faces were added using after-market decals.

Starter never provides a gear shift; I make then from a ball-headed pin (the kind you find in a new shirt) bent to shape. The most visible deficiency is seat belts. There's a good selection of photo-etched belts and belt hardware available and the belts can be simply cut from masking tape and painted in the appropriate color. I find it even easier to use Chart-Pak

tape, especially the crepe variety which really looks like fabric. It's available at good art supply stores in a variety of colors and widths. Finally, although the 1965 roll cage was pretty simple compared to those in today's stock cars, it should have a few more pieces than Starter included. I used Evergreen Plastic 1/16-inch plastic rod to make the outer perimeter bars, the internal diagonal brace and the rear braces which were added after the interior was attached to the body. It took less than an hour to make these simple additions but they add a *lot* of life to the interior.

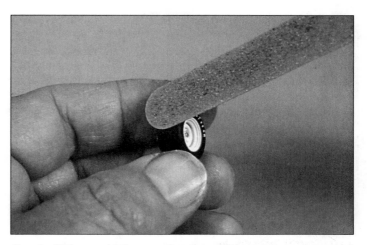

Sand off the mold line on the tires with an emery board. A few minutes spent painting the well-done details in Starter's wheels will enhance the looks of your finished model. (photo by Moyer)

Starter's wheels and tires are nice, but a few minutes' work will make them even better. After painting and assembling the wheels, I painted the lug nuts silver and the exposed hubs steel. A simple, but effective way to paint the tiny lug nuts is to wet the end of a toothpick in silver paint and lightly touch the raised lug nut. Just moisten the end of the toothpick; a visible drop of paint on its end is way too much. Sand away the mold line on the tire with an emery board and then apply the sidewall decals. When those are dry, brush a thin coat of acrylic (water-based) semi-gloss clear over the entire tire sidewall and decal. This serves two purposes—it seals the decal to the rubber tire so it won't fall off in a few months, and it blends the shiny decal into the less shiny rubber tire. If you can't find clear semi-gloss, mix a 60/40 ratio of clear flat and clear gloss. Realistic wheels and tires really improve a model, so these easy steps are well worth doing. Those who want even more detail can add wheel weights (a tiny dab of flat aluminum paint) and valve stems (stretched plastic sprue), though you'll probably break a few #75 drill bits making holes in the hard steel rims.

Current NASCAR racers have virtually no chrome, but back when the series started they really were *stock cars*, and it was all there. It didn't take long for NASCAR to realize that a 10-foot long chrome side-

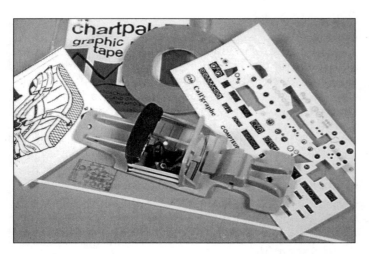

Chart-Pak tape can be used with after-market photo-etched hardware to make very realistic seat belts and decal gauge faces are available in several styles. Plastic rod is perfect for adding more roll cage bars. (photo by Moyer)

spear could become just that when it came off in a 150 mph crash. By the 1960s, most trim that could be torn off in a crash was required to be removed. Still, NASCAR's mid-1960s stock cars had chrome bumpers, grilles, window surrounds and door handles, even though the doors were welded shut. There are some pretty good chrome paints available, but since all those parts are molded integrally on a Starter body, they'd have to be brush-painted.

Bare-Metal foil can be used to chrome-plate the cast-in trim on a Starter body. With practice, even complex bumpers and tiny items like door handles can be very realistically plated with Bare-Metal foil. (photo by Moyer)

Nothing looks more like chromed metal than chrome metal foil, and that's where Bare-Metal Foil comes in. It's easy to do the window surrounds by applying wide strips of foil, buffing it down and then *very* gently running a sharp (new) X-Acto knife blade around the relief-cast trim. Then simply peel away the excess metal and buff the foiled trim again. With a little practice, more complex shapes can be plated with foil. The grille was done by laying a piece of foil over one half, buffing it down and then running the tip of a toothpick (indispensable little things) gently down each groove. The other half was done the same way with just a tiny overlap at the peak of the grille and a flat black wash was applied so that the grille didn't look like a solid chrome piece. Even the bumpers and door handles were plated with Bare-Metal, though the former had to be done with several small pieces due to the complex shape.

Until the mid-1990s, Starter's decals were simply superb. It wasn't unusual to cover more than half of the body with well fitting decals that were completely opaque and responded well to a strong decal solvent. Decals produced from 1995 on were often brittle and tended to break apart when dipped in water. Some of the older sheets may become brittle with age, too. Test a piece of the decal (Starter's name, for instance); if there's any doubt, coat the entire decal sheet with Micro Super Film. You'll then have to cut closely around each decal, but they will stay in one piece.

Starter's decals can be over-sprayed with clear gloss, but remember that race cars in the 1960s and 1970s didn't have the super-shiny finishes that are possible with today's catalyzed paints! I very gently waxed the body of Jarrett's Ford after the decals were dry, giving the decals virtually the same gloss as the body, and they really look right.

Micro Kristal Klear works very well for gluing clear glass in place. It doesn't get brittle like white glue and also fills any small gaps. (photo by Moyer)

Adding the most visible details, like the windshield braces, takes just a few minutes' work and makes a Starter kit look even more realistic. (photo by Moyer)

Later Starter kits (such as this Jarrett example) are made so that the vacuformed glass fits from the outside. Cut each piece oversize, then trim it carefully while checking the fit. When it just drops into place, paint a bead of Micro Kristal Klear around the opening and hold the window in place while the Kristal Klear sets up. Photos show two interior window braces in Jarrett's car; those were made from pieces of Plastruct's smallest tee and glued in place before the windshield was added. I used black dry-transfer stripes for the rear window straps, but decal stripes or pieces of tape will work equally well.

Final Assembly

Although some kits provide an assembly sequence, Starter's instructions are simply photos of the finished model. That's no problem since the kits are so simple; look everything over and think about what parts must fit where before gluing anything. I prefer to use super glues for assembly because they set quickly and need only a very thin film of glue between the pieces. Super glues can be hazardous—sloppy application can lead to fingers glued to the model (or worse places). I use the thickened super glues because their application can be controlled better and because their 30-second curing time makes it possible to tweak the alignment of a part (I always have a bottle of de-bonder on my bench!). Epoxy is the only other reasonable alternative—it's safer, but does take at least five minutes to set and leaves a noticeable thickness of glue between the pieces.

Ride height, the distance a model sits above the ground, is a subject that's too often ignored or over-emphasized for full-bodied cars. When building models of full-bodied cars, it's the relationship of the wheel/tire to the fender openings that really determine whether or not a model looks right when complete. The biggest villain here is the thickness of the fenders; on the real car they are only a few thousandths of an inch thick. Look at photos; tires are usually pretty much centered in the wheel arches and tucked up inside the lower edge of the fender. Glue the axle into one wheel, cut it slightly longer than the final length and test-fit the wheels to the body. I often enlarge the axle mounting hole both vertically and fore- and aft so that the wheel can be located within

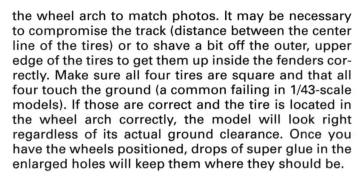

the wheel arch to match photos. It may be necessary to compromise the track (distance between the center line of the tires) or to shave a bit off the outer, upper edge of the tires to get them up inside the fenders correctly. Make sure all four tires are square and that all four touch the ground (a common failing in 1/43-scale models). If those are correct and the tire is located in the wheel arch correctly, the model will look right regardless of its actual ground clearance. Once you have the wheels positioned, drops of super glue in the enlarged holes will keep them where they should be.

Finished!

These few additional details make Starter's model look very realistic, though I spent less than 20 hours in building it. My finished model captures the look of Jarrett's car very well. With the chrome-plated bumpers and door handles, there's no clue to it's small size. Although the extra interior detail isn't visible from some angles, I enjoy knowing that it's there if someone wants to look closely.

It's easy to add even more detail; photo-etched hood pins are available in several styles, as are window clips and window nets for later cars. But Starter's kits give you the option of building a very good-looking display model right out of the box, adding just enough additional detail with a couple of hours more work or going all-out to build a competition masterpiece.

Chrome-plated bumpers, and grille and windshield trim, along with braces and detailed wheels, all help to make Starter's '65 Ford a very realistic miniature that gives no hint of its small size. (photo by Moyer)

With or without additional added details, Starter's '65 Galaxie makes a fine model of Ned Jarrett's last championship ride. (photo by Moyer)

Colorful, accurate, easy to build and very limited production—it's easy to see why Starter's NASCAR kits were so popular! (photo by Moyer)

Building a 1/43-Scale Multi-Medium Stock Car Kit

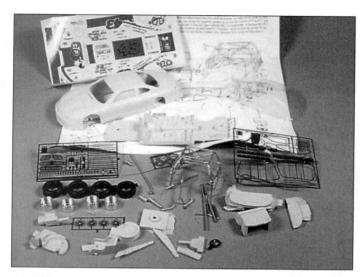

Multi-medium kits like this Renaissance Pontiac Grand Prix include white-metal castings and a wealth of photo-etched detail parts. (photo by Moyer)

Although it's probably a surprise to the typical American model car builder, photo-etched parts were first introduced in a 1/43-scale kit (Precision Miniatures' Ferrari Lusso) and p.e. after-market parts were available for 1/43-scale models long before they were introduced for larger scales. While 1/43-scale sports car and Formula 1 kits routinely included photo-etched wheels, seat belt hardware and small detail parts, none were included in stock car kits until the first Develotech kits were released. Sticker shock at Develotech prices decreased when modelers realized that the price of a multi-medium kit was less than that of a Starter kit plus the after-market sets of p.e. hood pins, window nets, windshield clips and retainers and seat belt hardware needed to bring a resin kit up to these new standards. We'll use one of the latest Renaissance kits, the 1996 STP Pontiac Grand Prix, to illustrate techniques for building multi-medium kits.

Preparation

Although the resin body, baseplate/interior and small parts are just like those of a resin kit, the Renaissance kit includes a white-metal roll cage and trees of both brass and chrome photo-etched parts. Some heavy brass trees may make it necessary to use sharp finger-nail scissors or miniature shears to cut the parts free, but using a flat surface and sharp knife to remove the pieces from thinner trees is less likely to result in damage to adjacent parts. I simply lay the tree on an old piece of 1/4-inch thick plate glass and cut the runner as close to the part as I can. Be *sure* to hold the part being cut free; otherwise it may simply disappear into the distance when the final runner is cut. A small paintbrush or a toothpick can be used to hold down parts that are too small for fingers.

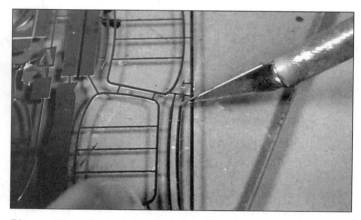

Place a tree of photo-etched parts on a smooth flat surface (plate glass is perfect) and carefully cut the part away from its runners with a sharp knife blade. (photo by Moyer)

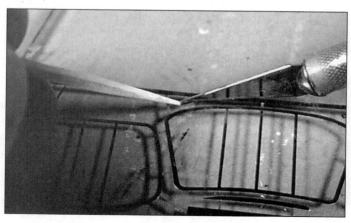

Always hold the part being cut free; if it's too small to hold with your finger, try a wooden toothpick. (photo by Moyer)

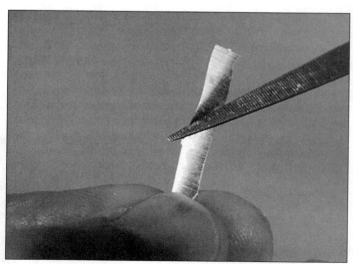

Unless the piece is very thin, you'll see a tag where the runner was cut. Take the time to file these smooth. (photo by Moyer)

It's almost impossible to cut loose any pieces (except for the thinnest p.e. pieces) without leaving a ragged tag at the cut. Take the time to file these smooth with modeling files *before* fitting them to the model.

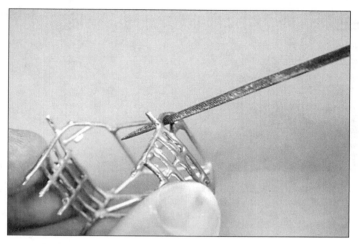

The very complex roll cage casting has both some thin flash and small mold lines on all the tubes. These can be easily removed with modeling files. (photo by Moyer)

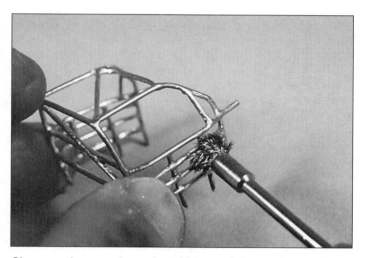

Clean-up time can be reduced by careful use of a small soft wire bush in a Dremel Tool. (photo by Moyer)

Any white-metal casting will have mold lines; the more complex the casting, the more mold lines you'll find. It's no surprise that the one-piece, three-dimensional roll cage casting in this kit has both some minor flash and mold lines. This is why you need a variety of file shapes; flat or knife files will do much of the clean-up on this casting, but there are places where half-round and round files are necessary. White-metal is soft and these tubes are tiny, so some care is needed not to bend them too much. However, a bent white-metal casting can be bent back to its original shape without breaking. A small, *soft* wire brush chucked into a Dremel Tool will remove small mold lines even more quickly than a file.

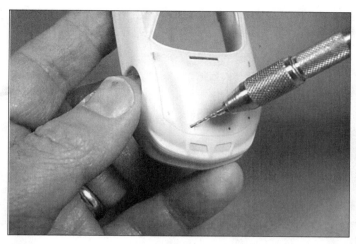

Open up any mounting holes before painting the model. The tiny indentations in the resin body were neither big enough or deep enough to let the machined hood pins sit flush with the hood. (photo by Moyer)

Don't assume that all those tiny parts will fit. In this case, the holes for the hood and trunk pins were simply indications of where they should go. The holes were made wider and deeper with a pin vise and bit to allow the tiny machined pin bases to set flush with the surface. You don't want to do this after all the painting is finished. Any small parts that will be painted in the body color should be attached before the first coat of primer, too.

NEVER apply super glue straight from the bottle when you're trying to glue a small piece in place. At best you'll wind up with a puddle of glue and more likely the part will wind up attached to your tweezers or your finger! A toothpick that's been sharpened to a chisel point (for applying a line of glue) or a point (for a small dot) makes a fine glue applicator. Put a drop of glue on a smooth surface, dip the toothpick in that and then use it to apply a *small* amount of glue just where you want it. If possible, I use tweezers to set the

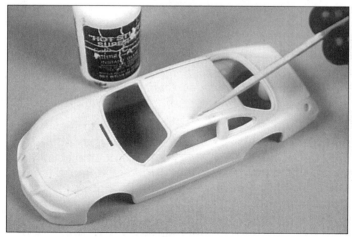

Small amounts of super glue can be neatly applied with a toothpick that's been cut to a chisel shape or point, as needed for the task. (photo by Moyer)

part in place. Using slower-setting thick super glue allows plenty of time to get the part in place and make sure it's lined up correctly.

Model-maker's pliers, especially a flat-nosed pair like this, are useful for folding photo-etched pieces. (photo by Moyer)

Many etched pieces will need to be bent to shape, and I've found that wide flat-nosed modeler's pliers are particularly useful for folding small pieces. Larger ones can be bent while holding a metal straight-edge along the engraved fold line.

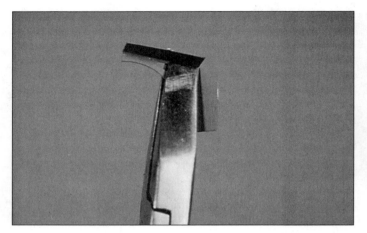

Renaissance provides beautiful 3-D photo-etched seat belt hardware, but no belt material. Chart-Pak tape is available in several colors and makes very realistic belts. (photo by Moyer)

Other parts like seat belts and instrument panels may be 3-D etched (put through the chemical milling process twice to produce 3-D surfaces) to make it easy to pop-out the chrome hardware. Do not prime these pieces, simply paint them flat or satin black; when dry, carefully scrape the paint from the raised surfaces with a knife blade. If you remove too much paint, touch the piece up and do it again. The kit's photo-etched seat belt hardware was used with Chart-Pak tape to make very realistic belts.

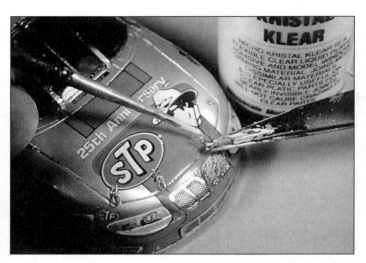

Larger photo-etched parts, like the nose screens, should be attached with super glue or epoxy, but Kristal Klear works very well for small pieces that won't be handled very much. (photo by Moyer)

Never use super glue on clear plastic pieces or anything that's glued to them. Kristal Klear was used to hold the windshield straps and clips in place, though small amounts of clear epoxy could also have been used. (photo by Moyer)

Final Details: The End Is In Sight!

Many of the smaller photo-etched detail pieces must be applied after the model is painted and assembled. I try to add larger photo-etched pieces first, then the smaller ones. If you aren't comfortable with super-glue, or are gluing something to a clear part, use small amounts of clear paint or Kristal Klear to glue the piece to the body. Neither is as strong as glue, but they are definitely easier to clean up if you make an error. Apply a small dot of Kristal Klear with a fine paint-brush and then carefully put the p.e. part in place. I never use anything but Kristal Klear to glue pieces like the windshield straps and hold-down clips to the clear glass pieces; super-glue will usually leave a large white spot on clear plastic.

Pieces that are too small to be handled with tweezers can be picked up with sticky sticks (small sticks with a gum on their end, or a toothpick with Blu-Tack or a similar sticky substance stuck on the end) or even with a toothpick whose point is wet. Lift the part carefully and then touch the part to the dot of glue and make any minor adjustments (30-second setting time, remember) with the point of a knife.

The beauty of these photo-etched pieces is their delicacy. If they are carefully applied (no glue smudges) there's no hint as to the model's scale. This 1/43-scale model is only about 4-1/2 inches long, but everything is very much in-scale, and there's no clue to its true size.

Multi-medium kits produce beautifully detailed models; this STP Pontiac is only about 4-1/2 inches long! Everything you see was included in the kit. (photo by Moyer)

The Future of 1/43-Scale Stock Car Models

There's little doubt that the good old days of 1/43-scale stock car modeling were the late 1980s, when Starter was releasing two to four new kits every month. It's not likely we'll ever see that again, even though building 1/43-scale models of other types of cars, both street and competition, continues to be a very active part of the model car hobby. The availability of quality diecast models like the Revell Collection Series also hurt the collector side of the hobby; why buy a $50 kit when you can get two very well made and detailed diecasts for the same price? However, the licensing problems now being encountered by the American after-market decal manufacturers and the sale of the Revell Collection series to another manufacturer may change this. Remember that almost all 1/43-scale kits are made in very small numbers (only 100-300 copies) by small shops in Europe. If it becomes impossible for American companies to fill the demand for 1/25 scale NASCAR stockers in a wide variety of markings, the small 1/43-scale manufacturers may once again step in to fill the void. Meanwhile, there's a new Renaissance kit every once in a while and a *lot* of older Starter kits still out there at bargain prices.

Happy 1/43-scale modeling!

Chapter 4

Stock Car Model Kits in 1/32nd Scale

Comparison of same subject in two scales. The R-M Cartoon Network/Flintstones Chevrolet Monte Carlo in two scales: 1/24th-scale kit No. 2484; and 1/32nd-scale kit No. 1707.

The R-M Olympic/Goodwrench Chevrolet Monte Carlo in two scales: 1/24th-scale kit No. 2483; and 1/32nd-scale kit No. 1706.

Among the popular model car building scales, the lack of interest in 1/32nd scale in the United States may be one of the great mysteries of our age. Like the other even-number scales that are divisible by the No. 2, 1/32nd scale is one of many architectural scales. Popular in England, Europe and Japan, this scale has never met with much success in the United States.

Undeniably the most popular U.S. scale is 1/25, which, by many perspectives, could be deemed as a "bastard" scale (indivisible by two). The 1/32 scale is neither too small, as many criticize the 1/43rd for; or too large, as some builders dislike about 1/24th.

This in-between scale remains very popular for static builders elsewhere in the world, but it is of greatest interest in this country by the legions of hardy diehards still engaged in slot-car racing. The greatest percentage of 1/32-scale stock car model kits sold today are bought by slot racers. The body and trim parts, along with the decals, are cannibalized from the kit and the remainder of the parts and pieces are discarded.

The first dedicated stock car model kits of note are a line of four items from Industro-Motive Corporation (IMC). Ironically enough, these first four 1965 models in 1/32nd scale were originally offered as body kits for slot racing. The quartet proved so popular that a tray-type interior with driver figure, a generic chassis, wheels and tires were developed as a common unit that would fit all four body shells. Though the bodies were dead-stock, the lack of stock interiors, wheel covers or correct chassis limited them to being only built as race cars.

This first grouping was followed up in the late-1960s with a pair of similarly appointed pieces from IMC. The same formula and concept was followed as before. A 1969 Charger 500 body shell along with a standard 1969 Ford Torino fastback were the choices. The generic chassis, etc., was used again for both items. The absence of authentic decals in either kit and the lack of any alternatives from the after-market pretty much limited the success of these excellent examples of the two primary corporate competitors on the race track. It is also puzzling that IMC would kit the limited production Dodge Charger 500 while ignoring the '69 Torino Talledaga in favor of the standard model. Go figure.

There was little activity in this scale for the stock car builder until the early 1990s. In an attempt to find a scale, a simpler degree of kit design and lower pricing, both Revell-Monogram and Ertl/AMT introduced a line of 1/32nd scale NASCAR stock cars.

Both lines have their plusses and minuses. R-M gets the nod for accurate looking body shells.

Ertl/AMT gets the nod for a parts layout more in line with the way larger stock car kits are designed. R-M uses a more realistic wheel/tire design, while Ertl/AMT is the choice of most builders since its kits feature genuine water-slide markings. The stickers contained in the R-M kits limit their appeal to the most novice builders.

Over the last 30 years, there have been a few items of note from MPC and some street-stock kits that could be converted into oval track race cars. The limiting factor for all but the really skilled and dedicated stock car modelers is the almost total lack of any accurate 1/32nd scale decals for virtually any racing era.

1/32nd-Scale Price Guide

Ertl/AMT

Stock #	Car #	Sponsor/Car	Value
8707	No. 4	92 Kodak Lumina	$16.00
8708	No. 22	92 Maxwell House Thunderbird	$15.00
8709	No. 43	92 STP Pontiac	$15.00
8712	No. 44	93 STP Pontiac	$16.00
8721	No. 21	93 Citgo Thunderbird	$15.00
8722	No. 10	93 Purolator Lumina	$15.00
8723	No. 26	93 Quaker State Thunderbird	$15.00
8727	No. 42	92 Mello Yello Pontiac	$15.00
8728	No. 18	92 Interstate Lumina	$15.00
8729	No. 6	92 Valvoline Thunderbird	$16.00
8730	No. 15	92 Motorcraft Thunderbird	$15.00
8799	No. 66	92 Phillips 66 Thunderbird	$15.00

Ertl/AMT 1/32nd-scale Snapfast Interstate Batteries Lumina kit No. 8728 and Motorcraft Thunderbird kit No. 8730.

A pair of Ertl/AMT 1/32nd-scale Snapfast Pontiac Grand Prix kits, STP No. 8709 and Mello Yello No. 8727.

IMC (Industro-Motive Corporation)

Stock #	Car #	Car	Value
181	No. 88	65 Ford Galaxie	$35.00
182	No. 54	65 Plymouth Fury	$35.00
183	No. 17	65 Pontiac Grand Prix	$35.00
184	No. 66	65 Chevrolet Impala	$35.00
185	No. 98	69 Ford Torino	$40.00
186	No. 6	69 Charger 500	$40.00

Built model of IMC 1/32nd-scale 1965 Ford Galaxie kit No. 181.

Built model of IMC 1/32nd-scale 1965 Plymouth Fury kit No. 182.

Built model of IMC 1/32nd-scale 1965 Pontiac Grand Prix kit No. 183.

Built model of IMC 1/32nd-scale 1965 Chevrolet Impala kit No. 184.

IMC 1/32nd-scale 1969 Dodge Charger 500 kit No. 186.

IMC 1/32nd-scale 1969 Ford Torino Cobra kit No. 185.

IMC kits No. 185 and 186, 1969 Dodge Charger 500 and 1969 Ford Torino Cobra.

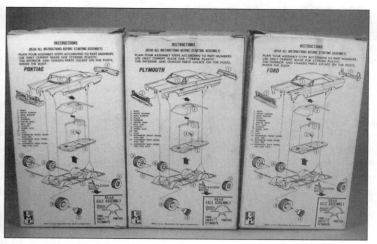

The building instructions for the IMC series of 1965 stockers is conveniently located on the back panel of the kit box as shown here.

The assembly is simple and the number of parts few in the typical IMC 1/32nd-scale 1965 stock car kit series as shown here.

Three of IMC's 1965 1/32nd-scale stock car kits: Ford Galaxie No. 181, Plymouth Fury No. 182 and Pontiac Grand Prix No. 183.

MPC (Model Products Corporation)

Stock #	Car #	Car	Value
1-3230	No. 77	82 Buick Regal	$30.00

MPC 1/32nd-scale mid-1970s Buick Regal kit No. 1-3230.

Revell-Monogram

Stock #	Car #	Sponsor/Car	Value
1086	No. 28	92 Texaco Thunderbird	$15.00
1087	No. 6	92 Valvoline Thunderbird	$12.00
1088	No. 3	92 Goodwrench Lumina	$32.00
1089	No. 12	92 Raybestos Lumina	$12.00
1090	No. 3	Goodwrench Race Set (tractor and trailer)	$55.00
1091	No. 28	Texaco Race Set (tractor and trailer)	$27.00
1094	No. 68	93 Country Time Thunderbird	$12.00
1095	No. 26	Quaker State Thunderbird (Brett Bodine)	$11.00
1095	No. 26	Quaker State Thunderbird (Steve Kinser)	$11.00
1700	No. 2	94 Penske Racing Thunderbird	$12.00
1701	No. 27	94 McDonald's Thunderbird	$11.00
1701	No. 27	95 McDonald's Thunderbat Thunderbird	$11.00
1702	No. 24	95 DuPont Monte Carlo	$15.00
1704	No. 24	DuPont Race Car Hauler (tractor and trailer)	$25.00
1705	No. 3	Goodwrench Monte Carlo	$12.00
1706	No. 3	Goodwrench/Olympics Monte Carlo	$15.00
1707	No. 29	Cartoon Network Chevrolet Monte Carlo	$12.00
1708	No. 88	Quality Care Ford Thunderbird	$10.00
1709	n/a	Goodwrench Service Race Rig (tractor and trailer)	$22.00
1712	n/a	Hot Wheels Race Rig (tractor and trailer)	$15.00
1713	No. 5	Monsters Chevrolet Monte Carlo	$11.00

Revell-Monogram 1/32nd-scale Quality Care/Red Carpet Leasing Ford Thunderbird kit No. 1708.

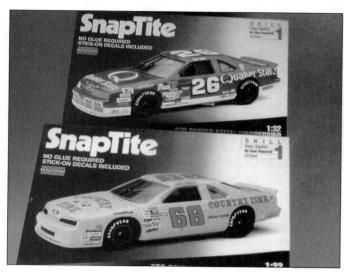

Revell-Monogram 1/32nd-scale DuPont Race Rig transporter kit No. 1704.

Revell-Monogram Snaptite 1/32nd-scale Ford Thunderbirds, Quaker State kit No. 1087 and Country Time kit No. 1086.

Revell-Monogram Snaptite 1/32nd-scale Ford Thunderbirds, McDonald Thunderbat kit No. 1701 and Quality Care/Red Carpet Leasing T-Bird kit No. 1708.

Built model of Revell-Monogram 1/32nd-scale Texaco Havoline Ford Thunderbird kit No. 1086.

Revell-Monogram Snaptite 1/32nd-scale Ford Thunderbirds, Valvoline kit No. 1087 and Texaco Havoline kit No. 1086.

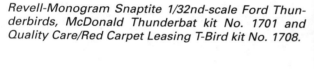

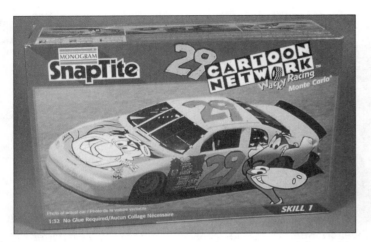

Revell-Monogram Snaptite 1/32nd-scale Cartoon Network/
Flintstones Chevrolet Monte Carlo kit No. 1707.

Built model of Revell-Monogram 1/32 scale Goodwrench
Chevrolet Monte Carlo kit No. 1088.

Revell-Monogram Snaptite 1/32nd-scale Chevrolet Monte
Carlos, Goodwrench kit No. 1088 and DuPont kit No. 1702.

Revell-Monogram Snaptite 1/32nd-scale Chevrolets,
Raybestos Lumina kit No. 1088 and Olympic/Goodwrench
Monte Carlo kit No. 1706.

The Revell-Monogram 1/32nd-scale Texaco Havoline Race
Rig transporter kit No. 1091.

The Revell-Monogram 1/32nd-scale
Hot Wheels Race Rig transporter kit
No. 1091.

Lindberg Stock Cars 500

(with generic racing accessories)

Stock #	Car #	Car	Value
391	No. 15	73 Pontiac Grand Am	$10.00
392	No. 21	73 Pontiac Grand Prix	$10.00
394	No. 7	73 Buick Century	$10.00

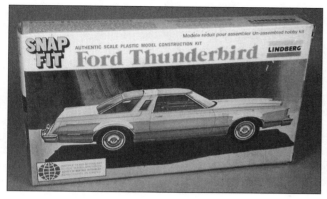

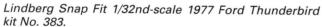

Lindberg Snap Fit 1/32nd-scale 1977 Ford Thunderbird kit No. 383.

Lindberg Snap Fit 1/32nd-scale 1977 Chevrolet Monte Carlo kit No. 365.

Revell

Stock #	Car #	Car	Value
H-1124	No. 23	76 Chevrolet Nova Snap-Together	$22.00

Other 1/32nd scale street-stock kits that could be modified into a race car:

Ertl/AMT

Car	Value
1955 Chevrolet Bel Aire	$5.00
1982 Chevrolet Camaro	$5.00
1982 Pontiac Firebird	$5.00

Revell-Monogram

Car	Value
1955 Chevrolet Bel Air	$5.00
1965 Pontiac GTO	$5.00

Lindberg

Model #	Car	Value
365	77 Chevrolet Monte Carlo	$12.00
378	77 Oldsmobile Omega	$8.00
383	77 Ford Thunderbird	$12.00
2112	No. 21, 69 Dodge Charger	$10.00
2113	77 Pontiac Grand Prix	$9.00

Pyro

Model #	Car	Value
C293	52 Chevrolet	$5.00

Building a 1/32nd Scale Stock Car

Leonard Carsner Works Wonders With a Revell-Monogram T-Bird

Probably the best approach for building a 1/32nd scale NASCAR Winston Cup car is to kit-bash the best parts from Revell-Monogram and Ertl/AMT kits. Admittedly this will require a bit more planning and more hand work but after all we do call ourselves model builders don't we?

Experienced builder Leonard Carsner agreed to build a 1/32nd scale stock car model and highlight the best approach to winding up with an attractive finished model. Carsner used a Revell-Monogram T-Bird as a basis for this project along with after-market paint and decals to wrap up the project.

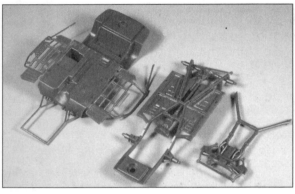

Shown here are the four main pieces comprising the typical R-M stock car kit engine. It is the same engine used in all makes of kit including both GM and Ford.

By contrast, the Revell-Monogram design bucks traditional stock car kit layouts with the roll cage molded to the floor pan and must be bent at an upright angle during assembly. Also combined into nontraditional subassembly groupings are the exterior floor pan with rear suspension attached and the lower front suspension, engine pan and exhaust system designed as a single unit.

An R-M Chevy Lumina is pictured with a T-Bird with a little added detailing. Study the picture carefully and see that subtle details can really add authenticity. These models were built by John Coulter and Leonard Carsner.

This finished specimen of the Revell-Monogram 1/32nd stock car kit line was built by Leonard Carsner. He describes it as a typical out-of-the-box effort. Similar models can be built using any other the various Thunderbird releases from R-M. The model features dry transfer tire lettering, wheel weights, valve stems and the requisite red line along each rim perimeter, window trim details and after-market markings.

A quick comparison of the chassis of a R-M stock car built straight from the box to the piece built by Carsner reveals how the detail painting of a few key components on the under side can add realism to the finished model.

The model with hood open (an advantage of the R-M series with a hinged hood). Though the R-M offerings feature a generic GM-style small block V-8, modifications to make it look more like a Ford engine are possible, as well as adding all the proper plumbing and electrical wiring.

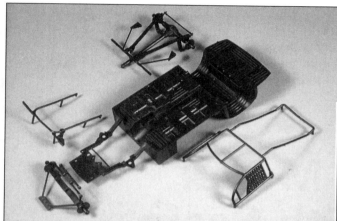

Inspecting the chassis and roll cage layout from a typical Ertl/AMT 1/32 scale stock car kit reveals the similarity of concept to such kits in larger scales. Here the roll cage, front hoop, suspension, etc., are individual assemblies which attach to the frame/floor pan.

Again, the parts arrangement and breakdown of the typical Ertl/AMT 1/32nd-scale stock car kit is very traditional with virtually all component pieces molded separately. By the way, there are two different engines in the Ertl/AMT kits: one for Fords and one for GM products.

Most serious stock car modelers agree that the R-M T-Bird body shell (top) is superior in proportions and accurate shape when compare to the Ertl/AMT offering (bottom).

Here the Ertl/AMT hood is on the left and the R-M hood is on the right. R-M has the advantage if you would like to be able to open and close the hood via hinges. The Ertl/AMT hood features registration pins allowing it to be snapped into place.

The R-M T-Bird shell is one piece with all panels, etc., molded onto the body. The Ertl/AMT shell comes in two pieces with the builder needing to attach the rear bumper.

One major limiting factor that many believe serious hampers building 1/32nd-scale stock cars is the lack of after-market markings. Here is a current project in progress by Leonard Carsner. Again the key element is the decal sheet pictured on the left.

Ertl/AMT kits feature water-slide decals while all Revell-Monogram kits contain peel-off markings.

Chapter 5

Stock Car Model Kits in 1/25th Scale

The actual plastic material to make model kits comes as a by-product from the distillation of petroleum. Just a few short decades ago, the cost-effective injection molding of polystyrene plastic was perfected, and the manufacturing of affordable plastic model kits became a reality for hobby product manufacturers and specifically the model building consumer.

Starting in the late-1940s and into the mid-1950s, companies like Monogram, AMT, Revell, Aurora, Lindberg, Palmer, Pyro, etc., were busy producing a wide range of plastic model kits of varying subjects in many different scales. But the big break for stock car model builders came with the introduction of what came to be called "annual kits" (those produced for a specific year and then updated annually), beginning with AMT in 1958. These model were done in 1/25th scale, which is the most popular and accepted building scale in the United States today. By many standards, 1/25th is a "bastard" scale, since virtually all other scales are even numbers, those divisible by 2.

The 1/25th scale came about for a number of reasons, including convenience and necessity. In the beginning, companies like AMT were first in the business of making sales promotional models for the auto industry. These plastic factory-built models were engineered from 1/10th-scale blueprints provided to AMT by each automobile manufacturer. This information was reduced 2.5 times to a size that would conveniently fit in a standard size paste-board box. That reduction was 1/25th scale and set the standard for a majority of the plastic model kits produced here for the next few decades.

The approximately 8-inch long models of a new '58 Chevy, Ford, Pontiac or Buick finally gave the race car model builder something substantial to work with in producing a NASCAR race car replica. Each kit contained a one-piece body shell, wheels and tires and interior, dashboard, steering wheel, chassis, bumper, grill and other accessories. Instead of working to convert an assembled plastic toy, the model builder now had a box full of separate parts that could be modified, painted and assembled to individual taste.

For at least another 10 years, building a model of an oval track racer would be solely the work of the individual hobbyist, since there were no specific race car kits. Models were brush-painted with whatever paint the builder could find. Any type of added detailing was up to the knowledge and imagination of each modeler. All markings were hand painted. There were no specific race car paints in spray cans or bottles, no kit or aftermarket decals, no accurate racing tires or wheels, etc. It remained a market segment yet undiscovered.

Building a stock car model was not something undertaken by anyone but the most skilled or daring builders. Eventually, some manufacturers included a roll bar, open wheels and generic water-slide numbers and sponsors decals…but these items weren't much help in building an accurate version of any specific stock car.

Things began to change a bit in the mid-1960s. Jo-Han Models (now owned by Seville) included the markings for Richard Petty's famous Daytona 500 winning race car in their 1964 Plymouth Sport Fury 1/25th scale kit. Richard Petty's Plymouth was actually a Belvedere, but the slight difference in body trim certainly didn't discourage long-suffering modelers. In 1965, AMT joined the fray. The original annual issue of AMT's '65 Ford Galaxie contained many racing hardware components. Most importantly, the kits included accurate markings for Fred Lorenzen's No. 28 Holman-Moody NASCAR racer!

By 1966, Jo-Han, MPC (Model Products Corporation, now merged with AMT under the Ertl banner) and AMT included in some of their kits various driveline, chassis and interior parts to aid NASCAR race car modelers. Occasionally, specific markings were part of the contents but this wasn't a general practice by the plastic kit manufacturers.

In 1972, stock car model builders got major league treatment from manufacturers like MPC. The relatively new company developed a continuing series of

1/25th-scale NASCAR stock cars which set new standards for this type of model kit. Included in the initial series were some 14 different, but specific, NASCAR race cars. There were three Richard Petty race cars, two Dodge Chargers and a Plymouth Road Runner. There was also a Jim Hurtubise Chevrolet Chevelle, a Coo Coo Marlin Chevy Monte Carlo, a David Pearson Pontiac GTO (with a clear plastic body shell), a Bobby Isaac '72 Ford Torino and a number of other variations on this basic tooling.

The MPC concept involved the use of a "one-size-fits-all" chassis. The whole line used body shells slightly modified from annual kit releases. The challenge here was that they all didn't have the same length wheel bases. A universal chassis with an adjustable length feature solved that problem. It was a neat concept, but the resulting chassis was not accurate. This expandable chassis was correct for the Ford Torino and Mercury Cyclone but incorrect for the Dodges and Plymouths as well as the Chevelles, Monte Carlos and Pontiacs. The final release in the original series ended with the sloped-nose 1976 Chevelle Laguna.

During this same period, AMT countered the new MPC releases with a Bobby Allison/Coca-Cola Chevrolet Monte Carlo. It was a popular subject but in its haste to get product on the market, the AMT 1972 Monte Carlo annual kit was literally "butchered" to make the race car. Today, this kit makes for a valuable collectible, but it's a hollow example of a true race car replica. This tooling was revised to kit a series of Chevelles through 1974 and 1975. AMT produced a decent likeness of the AMC Penske Matador in the mid-1970s. At best, the kit was a compromise, as the tooling was shared by the street-stock version of the car.

The mid-1970s also saw AMT produce three variations on the full-size Chrysler Kit Car concept in a 1/25th scale plastic kit. To represent the slightly different configurations between the NASCAR Sportsman and late model stock car chassis versions, AMT made both the 108-inch and 112-inch wheel base models as represented in the Dodge Dart Swinger and Dodge Dart Sport and Plymouth Duster. This series also included an ill-fated Petty race team release which contained the Dodge Swinger and a Ford conventional flatbed truck. These excellent kits were issued once and have not been seen since.

At the same time, Jo-Han Models developed a fairly accurate 1972 Ford Torino in 1/25th scale. The kit featured a flat hood which lacked the bulge representing the fake hood scoop which NASCAR rules would have required for the fastback body style. Many of the kit parts are well executed while others (the firewall, chassis and completely stock body shell) give the impression that this manufacturer took too many short cuts.

The 1970s saw a bonanza of stock-type race car kit series from both AMT and MPC. AMT produced a line of Eastern dirt track-style modified stock cars based around a Toby Tobias tubular chassis. There was a number of body shells available mounted on the

same chassis, roll cage and big-block Chevrolet drive line. These interesting kits were issued first in 1975 and weren't seen again until Ertl/AMT selectively reissued a few in original packaging as part of its Buyers Choice program. It's interesting to note that the Tobias chassis was originally developed for dirt track racing, but the kits all contain slick race tires.

MPC, not taking a back seat to anyone, brought forth an assortment of unique kit lines of stock-type race cars during this period. Four different kits in the series included a common chassis and drive line with a Pinto, Vega, '34 Ford and '36 Chevrolet body shells. These Southern-style NASCAR modifieds in miniatures featured '53-'57 Chevrolet passenger car-style chassis with either a GM or Ford big block power plant.

At about the same time, MPC brought out a series of short-track late-model stock cars called Super Stockers. The first releases were replicas of actual cars driven by name drivers like Don Gregory and Dick Trickle. Eventually the same standard chassis and drivetrain was used under a Pontiac GTO, Chevrolet Chevelle and Monte Carlo and Plymouth 'Cuda.

The fabricated perimeter-style chassis looked suspiciously like those built by Michigander Ed Howell's shops and the one constructed by Indiana's Ray Dillon. The engine was a late-model, big-block Chevrolet V-8 (not correct for the Trickle Mustang), which was used throughout the line. Again, one release is all these unique kits saw. Maybe the folks at Ertl can tell us if the tooling still exists.

During the late-1970s and early-1980s, while the popularity of NASCAR racing was growing rapidly, the domestic model kit market was stagnate due to the lackluster nature of annual production cars and the uncertainty of the availability of raw materials like plastic granules. When availability and the price of crude oil shot through the ceiling, it wasn't long before the shockwave was felt in the hobby industry. The 1979 energy crisis not only put a crimp in everyone's life style, it nearly put the plastic kit manufactures out of business.

In 1982, an ailing MPC made a feeble attempt to meet the increasing interest in NASCAR stock car models by adding current body shells to the old adjustable-chassis kits of the early-1970s and released them under the name "Southern Stockers." The first releases carried generic decals representing no particular race cars. Later, a Chevrolet Monte Carlo SS body shell was added to the line and specific race car versions were added. The regular rides of drivers like Rusty Wallace, David Pearson and Benny Parsons adorned the kit box art and water-slide decal sheets.

As a direst result of Revell-Monogram's initial release of new 1/24th scale stock car kit models, Ertl/AMT responded with a series of its own in 1/25th. At first, these kits were to be snap kits. Somewhere during the development stages, the assembly style was changed to glue kits. The kits were basic and simple to build, much like an unassembled promotional model. These crude miniatures (in the view of many) were no match for the competition. For the most part, consumers purchased many of these kits just for the water-slide decals, which, in some cases, depicted markings for race cars not available otherwise.

By the late-1980s, Ertl/AMT decided to commit to a series of full-fledged, glue-type kits of NASCAR stock cars. Many builders liked the attention to detail, such as the opening deck lid and full compliment of accessories in the trunk area (fuel cell, filler and overflow tubes). Some felt the kits fell short in the execution of the individual body shells. The 1989 through 1997 Ford Thunderbirds was one of the series that came off as the least accurate when compared to references.

When NASCAR debuted the Craftsman truck series, Ertl/AMT didn't wait long to respond with replicas of both Chevrolet and Ford race truck models in 1/25th scale. In many respects, the truck kits are more accurate in their execution and have received respectable praise from many builders and hobby magazine reviewers. Currently, in 1/25th scale, the next new trend in stock car models would appear to be the occasional vintage subject and snap together kits.

In 1997 a rejuvenated Lindberg surprised the stock car modeling public with the release of a decent representation of the 1964 Plymouth Belvedere Richard Petty drove to his first of seven Daytona 500 victories. This kit was not a rehash of some other similar tool but appears to be a brand new offering. What ever shortcomings the kit may have (small tires and skimpy racing suspension parts), the kit gets high marks for capturing the overall shape and proportions of the vintage Mopar body shell quite accurately.

AMT, in the first quarter of 1999, premiered a new series of Snapfast stock car kits. These elementary items not only feature easy assembly and very few parts, but have the correct body colors pre-painted and the larger markings pad printed accurately and cleanly. The kits all share a common one-piece undercarriage with all pertinent features represented in relief. There are no interior appointments and the front, side and rear one-piece window glass is opaque. Water-slide decals are used for the remainder of the body markings including all the proper contingency sponsors stickers.

1/25th-Scale Price Guide

AMT NASCAR Grand National Stock Cars

Stock #	Car #	Sponsor/Car	Value
T373	No. 12	73 Coca-Cola Chevrolet Chevelle	$125.00
T380	No. 88	74 DiGard Chevrolet Chevelle	$90.00
T391	No. 90	72 Ford Torino 2-door hardtop (a Jo-Han re-box)	$55.00
T395	No. 28	73 Pylon Wiper Blades Chevrolet Chevelle 2-door sedan	$125.00
T421	No. 12	72 Coca-Cola Chevrolet Monte Carlo 2-door coupe	$135.00
T429	No. 72	74 Kings Row Fireplace Chevrolet Chevelle Laguna 2-door coupe	$105.00
T430	No. 16	75 Penske/AMC Matador 2-door sedan (Bobby Allison)	$125.00
T430	No. 16	75 Penske/AMC Matador 2-door sedan	$125.00
T443	No. 54	74 Lenny Pond Chevrolet Malibu 2-door coupe	$125.00
T565		Penske Racing Team, Matador plus Chevrolet van and open trailer	$200.00
3030	No. 12	75 Bobby Allison AMC Matador NASCAR Sportsman	$40.00
8116	No. 12	75 Bobby Allison, Coca-Cola AMC Matador (reissue)	$15.00

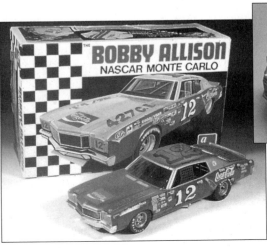

AMT Bobby Allison/Coca-Cola 1972 Chevrolet Monte Carlo built by Drew Hierwarter.

AMT Bobby Allison/Coca-Cola 1972 Chevrolet Monte Carlo kit No. T-421.

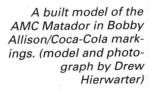

A built model of the AMC Matador in Bobby Allison/Coca-Cola markings. (model and photograph by Drew Hierwarter)

Two 1/43rd-scale Pontiac Grand Prix models built by Roy Vaughn. On the left is the Alka-Seltzer car driven by Jimmy Means, and on the right is the Country Time car driven by Michael Waltrip.

Two 1/43rd-scale models of car driven by Hershel McGriff. On the left is the 1950 Oldsmobile McGriff drove in both the first Mexican road race and the first Southern 500 at Darlington, S.C. On the right is the 1974 Dodge Charger he drove in the 1976 24 Hours of Lemans, France. Both models built by Wayne Moyer.

A 1/43rd-scale model of the 1965 Ford Galaxie driven by Ned Jarrett to the NASCAR championship that year. Model built by Wayne Moyer.

1/32nd-scale replica of the outlaw dirt track modified Chevy coach driven by Stan Westmore in the mid-1970s. This model is the work of Joel Naprstek.

Joel Naprstek built this 1/32nd-scale fictional '57 Ford Fairlane 500 convertible and the hand-built diorama on which it's displayed,

Dave Bauer built this 1/24th-scale '66 Chevrolet Chevelle late-model stock car replica from a stock street-driven Monogram kit. Photo by Glen Marek.

This is the big-block Chevrolet racing V-8 engine housed in Dave Bauer's '66 Chevelle. Photo by Glen Marek.

Dave Bauer built this 1/25th-scale '56 Chevy two-door sportsman from a Revell stock kit. Photo by Glen Marek.

This hand-built replica 1/25th-scale 1932 Chrysler Sportsman is the work of craftsman Doug Whyte. Photo by Doug Whyte.

This 1/25th-scale replica 1953 Oldsmobile was driven by Buck Baker to the series championship. The model, built from a resin kit, and photo are by Dave Dodge.

This 1/25th-scale '56 Chevrolet replica was built by Laverne Zachery using an MCW resin body and computer-generated decals. The car was driven by the late Gwyn Staley.

This 1/24th-scale 1950 Oldsmobile driven by Red Byron was built from a metal bank by Dave Dodge. The model was stripped and repainted with the decals made on his computer.

This 1/25th-scale replica was built by Dave Dodge from an AMT annual kit using Fred Cady decals. The model depicts the 1958 Chevy Impala driven by Buck Baker during that NASCAR season.

Dave Dodge used a resin kit from All-American Models to build a replica of Buck Baker's 1957 Chevrolet "Black Widow" two-door.

This model of the 1958 Buick Special driven by the Fireball Roberts was built by Dave Dodge from an original AMT annual kit.

Tom Dill started by modifying a 1/25th-scale AMT 1957 Ford Fairlane 500 kit into a NASCAR race car. Dill used Fred Cady decals.

This 1963 Pontiac was built by Dave Dodge from an MCW resin kit.

Dave Bauer built this 1966 Chevy II by carefully modifying an AMT stock kit.

This 1/25th-scale AMT Mustang Modified stock car was built and photographed by Drew Hierwarter.

Drew Hierwarter built and photographed this '36 Ford Sportsman coupe from an AMT stock kit.

This 1/25th-scale replica was built by Randy Derr from an AMT stock kit to depict Mario Andretti's winning Ford Fairlane from the 1967 Daytona 500.

Here's a pair of 1/25th-scale models of NASCAR stockers driven by Bobby Allison. On the left is the Coca-Cola Chevrolet Monte Carlo, and on the right is his 1969 Dodge Charger 500. Models by the author.

This 1/25th-scale 1975 AMC Matador is a replica of the car driven by Bobby Allison. Model by the author.

Drew Hierwarter built and photographed this 1/25th-scale replica of A.J. Foyt's 1976 Chevrolet Laguna. Hierwarter started with an MPC stock car kit and used Fred Cady decals.

The author built this 1/25th-scale replica of Richard Petty's 1972 Dodge Dart Swinger Chrysler Kit Car.

The author built this fictional 1/25th-scale winged asphalt modified starting with an AMT Early Modified kit.

Fred Bradley built this 1/24th Mercury Cougar replica using JNJ decals, an SMH resin body shell with a R-M T-Bird chassis.

Fred Bradley built this beautiful replica of Richard Petty's 1973 STP Dodge Charger from the MPC 1/16th scale kit.

The author built this 1/25th-scale replica of the 1965 Ford Galaxie driven by Dan Gurney to victory in the Motor Trend 500. The model is based on a Modelhaus resin kit and uses Fred Cady decals.

Robert Pizio built this 1/24th-scale Pennzoil Pontiac Grand Prix cutting away body panels to show off the considerable attention to detail.

Leonard Carsner used a pair of R-M '92 Pontiac Grand Prix kits to depict the STP Pontiac on display in the Indianapolis Speedway Museum on the right. At left is the car driven by Rick Wilson the year after Petty retired as a driver.

Mike Madlinger built this trio of Miller Buick Regals Revell-Monogram 1/24th-scale stock car kits.

Mike Madlinger built this 1/24th-scale replica of the Hooters Ford Thunderbird driven by the late Alan Kulwicki to the NASCAR championship in 1992.

The author built this 1/24th-scale replica of Ernie Ervin's 1988 rookie rider the Kroger/Pepsi Chevrolet Monte Carlo aero-coupe.

This 1997 Ford F-150 race truck replica was built by Daryl Huhtala using an AMT kit and Slixx decals.

Chevy Cavalier modified race car. Photo and model by Doug Whyte.

1969 K&K Dodge Charger. Photo and model by Doug Whyte.

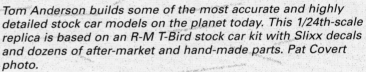

Tom Anderson builds some of the most accurate and highly detailed stock car models on the planet today. This 1/24th-scale replica is based on an R-M T-Bird stock car kit with Slixx decals and dozens of after-market and hand-made parts. Pat Covert photo.

The undercarriage of the Tom Anderson Texaco-Havoline T-Bird contains just about every detail possible—except the smell of motor oil and racing fuel! Pat Covert photo.

The attention to detail in the engine compartment of Tom Anderson's 1/24th-scale T-Bird almost defies belief. From the photo-etch hood hinges to the machine's aluminum belt pulleys, this is a most impressive piece of the model building art form. Pat Covert Photo.

This Pat Covert photo of Tom Anderson's Silver Anniversary Goodwrench Chevrolet Monte Carlo could pass for a shot of the full-size race car!

This view of the engine compartment of Tom Anderson's Silver Anniversary Goodwrench Chevrolet Monte Carlo looks like the pit crew are just on a coffee break. The attention to detail and authenticity is of the highest caliber as an example of stock car model building. Pat Covert Photo.

Joel Naprstek built and photographed this fictional 1/25th-scale model and diorama. The race car is based on an AMT Early Modified kit and features a '37 Chevy coupe body shell with a small-block Ford V-8 engine.

Bill Burtnet built this giant 1/8th scale replica of his Corvette-powered '32 Ford jalopy using a George Zurowski resin body shell mounted on a Revell-Monogram '32 Ford roadster chassis.

This 1937 Ford modified was built and photographed by Drew Hierwarter. The 1/25th-scale model is based on an Early Racing Classics resin kit with markings hand lettered.

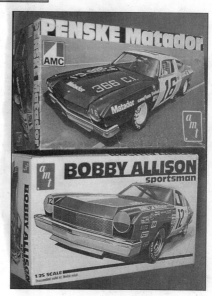

Two built model versions of the Ertl/AMT kit No. 373 Chevelle No. 11. It was driven by Cale Yarborough while car No. 52 was driven by Canadian NASCAR rookie of the year Earl Ross. Models by Wayne Doebling and Darel Huhtala.

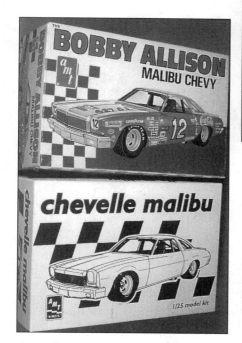

AMT Bobby Allison/Coca-Cola 1973 Chevrolet Chevelle kit No. 373 and the recent '74-'75 Chevelle reissue (done for Classic Hobbys by Ertl) kit No. 3688. Though the box art depicts a 1973 Chevelle, the kit is actually a later version but does have the S-3 Laguna nose clip included.

AMT kits of the '74-'75 Chevrolet Chevelle: Kings Row No. T-429 and Pylon No. T-395.

Two versions of the AMT AMC Matador in 1/25th scale: Penske No. T-430 and Bobby Allison Sportsman No. 3030.

AMT Annual kits (with stock car parts included)

Stock #	Car #	Sponsor/Car	Value
6125	No. 28	65 Ford Galaxie 500 XL 2-door	$100.00
6126	No #	66 Ford Galaxie 500 XL 2-door	$75.00
T328	No. 57	66 Ford Galaxie 500 XL 2-door, "Sweet Bippie" (reissue)	$35.00
6517	No #	66 Ford Galaxie 500 XL 2-door	$25.00
6893	No #	69 Ford Torino Cobra 2-door	$25.00
6889	No #	69 Ford Torino Talledaga 2-door	$25.00
T321	No. 99	70 Ford Torino Cobra 2-door	$120.00
T116	No. 71	71 Ford Torino Cobra 2-door hardtop	$120.00

A built model by Mike Madlinger based on the AMT '66 Ford Galaxie kit No. T-328 using JNJ after-market decals.

A 1/25th scale model built and photographed by Drew Hierwarter based on the AMT '69 Ford Torino Cobra kit No. 6983 and using after market paint and decals.

A built model by Wayne Doebling based on the AMT '71 Ford Torino Cobra kit No. T-116 using after-market decals. (Randy Derr photo)

Two annual AMT kits: 1966 Ford Galaxie kit No. T-328 and 1971 Ford Torino Cobra kit No. T-116 that include NASCAR stock car parts.

AMT Hardee's Chevrolet Monte Carlo kit No. 8045 and Valvoline Ford Thunderbird kit No. 8042.

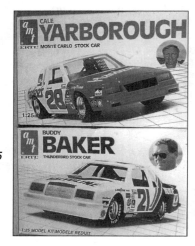

Ertl/AMT NASCAR Winston Cup Stock Cars (snap-style kits)

Stock #	Car #	Sponsor/Car	Value
8042	No. 21	83 Valvoline Ford Thunderbird 2-door coupe	$75.00
8043	No. 11	83 Pepsi Chevrolet Monte Carlo 2-door coupe	$80.00
8044	No. 43	83 STP Pontiac Grand Prix 2-door coupe	$75.00
8045	No. 28	83 Hardee's Chevrolet Monte Carlo 2-door coupe	$75.00
8046	No. 15	83 Wrangler Ford Thunderbird 2-door coupe	$100.00
8047	No. 7	83 7-Eleven Ford Thunderbird 2-door coupe	$80.00

Ertl/AMT NASCAR stock cars, special re-issue

Stock #	Car	Value
3688	1974-5 Generic Chevrolet Chevelle (Classic Hobby Distributors, Inc.)	$35.00

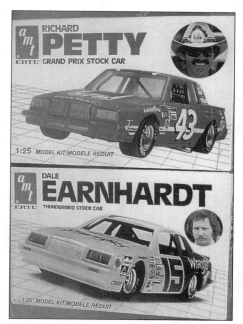
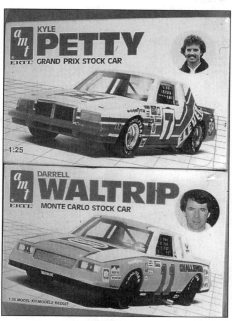
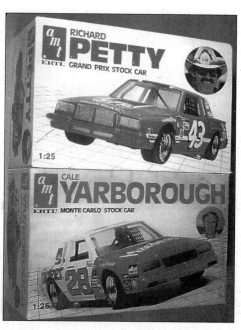

AMT STP Pontiac Grand Prix kit No. 8046 and Wrangler Ford Thunderbird kit No. 8044.

AMT 7-11 Pontiac Grand Prix kit No. 8047 and Pepsi Challenger Chevrolet Monte Carlo kit No. 8043.

AMT STP Pontiac Grand Prix kit No. 8044 and Hardee's Chevrolet Monte Carlo kit No. 8045.

Ertl/AMT NASCAR Winston Cup Stock Cars

Stock #	Car #	Sponsor/Car	Value
6162	No. 15	92 Motorcraft Ford Thunderbird	$15.00
6296	No #	97 Generic Ford Thunderbird (white, no decals)	$10.00
6297	No. 5	98 Kellogg's Chevrolet Monte Carlo	$12.00
6299	No. 4	98 Kodak Chevrolet Monte Carlo	$10.00
6372	No #	97 Generic Chevrolet Monte Carlo (white, no decals)	$10.00
6457	No. 22	91 Maxwell House Ford Thunderbird	$22.00
6727	No. 4	89 Kodak Chevrolet Lumina	$18.00
6728	No. 43	90 STP Pontiac Grand Prix	$30.00
6730	No. 15	91 Motorcraft Ford Thunderbird	$17.00
6731	No. 4	90 Kodak Chevrolet Oldsmobile	$22.00
6732	No. 30	90 Country Time Pontiac Grand Prix	$21.00
6733	No. 21	90 Citgo Ford Thunderbird	$27.00
6738	No. 94	91 Sunoco Oldsmobile Cutlass	$20.00
6739	No. 7	90 Zerex Ford Thunderbird	$80.00
6740	No. 9	90 Coors Ford Thunderbird	$30.00
6819	No. 68	91 Country Time Oldsmobile Cutlass	$17.00
6852	No. 24	95 DuPont Chevrolet Lumina	$42.00
6892	No. 44	93 STP Pontiac Grand Prix	$25.00
6894	No. 26	93 Quaker State Ford Thunderbird	$18.00
6961	No. 27	90 Miller Genuine Draft Pontiac Grand Prix	$50.00
6962	No. 9	90 Coors Ford Thunderbird	$50.00
8106	No. 42	90 Mello Yello Pontiac Grand Prix	$16.00
8160	No. 88	97 Quality Care Ford Thunderbird	$12.00
8161	No. 7	97 QVC Ford Thunderbird	$12.00
8163	No. 17	97 Parts America Chevrolet Monte Carlo	$12.00
8186	No. 18	95 Interstate Batteries Chevrolet	$14.00
8187	No. 5	95 Kellogg's Chevrolet Monte Carlo	$14.00
8188	No. 95	94 McDonald's Ford Thunderbird	$12.00
8189	No. 6	95 Valvoline Ford Thunderbird	$12.00

Stock #	Car #	Sponsor/Car	Value
8190	No. 24	95 DuPont Chevrolet Monte Carlo	$15.00
8191	No. 8	95 Raybestos Ford Thunderbird	$12.00
8200	No. 94	97 McDonald's Ford Thunderbird	$12.00
8403	No. 6	97 Valvoline Ford Thunderbird	$14.00
8404	No. 17	97 Parts America Chevrolet Monte Carlo	$14.00
8406	No. 7	96 QVC Ford Thunderbird	$14.00
8752	No. 18	91 Interstate/NFL/Marriott Chevrolet Lumina	$15.00
8753	No. 2	90 Wallace/Penske Pontiac Grand Prix	$15.00
8754	No. 66	92 Phillips 66 Ford Thunderbird	$14.00
8756	No. 6	91 Valvoline Ford Thunderbird	$22.00

AMT STP No. 44 STP Pontiac Grand Prix kit No. 6728 as driven by Rick Wilson and STP Pontiac Grand Prix No. 43 kit No. 6892.

The AMT kit No. 6727 Kodak Oldsmobile Cutlass as driven by Rick Wilson and the AMT kit No. 6731 Chevrolet Lumina as driven by Ernie Irvan.

Two versions of the Kellogg's Chevrolet Monte Carlo: kits No. 6267 and No. 8187.

Two AMT Motorcraft Ford Thunderbirds: kit No. 6730 and kit No. 6162.

Pair of Coors Thunderbirds driven by Bill Elliott: Coors kit No. 6740 and Coors Lite kit No. 6962.

Two DuPont Chevrolets driven by Jeff Gordon: Lumina kit No. 6852 and a Monte Carlo kit No. 8190.

A trio of Coors Thunderbirds built by the author for the sponsor. These replicas are built from AMT kit No. 6740.

Pair of Valvoline Thunderbird kits: (top) No. 8756 and (bottom) kit No. 8403.

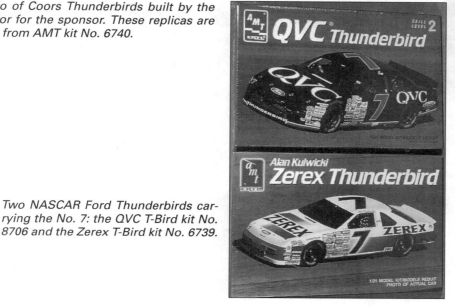

Two NASCAR Ford Thunderbirds carrying the No. 7: the QVC T-Bird kit No. 8706 and the Zerex T-Bird kit No. 6739.

A Kodak Chevrolet Monte Carlo, kit No. 6299 and a Quality Care Ford Thunderbird, kit No. 8160 both by AMT.

The Quaker State Ford Thunderbird kit No. 6894 and the Sunoco Oldsmobile Cutlass kit No. 6738 by AMT.

Miller Pontiac Grand Prix kit No. 6961 and the Country Time/Maxwell House Pontiac Grand Prix kit No. 6732 by AMT.

1989-90 Oldsmobile Cutlass driven by Harry Gant. The model was built and photographed by Drew Hierwarter and based on an AMT kit and aftermarket decals.

The Country Time Oldsmobile Cutlass driven by Bobby Hamilton kit No. 6819 and the Mello Yellow Pontiac driven by Kyle Petty kit No. 8106 both by AMT.

Pair of Ford Thunderbirds, Phillips 66 kit No. 8754 and Citgo kit No. 6733, both by AMT.

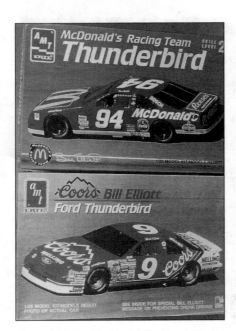

Top: AMT's McDonald's Ford Thunderbird kit No. 8188; bottom: AMT Coors T-Bird kit No. 6962.

Pair of AMT Pontiac Grand Prix kits in 1/25th scale: Miller kit No. 6961 and STP kit No. 6819.

Pair of AMT Oldsmobile Cutlass kits in 1/25th scale: Kodak kit No. 6731 and Country Time kit No. 6819.

Trio of AMT Coors Ford Thunderbirds built from kit No. 6740 by the author.

On the top is the AMT Interstate Batteries Lumina kit No. 8752 and on the bottom is the Western Auto Chevrolet Monte Carlo kit No,. 8404 by AMT.

A pair of AMT Ford Thunderbirds, at the top is the Maxwell House kit No. 6457 and at the bottom is the Raybestos kit No. 8191.

Ertl/AMT NASCAR Winston Cup Stock Cars (multi-car kits)

Stock #	Car #	Sponsor/Car	Value
8910	No. 22	90 Maxwell House Ford Thunderbird	$70.00
	No. 4390	STP Pontiac Grand Prix	
	No. 4	91 Kodak Chevrolet Lumina	

Ertl/AMT Snap Fast stock cars in 1/25th scale: Cheerios Taurus kit No. 30022 and kit No. 30024 the McDonald's Taurus.

Ertl/AMT 1/25th scale pre-decorated stock car kits feature water-5-decals, one-piece chassis, no interior detail and blackened windows.

Ertl/AMT NASCAR Snap Fast kits

Stock #	Car #	Sponsor/Car	Value
30022	No. 26	98 Cheerios Ford Taurus Snap Fast Plus	$8.00
30023	No. 6	98 Valvoline Ford Taurus Snap Fast Plus	$8.00
30024	No. 94	98 McDonald's Ford Taurus Snap Fast Plus	$8.00

Ertl/AMT NASCAR Winston Cup Transporter

Stock #	Car	Value
6019	Coors transporter trailer	$75.00
6802	Kodak transporter trailer	$50.00

A built model based on the AMT 1936 Plymouth Earl Modified kit No. T-165 with some additional hand-made parts added. (model by the author)

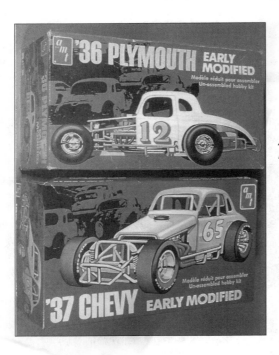

Two examples of AMT's 1/25th scale Early Modified kits: 1936 Plymouth No. T-165 and 1937 Chevrolet No. T-166.

Two examples of AMT's 1/25th scale Early Modified kits: 1965 Ford Mustang No. T-180 and 1975 AMC Gremlin No. T-175.

Ertl/AMT Early Modifieds

Stock #	Car	Value
T165	36 Plymouth 2-door Coupe Early Modified	$85.00
8667	36 Plymouth 2-door Coupe Early Modified (reissue)	$15.00
T166	37 Chevrolet 2-door Coupe Early Modified	$85.00
6087	37 Chevrolet 2-door Coupe Early Modified (reissue)	$20.00
T167	40 Ford 2-door coupe Early Modified	$80.00
T175	75 AMC Gremlin 2-door sedan Modified	$80.00
T180	65 Ford Mustang 2-door hardtop Modified	$80.00
T181	35 Chevrolet 2-door sedan Early Modified	$85.00
T390	53 Ford F-100 pickup and open trailer, Early Modified Series	$55.00
T566	Modified Ford Race Team, 40 Ford modified plus 75 F-150 and open trailer	$85.00

AMT Modified Stockers

Stock #	Car	Value
T186	65 Chevrolet Chevelle 2-door hardtop	$85.00
T187	65 Pontiac 2-door hardtop	$75.00
T188	69 Ford Falcon 2-door sedan	$60.00
T189	66 Buick Skylark 2-door hardtop	$55.00
T190	65 Oldsmobile 88 2-door hardtop	$55.00
T191	65 Ford Fairlane 2-door hardtop	$85.00
T192	66 Chevrolet Impala hardtop	$65.00
T193	64 Ford Galaxie hardtop	$75.00
T194	69 Ford Torino 2-door hardtop	$85.00
30142	69 Ford Falcon 2-door sedan	$10.00
30143	65 Oldsmobile 2-door	$10.00
30147	65 Buick Skylark 2-door	$10.00

1965 Chevelle #T186

AMT Chrysler Kit Cars, etc.

Stock #	Car #	Sponsor/Car	Value
T229	No. 43	72 Petty 72 Dodge Dart Swinger NASCAR Sport man	$125.00
T230	No. 8	75 Ohio Air National Guard Plymouth Duster	$105.00
T231	No. 60	73 Warren Stewart Dodge Dart	$100.00
T233	No. 2	72 Plymouth Valiant Scamp (actually a 72 Dodge Dart Swinger)	$85.00
T569	No. 43	Petty Racing Team (Ford LN8000 and 72 Dodge Dart Sportsman)	$175.00

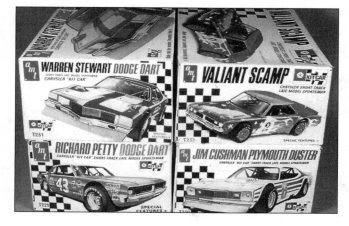

The four Chrysler Kit Car kits from AMT in 1/25th scale: Stewart Dodge Dart No. T-231; Plymouth Scamp No. T-233; Warren, Petty Dodge Dart Swinger No. T-229; and Cushman Plymouth Duster No. T-230.

Richard Petty Race Team kit #T569.

Ertl Grand National Stock Cars

Stock #	Car #	Sponsor/Car	Value
8105	No. 43	1977 STP Chevrolet Caprice 2-door sedan (metal and plastic)	$85.00
8109	No. 88	1977 Gatorade Chevrolet Caprice (metal and plastic)	$75.00

Ertl metal kit of the Petty Chevrolet Caprice No. 8105 shown along side of the factory assembled version.

AMT Super Trucks (NCTS: NASCAR Craftsman Truck Series)

Stock #	Car #	Sponsor/Car	Value
6206		Generic 97 Ford F-150 Supertruck	$9.00
6301		Generic 97 Chevrolet C-1500 Supertruck	$9.00
8164	No. 98	96 Raybestos Ford F-150 Supertruck	$15.00
8241	No. 24	96 DuPont Chevrolet Supertruck	$20.00
8242	No. 98	96 Raybestos Ford F-150 Supertruck	$15.00
8243	No. 3	96 Goodwrench Chevrolet Supertruck	$20.00
8244	No. 17	96 Sears Chevrolet Supertruck	$12.00
8304	No. 21	96 Ortho Ford Supertruck	$10.00
8305	No. 52	96 AC-Delco Chevrolet Supertruck	$10.00
8406	No. 24	97 Quaker State Chevrolet Supertruck	$20.00
8451	No. 3	97 Goodwrench C-1500 Chevrolet Supertruck	$12.00
8453	No. 17	97 Sears Diehard C-1500 Chevrolet Supertruck	$12.00

Top: Kenny Irwin Jr. Raybestos Ford kit No. 8164; bottom: Butch Miller Raybestos Ford kit No. 8242.

The Kenny Irwin Jr. Raybestos Ford F-150 by AMT, kit No. 8164.

A pair of generic AMT race truck kits, No. 6206, a Ford and No. 6301, a Chevrolet.

The No. 1 Diehard Chevrolet truck built by Daryl Huhtala based on an AMT kit using aftermarket decals.

A model of a 1996 Ford race truck built by Fred Bradley, based on an AMT kit, using an aftermarket resin body shell and decals.

MPC NASCAR Grand National Stock Cars

Stock #	Car #	Sponsor/Car	Value
731	No. 71	69 K&K Insurance Dodge Charger Daytona (2 boxes, 1-stock chassis)	$210.00
731	No. 71	69 K&K Insurance Dodge Charger Daytona (2 boxes; 1 adjustable chassis)	$200.00
1-1701	No. 43	72 Petty Plymouth Roadrunner 2-door	$175.00
1-1702	No. 11	72 Petty Enterprises Dodge Charger 2-door	$175.00
1-1703	No. 56	72 Miller High Life Chevrolet Chevelle 2-door	$125.00
1-1704	No. 21	72 Purolator Mercury Cyclone 2-door	$130.00
1-1705	No. 22	69 Golden Products Dodge Charger Daytona 2-door	$125.00
1-1706	No. 33	71 C.V. Enterprises Pontiac GTO 2-door	$125.00
1-1707	No. 14	72 Cunningham-Kelly Chevrolet Monte Carlo 2-door	$120.00
1-1708	No. 43	73 STP Dodge Charger 2-door	$185.00
1-1709	No. 11	73 Kar Kare Chevrolet Chevelle Laguna 2-door	$125.00
1-1710	No. 15	72 Sta-Powr Ford Torino 2-door	$115.00
1-1711	No. 71	73 K&K Dodge Charger 2-door	$150.00
1-1712	No. 39	75 Pepsi Chevrolet Chevelle Laguna S3 2-door	$110.00
1-1713	No. 43	74 STP Dodge Charger 2-door (75-76 season)	$175.00
1-0681	No. 1	75 Hawaiian Tropics Chevrolet Chevelle Laguna S3 2-door	$110.00

Two MPC Richard Petty kits: Plymouth Road Runner kit No. 1-1701 and the STP Dodge Charger kit No. 1-1713.

A pair of MPC Chevrolet stock cars: Miller Chevelle kit No. 1-1703 and a Monte Carlo kit No. 1-1707.

A model built by the author of Richard Petty's 1971 Road Runner based on MPC kit No. 1-1701.

A replica of the Cotton Owens/Buddy Baker Dodge Charger Daytona built from MPC kit No. 731 using aftermarket decals by the author.

Two MPC Chevrolet stock car kits: Car Care Chevelle kit No. 1-1710 and the Pepsi Chevelle Laguna kit No. 1-1712.

Two MPC Dodge Charger Daytona stock car kits: K&K kit No. 731 and the Golden Products kit No. 1-1705.

A built model of the K&K Dodge Charger MPC kit No. 1-1711 by the late Jerry Kathe.

Pair of MPC Dodge Charger stock car kits—top: K&K kit No. 1-1711; bottom: Buddy Baker/Petty Enterprises kit No. 1-1702.

Top: Cannon Ball Run Chevrolet Laguna kit No. 1-0681; bottom: CV Enterprises Pontiac GTO kit No. 1-1706, both by MPC.

A model built and photographed by Drew Hierwarter of the Purolator Mercury based on an MPC kit No. 1-1704.

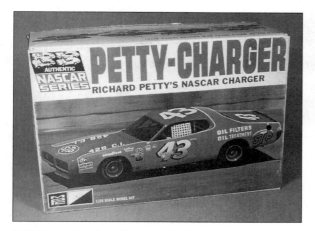

MPC Petty Dodge Charger kit No. 1-1708.

A pair of MPC kits of Ford products: bottom: Purolator Mercury kit No. 1-1704; top: Sta-Power Ford Torino kit No. 1-1710.

A model built by the author of the Petty/STP Dodge Charger driven to the 1972 NASCAR title, based on kit No. 1-1708.

A model of the Gatorade Laguna built and photographed by Drew Hierwarter, based on MPC kit No. 1-0681 using Fred Cady decals.

A model built by Tom Dill of the Kings Row Laguna based on MPC kit No. 1-0681 using aftermarket decals.

MPC kit of the Cannon Ball Run Laguna No. 1-0681.

MPC Annual kits (with stock car parts included)

Stock #	Car #	Sponsor/Car	Value
7	No. 5	66 Dodge Charger R/T	$175.00
763	No. 5	67 Dodge Charger R/T	$75.00
768	No. 6	68 Dodge Charger R/T	$250.00
769	No. 6	69 Dodge Charger R/T	$275.00
1-0661	No. 01	69 Dodge Charger (The Dukes of Hazard "Gen. Lee"), original issue	$50.00
8597	No. 01	69 Dodge Charger (The Dukes of Hazard "Gen. Lee"), re-issue	$15.00
0770	No #	70 Dodge Charger R/T	$100.00
1-7319	No. 55	73 Chevrolet Camaro Z-28 (Tiny Lund NASCAR Grand American decals)	$70.00
1-7415	No. 9	74 Pontiac Firebird 400	$55.00
1-7515	No. 5	75 Pontiac Firebird 400	$50.00
1-7615	No. 35	76 Pontiac Firebird 400	$35.00
1-7315	No. 87	77 Pontiac Firebird T/A (Buck Baker NASCAR Grand American decals)	$45.00
1-7815	No #	78 Pontiac Firebird T/A	$40.00
1-0735	No #	79 Pontiac Firebird T/A	$25.00
1-7819	No. Z28	78 Chevrolet Camaro Z-28	$30.00
1-0786	No. Z28	79 Chevrolet Camaro Super Z	$30.00

MPC Southern Modifieds

Stock #	Car	Value
1-0710	71 Ford Pinto 2-door, Rough Rider	$75.00
1-0711	34 Ford 2-door, Slammer	$75.00
1-0712	71 Chevrolet Vega 2-door, Rat Trap	$75.00
1-0713	36 Chevrolet 2-door, Wild One	$75.00

Pair of MPC Southern Modified kits: Rat Pack Chevrolet Vega No. 1-0712 and the Rough Rider Ford Pinto No. 1-0710.

MPC Super Stockers

Stock #	Car #	Sponsor/Car	Value
1-2750	No. 7	70 Pontiac GTO 2-door hardtop	$70.00
1-2751	No. 7	69 Jegs Chevrolet Camaro 2-door hardtop	$80.00
1-2752	No. 99	70 Chevrolet Chevelle 2-door hardtop	$65.00
1-2753	No. 99	69 A&W Ford Mustang 2-door hardtop	$85.00
1-2754	No. 03	72 Chevrolet Monte Carlo 2-door coupe	$60.00
1-2755	No. 72	73 USAC Plymouth Barracuda 2-door hardtop	$80.00

Two MPC Super Stocker kits: Camaro No. 1-2751 and Mustang No. 1-2753.

Pair of MPC Super Stocker kits: Chevelle No. 1-2752 and Plymouth Barracuda No. 1-2755.

MPC Southern Stockers

Stock #	Car #	Sponsor/Car	Value
0738	No. 37	83 Generic Chevrolet Monte Carlo	$65.00
0845	No. 58	83 Buick Regal	$65.00
0846	No. 20	83 Generic Pontiac Grand Prix	$65.00
1301	No. 21	Chattanooga Chevrolet Monte Carlo	$75.00
1302	No. 55	Copenhagen Chevrolet Monte Carlo	$75.00
1303	No. 2	Alugard Pontiac Grand Prix	$75.00
1304	No. 66	Skoal Chevrolet Monte Carlo	$75.00

MPC Southern Stockers Skoal Monte Carlo kit No. 1304.

Pair of MPC Southern Stockers kits: Alugard Pontiac Grand Prix kit No. 1-1303 and a generic Monte Carlo kit No. 1-0738.

Pair of MPC Southern Stockers: generic Buick Regal kit No. 0845 and generic Pontiac Grand Prix kit No. 0846.

The Copenhagen Monte Carlo MPC kit No. 1302 and the Chattanooga Monte Carlo kit No. 1301 both by MPC.

Pair of MPC Chevrolet Camaros: 1978 kit No. 1-7819 and 1973 kit No. 1-7319.

Dodge Charger built and photographed by Drew Hierwarter based on the MPC kit and using aftermarket decals.

Dodge Charger driven by the late Neil Bonnett, built and photographed by Drew Hierwarter based on the MPC kit a featuring hand-drawn markings.

Model of the Bobby Allison 1969 Dodge Charger 500, built by the author based on the MPC General Lee kit using aftermarket decals.

1966 Dodge Charger as driven by David Pearson to the NASCAR title that year. This replica was built by Tom Dill and is based on an MPC kit with aftermarket decals.

Jo-Han NASCAR Grand National Stock Cars

Stock #	Car #	Sponsor/Car	Value
GC372	No. 27	72 Ford Torino 2-door hardtop (generic decals)	$50.00
* GC-964	No. 43	64 Petty's Plymouth Belvedere 2-door hardtop	$80.00
GC-964	No. 43	64 Richard Petty's Plymouth Belvedere (rectangular box)	$75.00
C-1170	No. 27	70 AMC Javelin NASCAR GT Racer (with funny car option)	$75.00

* (Golden Commandos funny car option, flat box)

Pair of Jo-Han 1964 Petty Ply-mouths, both carry the kit No. GC-964.

Two Jo-Han Ford Torino kits, the snap kit No. CS-502 and the NASCAR kit No. GC-1470.

Model built by the author based on the Jo-Han Petty '64 Plymouth using Fred Cady decals.

Model built by Wayne Doebling based on the '64 Petty Jo-Han kit using Fred Cady Decals.

Model built by the author based on the Jo-Han Torino kit using an All-American Models resin body shell and Dave Romero decals.

Model built by the author of the Petty '64 Plymouth based on the Jo-Han kit using aftermarket decals.

Model built and photographed by Drew Hierwarter based on the Jo-Han Torino using Fred Cady decals.

Jo-Han Annual Kits with stock car parts

Stock #	Car #	Sponsor/Car	Value
C-164	No. 43	64 Plymouth Fury Hardtop (original issue, R. Petty decals)	$175.00
C-264	No. 6	64 Dodge Polara 2-door hardtop	$175.00
C-1565	No. 43	65 Plymouth Fury III 2-door hardtop (Richard Petty decals)	$135.00
C-1266	No. 2	66 Plymouth Fury III 2-door hardtop (Norm Nelson/Hub Motors decals)	$75.00
C-1669	No. 43	69 Plymouth Roadrunner (original issue)	$125.00
GC220	No. 22	69 Plymouth Roadrunner 2-door coupe (reissue, generic decals)	$45.00
C-1470	No. 25	70 Plymouth Roadrunner 2-door hardtop	$85.00
GC1470	No. 43	70 Petty Plymouth Superbird 2-door hardtop	$100.00

Model built by Daryl Huhtala based on a Jo-Han '64 Dodge kit using aftermarket decals.

Two original issue 1969 Plymouth Road Runner kits by Jo-Han No. C-1669.

Pair of Jo-Han Plymouth Superbird kits, one is molded in white and one in blue. Both carry the same kit No. GC-1470.

1965 Jo-Han Plymouth Fury kit with some stock car parts included, No. C-1565.

Model by the author based on the Jo-Han Petty Superbird kit using aftermarket paint and decals.

1966 Jo-Han Plymouth Fury kit with some stock car parts included, No. C-1266.

Lindberg NASCAR Grand National Stock Cars

Stock #	Car #	Sponsor/Car	Value
72164	No. 43	1964 Richard Petty's Plymouth Belvedere 2-door hardtop	$10.00

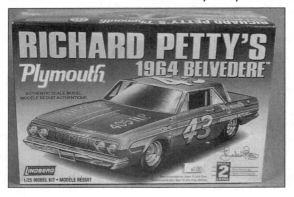

The Lindberg 1964 Richard Petty Plymouth Belvedere, No. 72164.

Revell ASA Stock Cars

Stock #	Car #	Sponsor/Car	Value
7138	No. 84	89 Pro-Am Leasing Chevrolet Camaro	$35.00
7141	No. 52	89 LAI-Lane Automotive Chevrolet Camaro	$40.00
7145	No. 17	89 Superflo Chevrolet Camaro	$35.00
7445	No. 5	90 Zerex Ford Thunderbird	$35.00
7448	No. 0	90 Fel-Pro Ford Thunderbird	$35.00

1/25th-scale street-stock kits that could be modified into an oval track race car

Revell Camaro driven by Butch Miller to an ASA championship, kit No. 7141.

Revell ASA Zerex Ford Thunderbird in 1/25th scale kit No. 7445.

Pair of Revell ASA Chevrolets: Superflo Camaro kit No. 7145 and the Pro-Am Leasing Camaro kit No. 7138.

Revell ASA Fel Pro Ford Thunderbird in 1/25th scale kit No. 7448.

Ertl/AMT

Car	Value
34 Ford 2-door coupe	$10.00
36 Ford 2-door coupe	$10.00
39-40 Ford 2-door sedan	$20.00
40 Ford 2-door coupe	$12.00
49 Ford 2-door coupe	$10.00
57 Chevy Bel Air	$10.00
56 Ford Fairlane	$12.00
57 Ford Fairlane	$12.00
58 Chevy Impala 2-door hardtop	$15.00
62 Chevy Bel Air 2-door hardtop	$15.00
63 Chevy Impala 2-door hardtop	$15.00
66 Ford Fairlane	$20.00
67 Chevrolet Chevelle	$15.00
68 Plymouth Road Runner	$20.00
69 Chevy Chevelle 2-door hardtop	$20.00
69 Dodge Charger 500	$25.00
70 Chevy Chevelle 2-door hardtop	$20.00
70 Chevy Monte Carlo	$12.00

A 1957 Wood Brothers Ford 1/25th model built and photographed by Drew Hierwarter. The replica is based on an AMT 1957 Ford Fairlane with Fred Cady decals.

A 1/25th scale model built and photographed by Drew Hierwarter. This replica is based on AMT's 1963 Chevrolet Impala kit No. 6834 using Fred Cady decals.

A built model of a typical early NASCAR Strictly Stock race car like those raced on the beach at Daytona. The model was built by the author and based on AMT kit No. 6830.

Revell-Monogram

Car	Value
55 Chevrolet Bel Air convertible	$12.00
56 Chevrolet Del Ray 2-door sedan	$18.00
59 Chevrolet Impala	$12.00
60 Chevrolet Impala	$12.00
65 Chevrolet Impala	$15.00
67 Chevrolet Chevelle	$15.00
67 Plymouth GTX 2-door hardtop	$15.00
69 Pro Modeler Dodge Charger R/T 2-door hardtop	$18.00
69 Pro Modeler Dodge Charger Daytona 2-door hardtop	$18.00

Lindberg

Car	Value
1961 Chevrolet Impala	$12.00
1964 Dodge 330	$12.00

A Bull by the Tail

Building the Penske/AMC Matador NASCAR Grand National race car in 1/25th scale

The History: With a competitive Indy car program in place and great success in the Sports Car Club of America's Trans-Am pro-racing series, Roger Penske sought new challenges in 1972. The Penske team ran Chevrolet Camaros from 1967-1969, switching to AMC Javelins for the 1970 and 1971 season. American Motors decided to leave T-A for the higher profile NASCAR Grand National (now called Winston Cup) series.

One major reason for this move was the fact that American Motors had a brand new swoopy intermediate coupe on the drawing board set for introduction as a 1974 model. Management and marketing saw stock car racing as an avenue to promote the new model. AMC approached Penske with the idea of fielding a competitive Grand National race car. Penske contracted with Hutchison-Pagen race car constructors in Charlotte, N.C., to build a couple of 1973 Matadors for a few selected NASCAR events. These cars carried the old sheet metal. But this was to be a "shake-down" cruise in preparation for the new Matador. Once the primary work was completed on the two Matadors, final touches were applied in the Penske fabrication shops in Pennsylvania.

Drawing from its T-A experience, Penske contracted with Traco Engineering in California to build some race-worthy AMC small-block V-8s, according to NASCAR specifications. This was the same outfit that was responsible for the potent muscle under the hood of the Penske/Sunoco Javelins driven to the Trans-Am title in 1971. All the elements were now in place for Penske racing to compete on the highly competitive NASCAR circuit.

The Penske NASCAR team entered 11 races in 1973. The late and legendary driver Mark Donahue piloted the car on its maiden voyage as he covered the field, winning handily in the Winston Western 500, Riverside, Calif. In that inaugural race, the "old" Matador carried No. 16. In the remaining 10 events of that first season, Dave Marcis drove the car, using the No. 2, which he used on his Dodge when not at the wheel of the "Bull Tamer." The best finish for the Wisconsin native came at Rockingham, N.C., in the American 500 near season's end, where he took fifth place. The other nine races saw the Matador either near the back of the pack or not finishing (because of mechanical difficulties).

With the coming of the new season, AMC introduced its new "swoopy" Matador, the lines of which were reportedly penned by the late Dick Teague, long-time head of the design department at America's smallest auto builder. The new Penske/AMC racers now rode on new Holman-Moody chassis with fresh Traco-built 358 cid V-8s based on AMC's production 360 engine.

Penske racing again did not commit to running the full schedule for the 1974 season. The team's first outing came at the Daytona 500 where United States Auto

The finished model of AMC Matador driven by Bobby Allen built by author.

Club (USAC) star Gary Bettenhausen brought the new car home to a respectable 12th place finish. The next event for the Penske team came at Atlanta where Bettenhausen finished in ninth. In the spring Darlington race, super-sub Dave Marcis was back at the controls for this event and managed to capture a sixth place. Bettenhausen was back in the car once again for the early race at Talladega, Ala. Bettenhausen, after starting on the front row, retired early with mechanical problems and wound up in 37th place.

When the series rolled into Riverside, Penske had lined up road-racing expert George Fulmer to drive the Matador. Fulmer put the red, white and blue racer on the pole but retired early, scoring only a 33rd place finish. Then in the June race at Michigan International Speedway, Bettenhausen was back in the car and battled the series regulars to a fourth place.

Before the series moved to Daytona for the Firecracker 400 in July, Penske signed struggling-independent Bobby Allison to a regular contract. Allison drove the Matador in eight races during the second half of the 1974 season. Allison brought with him Coca-Cola sponsorship for the DIS event and came in fifth. This was the only one of the eight races with Allison at the wheel of the Matador using the No. 16. From Atlanta in July until Bobby won the final race of 1974 at Ontario, Calif., the car would carry Allison's familiar No. 12. The victory at Ontario was sweet but bittersweet as the car did not pass post-race inspection. The Penske team was fined $9,100 (the largest ever for a NASCAR Grand National infraction at the time) though Allison was allowed to keep the victory and the accompanying championship title points.

The season concluded for the Penske team, Allison and the new Matador showing one victory, 17 top-five and 17 top-10 finishes. Allison had finished fourth in the title chase behind Richard Petty who recorded his fifth championship title.

Allison again returned to the Penske/AMC operation for the 1975 Grand National series. Right out of the box, Allison won at Riverside and followed that up with a second place at Daytona. However, Penske again did not choose to contest the entire schedule, which didn't sit well with Allison. In spite of everything, the Matador (with Allison at the wheel), captured its second win of the season at Darlington in the Rebel 500. The Allison/Matador combination must have liked something about the "Lady in Black." When the series returned to Darlington for the Southern 500, it was Allison and the Penske Matador in victory lane once more. At the conclusion of the 1975 season, the record book showed the Allison/Penske/Matador combination had recorded the three victories previously mentioned along with 15 top-five and 19 top-10 finishes.

During the off-season, a cash-strapped AMC reluctantly decided to withdraw its support from the Matador-based Penske operation. The decision was made to switch to Mercurys as early as possible into the 1976 season. Allison handled the Penske Matador for the season opener at Riverside where he started the race from the pole but managed only a 15th place due to mechanical problems. This was the final ride for Allison in a Penske-owned AMC Matador, but not his last ride ever in the marque.

At the conclusion of the 1976 season, Allison announced his departure from the Penske team. Marcis was immediately hired away from the K&K Insurance Dodge team to drive Penske's Mercurys.

Allison returned to Hueytown, Ala., determined to jump-start his own independent operation again and campaign Chevrolet Chevelles. But prior to the start of the season, Allison decided to let his many fans choose what make of car he would race. Overwhelmingly, the fans said they wanted him back in the Matador! After discussions with AMC management, the Allison shop quickly got to work preparing red, white and blue Matadors for the new season. Allison had also been successful in persuading Citicorp to back his operation under its First National City Traveler's Checks product line.

Allison was able to run the entire 1977 series but managed only five top-10 finishes and no victories. His best finish was a second place in the first visit to Nashville in 1977. All but one of the other top-fives came on short tracks like North Wilkesboro and Richmond. After the 1977 season concluded, it wasn't the last time we would see a Matador in a NASCAR race or Allison at the wheel.

Rather than Penske having an entirely new race car built, some stories have the AMC Matadors being reskinned as CAM 2 Mercurys. If this story is true, those original Penske Matadors were sold to the Elliott family, Dawsonville, Ga. It is a fact that some '77 Mercurys were purchased by the Elliotts from Roger Penske. To further muddy the waters, one must ponder the origin of the Allison-owned Matadors. Were these cars refitted having worn Chevy sheet metal or did any of them come from the Penske shops?

Even after Allison went to work for Bud Moore driving the new 1978 Norris Industries Ford Thunderbirds, he continued to compete in the old Sportsman series (renamed Busch Grand National in 1982). His choice of race car was the Matadors he'd driven the year before. Allison was a veritable terror on the NASCAR Sportsman circuit during the 1978 season, winning many races.

The Penske-campaigned Matador race cars will best be remembered for introducing four-wheeled disk brakes to the NASCAR series. It didn't take long before all of the other competitors and the sanctioning body saw the benefits of this system.

In the manufacturer's championship chase, the Matador garnered only four points in 1972, 11 in 1973, then jumped to 26 in 1974 and catapulted to 57 in 1975. It finally fell back sharply in 1977 to only 19. Contrary to the information given in the Ertl/AMT Matador instruction sheet, the car scored victories in the following years: one in 1973, one in 1974 and three in 1975.

The Model Kit: The Matador NASCAR race car model currently available from Ertl under the AMT name was first produced in 1975. The race car version has been available in a few different forms, namely the Gary Bettenhausen original issue, a Penske race team that included trailer and Chevrolet van and the Allison Sportsman issue.

The current reissue is certainly welcomed by the race car modeling community. It is a shame that the box art is so uninspiring. There is also nothing to hint to the potential buyer that there are indeed variations of markings available on the new decal sheet.

Ertl could also have assisted builders with a little identification of paint colors or recommendations. Early versions may have used the Sunoco-like dark blue on the nose, but most of the time medium blue (a Process Blue shade) was prevalent. At step number 12 Paint and Decal Information on the instruction sheet, it would have been nice if Ertl could have recommended something like Testors French Blue (bottle) or Racing Blue (spray can), Gloss White and number three red.

Remember, the original tooling was designed to produce a race car as well as a street-stock annual kit. This forced some compromises, primarily to the race car version. The roll cage and other interior appointments are nicely done when you consider this is a conversion from a production interior. There appears to be most of the right pieces as well as the padding included. The replacement of stock inner fender panels with a race car-type structure under the hood is a welcome touch. There is no window net included, but that doesn't create a major problem as there are many after-market ones to select.

Does the chassis resemble a Holman-Moody product? Not exactly. The rear suspension includes a Watts link, but should have dual shocks instead of singles on either end of the rear end housing. There is very little in the way of front suspension detail. The tires and wheels look pretty close to the right choice for 1977 and later, as Goodyear had made the move to slicks by then. The wheels resemble the kind used on Allison's Sportsman Matador in 1978 when he won the race in Charlotte, N.C. However, for earlier versions of the car, the treaded tires from the old MPC stockers are the most accurate. Also, Weld five-slot wheels like those used on the Penske Matador are available in plated resin from the Modelhaus.

Again, it would be very helpful to the younger modelers if Ertl/AMT had shown the other decaling versions of the Matador in color on the box art. The clear areas surrounding the numbers and letters on the kit decal sheet appear a bit milky. I have no idea if this will carry over onto the finished model once the decals are dry and in place. It might be an excellent idea to trim these decals as close and tight as possible before application.

Some adjustment to ride height may be necessary. Also later versions of the car show some gentle reshaping of the wheel openings. Study reference photos carefully before getting carried away with removing plastic from these areas.

The reissued kit like the original has an excellent representation of the 358 cid small-block AMC racing engine including a dry sump and headers. I found no photos showing the type of dump pipes included with this kit. All the pictures I looked at would lead me to believe the Matador dumps should be made from aluminum or plastic tubing and probably resembled those found on current stock car kits.

This is not a "slam-dunk" kind of project, though the Ertl/AMT Matador kit will build a decent (though not especially accurate) model out-of-the-box. Thorough research and an understanding of how stock cars were being built during this period in history helps immensely to replicate this important race car. What you desire as the final finished replica is the only limitation to that end.

Reliable sources of reference material for the Matador are available in the following:

• *Motor Racing Replica News* (now *Motor Racing Models*), Issue No. 26, July-August, 1995, UMI-Model-werks, 408-266-8143.

• *Vintage and Historic Stock Cars*, Dr. John Craft, Motorbooks International

• You can always get a first hand view of the AMC/Penske Matador as it is on permanent display at the International Motorsports Hall of Fame at the Alabama Motor Speedway in Talladega.

Body work includes the deluxe window treatment. Here the insert is glued into place for both quarter windows first. Then the seams around the inserts need to be finished off. I recommend using micro-balloons along with super glue. Make sure to work with this stuff in a well-ventilated area as the chemical reaction can result in an unpleasant aroma.

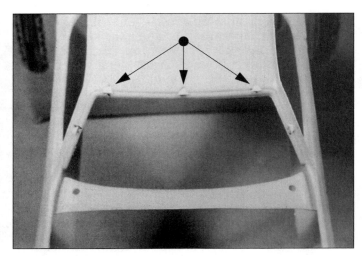

Use .010-inch sheet plastic to cut out small triangles of material which are glued into place around the windshield perimeter to represent retainer clips.

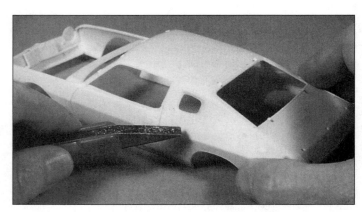

The Revell-Monogram Pro Modeler sanding stick makes quick work of blending in the area that was filled in around the quarter windows.

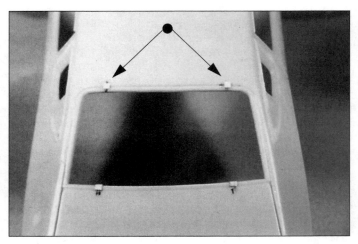

Using .010-inch sheet plastic, cut out small squares of material to represent the retainers for the rear window safety straps that will be added during final assembly.

Material will need to be removed from both front fender wheel openings. I found that a standard 35mm film canister was just about the right diameter. Simply wrap a piece of 360 grit automotive sand paper around the canister and rotate the combo in the opening to achieve the proper radius.

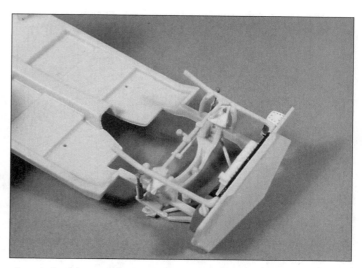

A set of resin upper control arms was added.

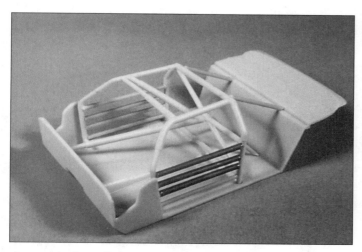

Assemble the roll cage according to kit instruction sheet. The kit cage falls far short of meeting the requirements of the period according to the rule book. I included additional side bars on both sides of the cage using .125-inch diameter tubing and .080-inch diameter plastic rod cut to fit.

Next, a complete rear steer, lower suspension assembly from an Ertl/AMT Thunderbird was dropped into place on the front of the Matador chassis. Very little cutting and filing were required to get the parts to fit properly.

Once the kit front chassis parts were assembled, I determined that more detail and accuracy could be added. First I replaced the kit front shocks with units from a Monogram stock car kit as shown here.

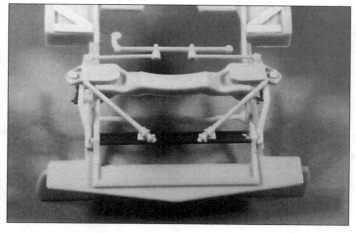

To support the Thunderbird's front strut rods, a cross brace was added from Plastruct channel-style bar stock.

Finally, a resin oil cooler and reservoir along with a scrap parts box radiator were attached in place to the front core support.

Kit wheels and tires were discarded in favor of this set of MPC treaded Goodyears along with plated resin Weld wheels and plain wheel backs from the Model Haus.

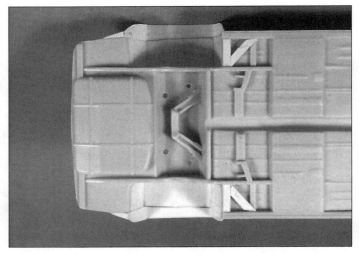

Thin sheet plastic was used to "box-in" the rear inner fender panels. A bit of trial and error test fitting will be required to ensure a good fit once the chassis and interior are inserted into place in the body shell.

The periodic test-fitting of parts and sub-assemblies is a necessity. It's always preferred to find out about misfit pieces before final assembly.

This front and rear view shows the primary parts to check the stance of the Matador as it sits on all fours.

A strip of 3/32-inch bar stock was shaved to a triangular cross section and added to the base of the rear deck spoiler.

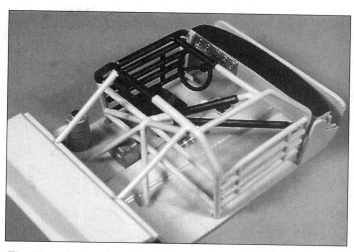

The Matador interior is taking shape. The interior panels and the assembled roll cage were painted with Tru-Match Roll Cage Gray spray paint. A more correct instrument cluster was taken from the spare parts box and fitted into place on the dash panel.

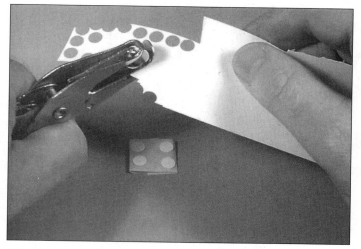

The kit contains no parking light or tail light metal covers. I used a single hole paper punch and trimmed out round pieces from .010-inch sheet plastic.

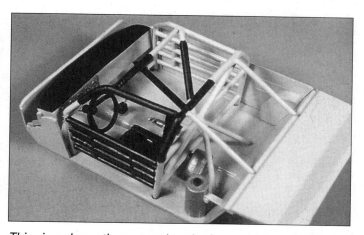

This view shows the rear-end cooler fan and primary engine oil storage tank for the dry-sump system painted, plumbed and glued into the proper location in the left rear of the cockpit.

This view shows the hole punch circles in place in the Matador grill.

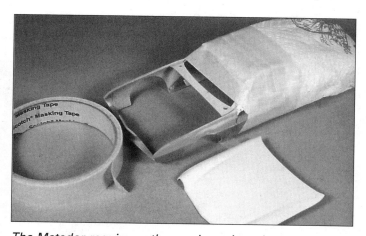

The Matador requires a three-color paint scheme. The front section of the body shell is being prepared for the blue paint. I use Bare-Metal chrome foil to mask the fine edge between colors. Then I use masking tape along with household paper hand towels to complete the task.

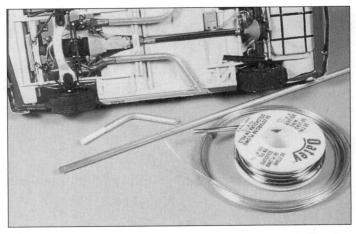

Accurate exhaust dump pipes can be constructed using 3/32-inch diameter aluminum tubing and .090-inch diameter solid core solder wire. Once the solder is inserted into the tubing it can be carefully bent to the proper angle. Follow this up by making dump hangers from small diameter aluminum wire.

This view of the completed engine compartment reveals the abundance of detail. Included here are all the fuel, electrical and cooling lines.

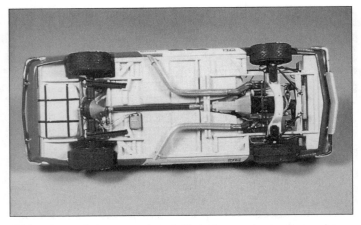

This view of the completed Matador undercarriage shows the use of various shades of black and metal paint colors to enhance realism. This view also shows the rear end plumbing, including the cooling pump driven off the driver shaft. At the front can be seen the bottom end engine plumbing and the exhaust dumps hung in place.

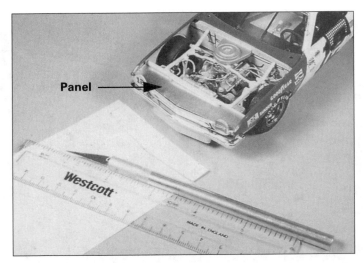

The finished model results in a rather large gap between the core support and the back of the grill. I cut a panel from file card stock and covered it with Bar-Metal chrome foil. The finished panel was attached into place with white craft glue.

Finished! Final details include photo-etch hood pins by Pro-Tech and an excellent decal package from Dave Romero design.

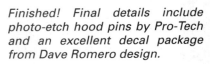

Short Track Stormer that Comes in a Box

Building and Detailing the 1/25th scale Chrysler Kit Car Kits

The History: In the early 1970s, General Motors' Chevrolet Division had an absolute lock on the short-track stock car racing game in this country. The No. 3 auto maker, Chrysler Corporation, decided to take a crack at producing a competitive race car for the competitor on a budget. Larry Rathgeb, chief engineer at Chrysler, stopped to visit his old friend (the late) Harry Hyde at the Charlotte, N.C., headquarters of K&K Insurance's NASCAR racing facilities. The duo agreed to take in an evening of dirt track racing at Concord Speedway.

Rathgeb was surprised that night at what he saw on the race track. Yes, there was a full field of race cars…29 Chevrolets and one Ford! "Where are the Mopars, Harry?" asked Larry. Harry told him there were no Mopar short track race cars. In fact, the lack of a ready supply of parts simply made it impossible. Rathgeb departed Charlotte the next day. He had gotten an idea that he simply couldn't put out of his head!

Rathgeb's burning idea resulted in what was officially known as the Chrysler Kit Car Program. It was a simple concept: put all the best competition-tested parts—literally everything needed to construct a race car—in a large shipping container along with a set of easily understood instructions. After the budget-minded racer assembled the parts (and with a bit of tweaking) he would be ready to take on those pesky Chevrolets. What a great concept! An unassembled race car in a box with instructions on how to put it together correctly. It sounds exactly like building a model car kit, except this thing was 25 times bigger and it didn't just sit there on the shelf…it would literally fly!

As in every good yarn, there's a downside. In this instance, it was poor timing. Late In 1972, the United States experienced the first major energy crisis in its history. The American auto industry was awash in red ink as the result of poor sales. Of the Big 3 Auto Makers, Chrysler was in the worst shape. At this time, Chrysler was not able to supply their major racing operation, Petty Enterprises. It had all it could handle just keeping the corporation's doors open. So it's no wonder the Kit Car program slowly faded into history. By 1978, save for government intervention, Chrysler came within a heart beat of extinction.

When I was told about the kit car program by a friend at Petty Enterprises, it occurred to me this might be a great idea if there was a model of the kit car to aid Chrysler in promoting the concept. Since Chrysler hoped to sell all the parts and pieces, including a complete race car through neighborhood Mopar dealer parts departments, what if they had a model kit to also sell to promote the program?

We didn't get too far with the big boys at Chrysler, but I did manage to convince the original AMT man-

agement that a model kit would be a good idea. A hand shake between Bill Brown, AMT VP of marketing, and Richard Petty in the Michigan International Speedway garage during a race weekend got the whole thing into motion.

As is common practice, multiple versions of this model stock car kit would need to be produced to make the whole thing profitable for AMT. The stock car fans working at AMT were already aware of the Warren Stewart Dodge Dart Sport running on tracks around the southeast part of Michigan. I had already spotted the Ohio National Guard-sponsored Plymouth Duster driven by Buckeye short track legend Jim Cushman at Kil-Kare, Columbus and Shady Bowl speedways in Ohio.

Current Ertl/AMT engineering manager John Mueller (who worked at the original AMT in those days), traveled to Level Cross, N.C. (home of Petty Enterprises), intent on measuring and photographing Petty's own Dart Swinger kit car. In the interim, Petty employee Joe Milikan had been campaigning the car with a bit different markings. What Mueller saw at Petty Enterprises was the same electric blue Dodge, but now carrying the number 04 with major sponsorship by Hayes Jewelers. Those changes were minor compared to the situation Mueller was confronted with when he got to work. I got a hurried phone call from a thoroughly stressed Mueller that really startled me. He asked me which one of the cars was AMT doing? Of course, I said all three of them!

Unknown to me, there was a split now developing between Chrysler and Petty Enterprises over which type of racing the kit car was intended for. Chrysler wanted a "Saturday Night Special" intended for the local short tracks located all over North America. By contrast, the Pettys didn't see much point in building a race car that would not meet NASCAR Sportsman (now Busch Grand National) specifications. What then developed was both a 108-inch wheel base Dart/Duster and a 112-inch wheel base Swinger/Scamp. NASCAR Sportsman rules dictated a minimum 112-inch wheel base, so only the Swinger/Scamp configuration was eligible to compete in that series. The larger heavier race car, built to NASCAR specifications, could not be competitive running the nation's local short tracks.

For both Chrysler and the Pettys, the two different race car concepts combined with the economic climate went along way to kill the program by the early 1980s. The two different concepts also nearly killed the scale model-kit project, as well. Add to this the complexity of the paint scheme on the Ohio Air National Guard Duster (and the prohibitive cost associated with developing the decal sheet), and the whole model kit project nearly was scrapped.

The Model Kits: The model kit project survived, and AMT released four model kits of four different race cars by 1975. Also, a double kit was released later featuring a Ford truck race car hauler and a repop of the Petty Dart.

Three of the original four releases featured scale versions of actual full-scale race cars. The fourth release, touted as a Plymouth Valiant Scamp, was actually the Petty Dart Swinger with a convoluted paint scheme. The box art model was the winner of a hobby shop contest in Lafayette, Ind. The top prize was having your winning model featured as an AMT kit release. Ironically, it is the hardest (most expensive) one of the four releases to find today.

The final release in the Chrysler Kit Car series was the Richard Petty Race Team comprised of the Petty Dart with a conventional Ford truck race car hauler mentioned earlier. There may have been fewer of this combo kit made than any of the other four. Poppa Lee Petty blew a gasket when he saw the box art featuring a Ford product and Dodge! A hasty call from the Pettys was made to AMT and production of the kit was stopped. Eventually, an agreement was reached permitting AMT to produce whatever number of kits that they had received pre-printed boxes for. That number could have been as few as 20,000 or as many as 60,000—no one really knows.

The two basic kits (Swinger/Scamp vs. Dart/Duster) differ a bit. The (Chrysler) short track car has a slightly different roll cage and rear end setup. The Dart/Duster rides on a quick change, while the Swinger/Scamp runs a Dana differential.

The front part of the roll cage is basic to all four kits; that's why, if built from the box, the cage sits back a bit from the windshield header and the A pillars in the Petty Dart. When building the Petty Dart, for example, this can be fixed easily by adding some extra plastic rod to the length of the upper side bars and adjusting the front uprights to become parallel with the angle of the A pillars.

The AMT Kit Car kits are fairly faithful to the original race cars, even by today's high standards. Admittedly, the kits don't go together like a typical Monogram stock car model. Assembly would be less frustrating if there were an abundance of locator pins typical in current plastic kits. This system in common use today for positively attaching assemblies would also help the builder to know exactly where each part should be attached. Detail of some of the suspension components is rather nondescript: for example, the shock absorbers. They need work.

The assembled components, when compared to my reference material on the Kit Car, indicate that Mueller (and AMT) did a respectable job engineering these model kits.

The Cushman Duster: The Cushman Duster pictured on page 112, is the second one I built, shortly after the kit was released. The first built model was presented to Jim Cushman during special ceremonies at Columbus Motor Speedway, Columbus, Ohio, in 1976. Since the decision was made to short cut the marking on the decal sheet, I had to draw a template and then hand-cut the markings from Mystic vinyl tape. The kit decal sheet contains only the numbers, Ohio Air National Guard shields and incidental sponsor decals. By the time development of this kit was nearing completion, the paint scheme had changed to what you see here. As I said, it nearly brought the whole project to a halt. A completely accurate decal layout was deemed too expensive to produce.

The K&K Dodge Dart Sport: This K&K Insurance Dodge Dart Sport was built from the Warren Stewart kit with some modifications. The car, as pictured on page 112, competed only twice in this color scheme and graphics. Harry Hyde decided after the Pettys built their own Kit Car that K&K should have one of its own. The car was built originally for Bobby Unser to compete in the Pikes Peak Hill Climb event. As he has done frequently, Unser blew them away, setting new records in the process in the K&K Dart.

After the thrill of victory had worn off a bit, Larry Rathgeb pointed out to Hyde that it wasn't really the hill climb competitors this race car concept was designed for. So Hyde tweaked the car thoroughly, loaded up and headed back to Concord Speedway where this whole story began. Upon arrival, Hyde didn't arrange for the track champion to drive the car. Quite the contrary. He looked around the pit area for someone who was struggling to run in the middle of the pack. Chuck Piazza got the honors that very special Saturday night. Piazza surprised everyone but Hyde as he went out and took the pole, won his heat and ran away and hid from the field of Chevys in the feature.

After the night of racing was over, Hyde and crew rolled the little Dodge back towards the trailer when they were stopped by the guy who owned Piazza's regular race car. He asked what it would take to get Hyde and the boys to go home with an empty trailer and leave the hot-red Dodge right where it sat. Hyde finally sold the car and Piazza went on to mow 'em down the rest of the season at Concord Speedway.

This model was built pretty much straight from the box with a few modifications. I was never pleased with the molded-in grill in the Stewart kit. No suitable grill could be found for a 1973 Dart, so I got creative and modified an MPC '73 Duster grill to resemble the Dart. The two units are pretty close in appearance and the protective screen serves to cover up some of the obvious differences.

The model was painted with '86 GMC truck red-orange, which looked to me to be a pretty close match to the red used on K&K race cars. MCW stocks an accurate color for these cars, also. The markings are a combination of JNJ decals and Woodland Scenes dry transfer lettering.

The Petty Dart Swinger: The Swinger, Dart or Duster body shells can all be improved with a little tweaking. The Swinger needs to have the body seams filled and rescribed around the tail lights and rear bumper. Once this is done, the rear corners of the body more closely resemble the configuration of the full-size race car. The engraved lines representing panel lines in this area are in the wrong place.

The Dart/Duster body shell's front fender "eyebrows" were molded with extra material that needs to be removed. This is done for very obvious reasons. The leading edge of the front fenders would have drooped severely when removed from the mold had thinner more accurate flares been tooled for the kit. Removing material from this part of the fender flares will require adjusting the overall ride height downward. The nose of this type race car should hug the ground. If left in the box-stock location, once the fender flares are opened up, it results in way too much clearance between fender and tire.

A quick and simple solution requires notching the firewall in two places directly above the main side frame rails. This permits the body platform to rest a bit lower on the chassis. Some experimentation may be necessary. Make the adjustment a little at a time until you get the ride height that satisfies your eye. The front spoiler will also need to be raised up approximately 1/8 inch. Provide a small bit of ground clearance. But just as important, the finished model should display an aggressive, ground-hugging stance.

Building the Petty Dart is pretty straight forward from here. Remember that the outside, inside and underside of this car should be painted Petty Blue. I contrasted this by finishing the suspension components in metallic and semi-gloss black bottle paints.

You may also wish to play a bit with the track width, both front and rear. On the Petty car, I reduced the front track width by removing material from both inner wheel backs. You can also make some adjustments by shimming the rear track with thin washers made by slicing various thickness wafers from plastic tubing. Simply add these wafers to the wheel backs where they attach to the ends of the rear axle until you are satisfied with how far the tires protrude from the fender openings. In those days, NASCAR Sportsman rules permitted the tires to extend beyond the edge of the fenders.

The wheels, tires and power train for all the Chrysler Kit Cars kits are identical, Actually, the wheels and tires in these kits are quite appropriate for the larger Grand National cars (now Winston Cup) used during the late 1970s and pre-Eagle markings. Ertl/AMT has used these same tires in its line of Winston Cup stock car kits.

I built a prototype Dart Swinger for AMT's exhibit at the annual Chicago and New York hobby shows in 1975. This was built as a curbside model. Parts of an MPC Schrewsberry Dart Swinger drag car were combined with the nose of an MPC '71 Demon to make the body shell. Various other kits gave up their wheels, tires, interior, roll cage, etc., to finish the model. Unexpectedly, this model was returned to me some years ago when Lesney (former owners of AMT) went bankrupt and liquidated everything at AMT.

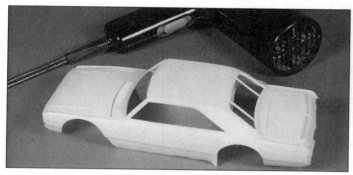

Upon opening this 25-year-old kit I found the body was slightly warped. It was twisted diagonally across the body from right front to left rear corner. No sweat! This is a common occurrence and can be fixed quickly. Carefully apply heat with a hair dryer to the affected areas of the body.

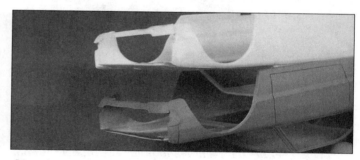

Glue the pan to the lower front of the body shell. Fill in and file to the shape of the body seam. Priming the work surfaces will help determine the extent of the effort required. Likewise, mold in the rear pan to the lower rear of the body shell. Reshape the lower corner of the fender.

When the plastic is very warm to the touch, twist the body shell in the opposite direction of the problem. You may need to repeat the process until the body shell is square or will sit level on a perfectly flat surface.

Remove the molded-in hood pins from the leading edge of the hood. Repeat the process for the moded-in hood pins on the rear deck lid. Also fill in the gap between the two sides of the rear spoiler where it attaches to the deck lid.

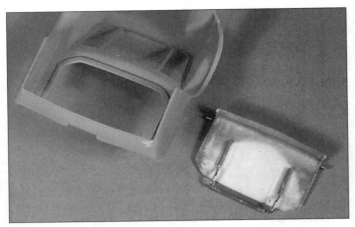

Make a pair of deck lid hinges by bending .045-inch diameter copper wire to shape as shown. Insert the long ends of the two wire hinges into lengths of .065-inch diameter plastic tubing. Insert the short ends of the wire hinges into 1/2-inch lengths of .065-inch diameter plastic tubing. Glue this assembly into place on the underside of the rear of the deck lid. The portion of the hinge protruding from the rear of the deck lid will be glued into place under the rear cowl as part of the final assembly.

This wire coat hanger paint stand holds the model for both priming and painting. I used Plasti-Kote T-235 primer and Tru-Match No. 43 Petty Blue automotive enamel for model application.

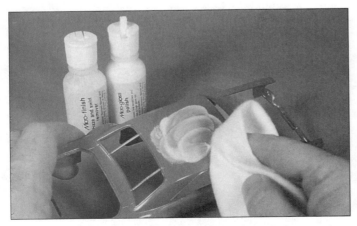

Once the automotive enamel has had sufficient time to thoroughly dry and properly cure (7-10 days), rub out the paint finish using an LMG polishing kit.

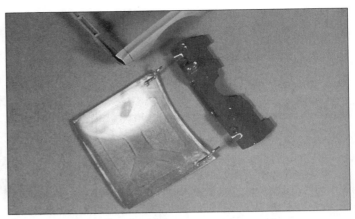

.060-inch diameter copper wire was bent to shape to make a pair of hinges for the hood. Corresponding notches were cut in the firewall, which will allow the hood to open and close properly.

Mount all parts and pieces to be sprayed with primer on a pieces of cardboard or card stock. Use small loops of masking tape to attach each piece. I recommend using Plasti-Kote T-235 light gray sanding primer which will not harm styrene plastic.

Bare-Metal chrome foil is carefully applied to the metal trim surround on the front windshield. Burnish the foil into all the surface details with a clean cotton swab.

After carefully trimming around the edges of the windshield surround with a fresh X-Acto blade, slowly peel the excess foil away from the window trim with fine tweezers.

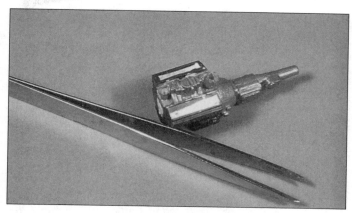

The W-2 355 cid Chrysler small block V-8 racing engine can benefit with the removal of some molded-in features like the carburetor and distributor. Here the kit distributor has been replaced by an other eight cylinder unit from the parts box.

The partially assembled engine is test-fitted into the chassis. Note the new carb with fuel line, the replacement distributor with spark plug wire and the painted accessory belts and pulleys.

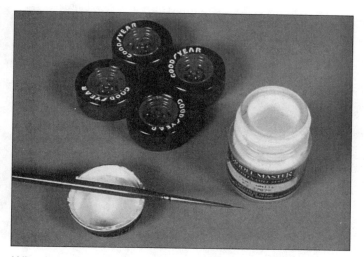

Wheels are painted to match the body etc., with Tru-Match Petty Blue. First, sand the slick tread and carefully paint the raised lettering on each tire using a 000 brush and flat white bottle paint.

The brass wire hinges that were fabricated from the hood and rear deck lid now allow the finished model to be posed with these two panel open as shown. As part of the final assembly, Pro-Tech photo-etch hood pins were added fore and aft; a Scale Speedways window net was assembled and installed draped out the driver's window, and a Race Ready Replicas dry break gas filler and overflow tube were added.

These two view of the finished engine compartment feature all the proper electrical, fuel and cooling lines in place.

The undercarriage of the finished Petty Dart displays the correctly plumbed rear-end cooling equipment and features the variety of metallic paint finishes that adds realism to the suspension and drive line elements.

The Petty Dodge Dart Swinger was only available twice in the mid-1970s, once as a stand-alone kit and again as part of the Richard Petty race team. Rumor has the '72 Dart being reissued early in the new millinium.

A built model of the Jim Cushman-driven Ohio Air National Guard '75 Plymouth Duster. (model by the author) A template was drawn to replicate the patriotic paint scheme on the Jim Cushman Plymouth Duster. In this case red and blue mystic vinyl tape was cut from the templates and applied to the Duster body over testor gloss white enamel. The Cushman Plymouth Duster 1/25th scale kit was issued in 1975 and has not been available since. Though not on a level with today's kit technology, this kit car builds into a stricking replica.

The K&K #71B Dodge Dart Sport was an easy conversion from the Stewart kit. Yesterdays Vintage Decals has recently released K&K decals. Note that the treaded tries on this Dodge mark it as a non-pavement racer. "Down in the Dirt" shows how to convert slicks to treaded tires.

Down in the Dirt!

I started the No. 71B Dodge project (see page 112) many years ago after seeing an article on the car in *Stock Car* magazine. There was one stumbling block that always kept me from finishing it...no dirt track tires for short track stock cars! Thanks to master modeler Randy Derr, I was shown the technique for grooving a set of slick tires, turning them into just what I needed.

Derr made a tool for this purpose by first, cutting a piece of 3/4 in. thick wood to the dimensions of 2-1/2 inches x 1-1/2 inches. In the center of the wood block, he drilled a 5/8-inch diameter hole to a depth of 1 in. On the top edge (2-1/2 in. side) Randy cut two grooves at an oblique angle (about 30 degrees off the center line). Cut these diagonal grooves 1/8 in. off the center line of the hole. Make guide marks at 1/16th-inch increments off the same center line. Finally, insert a 1-9/16-inch length of tubing or wooden dowel rod into the hole in the side of the block. Make sure at least

9/16 inches of the tubing or dowel rod extends from the side of the block. Now you are ready to make treaded racing tires.

Insert the tire in a sanding tool mounted in a 3/8-inch drill, spin the tires slowly while holding a piece of coarse sand paper against the tread surface. Next, using a razor saw, cut evenly spaced concentric grooves (approximately 3/32 inches apart) across the tread surface of the spinning tire. Then mount each tire onto the jig and start by cutting a single oblique groove with the razor saw. Slowly rotate the tire clockwise around the tubing or dowel one incremental mark at a time before cutting the groove. The determining factor will depend on whether you want the cross grooves on the finished tire to be fine or coarse. Proceed to cut each successive groove until you have worked your way completely around the circumference of each tire.

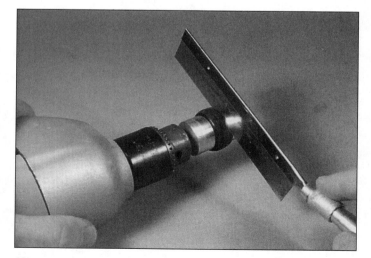

Shown here is a Mike Dowd tire sanding tool, Randy Derr's grooving tool, a screw driver and a slick (treadless) racing tire.

It is recommended the tire grooving tool be used with a bench vice. Work cautiously and carefully as this is a tedious step and repeat procedure. However, the final results are worth the effort.

Here grooves are being cut around the circumference of the tire across the contact surface. Space cuts equal measurements apart depending on how many grooves you would like. Use a variable speed drill to rotate the tire slowly. You may wish to clamp the drill to a hard work surface or in a bench vice.

From left to right are four tires demonstrating the various stages of this grooving procedure: sanded tire tread surface; the first perimeter cuts; half-way there; and the grooved tire finished and ready to mount on the model.

Building a 1967 Ford Fairlane

Randy Derr builds a replica of Mario Andretti's
Holman-Moody half-chassis winner from the Daytona 500

The History: From the late 1950s, Ford Motor Company had remained a major force on the nation's race tracks. Fords and Mercurys had no problem matching equipment and driving talent with any combination from General Motors and Chrysler. That was true until 1964 when Chrysler, tired of being an also-ran, released the mighty and legendary late-model 426 Hemi V-8 engine. With awesome horsepower and stump-pulling torque, Hemi Plymouths and Dodges muscled their way to the front of the pack quickly and often.

Ford moved to match the Chrysler twins for the 1966 season by engineering a monster motor of its own, the overhead cam 427. Ford withdrew its factory teams from NASCAR competition after the eighth race of the 1966 season at Atlanta Motor Speedway when the sanctioning body refused to allow Ford to race its new engine.

Chrysler had withdrawn its factory teams in 1965 when NASCAR temporarily disallowed the Hemi. Attendance and race car fields dwindled in 1965 but that disaster was not repeated when Ford countered for 1966. Many Ford factory drivers found competitive rides with other teams (Ford and Mercury drivers needed to stay employed!). Ford could feel the pressure that resulted from being off the track and out of view.

In the fall of 1966, Bud Moore built a new 1966 Mercury Comet and hired Darrell Derringer to drive it. At first, NASCAR inspectors sent the new car home. It was obvious there wasn't much "stock" on the Bud Moore Comet. Production model Fairlanes and Comets rolled out of the factory on a unibody platform. Here, the body and chassis are constructed of numerous sheet metal stampings welded together, forming a single structure, hence the term "unibody." Previously, Ford and Mercury race cars had been built body-over-frame like their full-size production cars used.

On these new concept stock cars, the entire front snout, upper and lower control arms, dual shock absorber, etc., were transplanted from the 1965-1966 Galaxie which was attached to the Ford intermediate unibody platform ahead of the firewall. Fabricated L-shaped side beams were welded to the new front snout, around the perimeter of the production intermediate platform then attached to the rear sub-frame. This new structure tied the whole thing together and closely resembled the larger Ford's body-over-frame design.

Though NASCAR gave a thumb's down to the new creation, hundreds of empty seats in the grandstands hit everybody in the pocketbook. Eventually, NASCAR saw the light and approved the new hybrid (referred to as "half-chassis"). From that point on, any reference in the Grand National rule book requiring race cars to be based on production components disappeared forever.

This new hybrid platform used under NASCAR 1966-1967 intermediate Fords and Mercurys, except for rear suspension, set the standard for the next 30 years of race car construction. Small evolutionary improvements and changes for safety reasons have been incorporated over the years, but the current NASCAR stock car chassis is a close relative to those first half-chassis race cars.

The Project: Randy Derr built a 1/25th replica starting with a street-stock Ertl/AMT 1966 Fairlane kit. Unlike purpose-built kits of current stock car subjects, there is currently no such kit of stock cars of this era. The techniques presented here are typical of those employed when converting street-driven model car kits into race cars.

The stock kit interior panels were replaced by items made from plastic sheet stock. The new side panels represent the appearance of a stripped or gutted interior typical of a 1960s-era stock car. The new side panels are cut 1/16-inch lower in height than the stock panel to allow the body to set lower over the chassis of the finished model. Once the stock rear seat was separated from the kit package shelf, Derr made a new rear bulkhead panel and attached it to the kit package shelf. Randy used the stock Fairlane kit dashboard for the race car. He removed the gauge panel from a Monogram stock car kit dash and trimmed it down to fit in place of the Fairlane instrument cluster. Now is a good time to test-fit the interior into the body shell.

The stock kit firewall was cleaned by carefully removing all surface detail, including the heater and molded-in windshield wiper motor. Automotive body putty was used to fill in the angled channels where the stock inner front fender panel would be located. Next, the height of the firewall was reduced by 1/16-inch in height as was done for the interior panels.

Derr built an accurate race car roll cage by first inserting lengths of .060-inch diameter brass rod inside 3/32-inch diameter plastic tubing. The soft wire allowed him to bend the plastic tubing at right angles easily. Inserting the rod into the tubing helps maintain the tubing wall integrity and shape, as it will not collapse when bent.

Next, Derr built the front hoop using 3/32-inch Evergreen tubing with .060-inch brass rod inserted inside like the roll cage. Structural uprights on the left and right sides of the chassis were added that form the dual shock towers. A 3/4-inch length of .030-inch diameter rod was laid horizontal to make the actual attachment points for the dual shocks. Finally, he used two lengths of .040-inch sheet plastic to form the "ears" which serve as fender supports and attachment points for the oil cooler and tank. Finally, test fit the finished roll cage into the interior. Some adjustment to width, height and length may be required for a good fit.

Then, 1/16-inch square bar stock was used to form the structure that represents the radiator support. Derr used a small rectangle of .020-inch sheet stock to form the base plate for the battery tray. Next, the lower shock mounts were made from .060-inch diameter rod. These pieces were attached horizontally across the lower control arms next to the ball joints. The steering arm was then attached to the spindles which were made from .030-inch diameter brass rod. Scratch-built coil springs were added to the front suspension. Derr formed these coil springs by winding .020 wire-wrap wire around a piece of small diameter tubing.

Four pairs of adjustable shock absorbers were made next. He used .060-inch diameter Evergreen rod for the shock absorber body and .030-inch diameter silver wire for the shaft. He also made the upper and lower mounts from short lengths of tubing. The rear shocks were made in the same fashion and attached on either side of the rear leaf spring mounting pads. The four rear shocks were attached to the rod extensions. Finally, Derr added a rear end cooling pump between the rear universal joint and the drive shaft and the snout of the differential.

Next, he built two pairs of rear spring shackles from .020-inch sheet plastic. The spring shackles were glued in place to the sides of each rear spring perch. On the full-size race car, they were used to adjust ride height. Finally, he constructed (from sheet plastic) a rectangular-shaped box that fit around the existing kit fuel tank to form the fuel cell.

For added detail, Derr removed the U-joint from the kit drive shaft. He replaced the kit drive shaft with a 2-1/4-inch length of 3/32-inch diameter aluminum tubing, reattaching the kit U-joints to either end. Additional realism was applied to the engine oil cooler by attaching rectangular sections of Dr. Micro Tool fine mesh screen to the front and rear surfaces.

He found the production body shell required many small modifications to make it better resemble a NASCAR stock car. The hood depressions were filled in, the windshield wipers were removed and a 1/8-inch diameter hole was drilled for the new fuel filler neck in the left rear fender. Then a short length of aluminum tubing was inserted into the hole to represent the fuel filler neck. He filed and sanded off the molded-in windshield wipers making sure not to remove too much material from the cowl area. He worked carefully, making sure he retained the air-vent detail in the cowl panel.

The front wheel wells were enlarged by approximately 1/8-inch for better tire clearance. First, Derr used an X-Acto knife to carefully enlarge the wheel arches. He then wrapped a piece of 320 automotive sand paper around a common 35mm film canister and trued up the wheel opening shape. He formed the lip of the new wheel opening by first gluing a strip of 1/16-inch bar stock into the opening. When the glue was dry, he filed and sanded the bar stock, inside and outside, to the proper shape. Then he used automotive body putty to blend the lip into the exterior surface of the fender. He repeated this process for the rear fender opening lips. He found that the arch of the new rear fender opening should be much flatter than the one on the front fender.

Final comments: Derr completed this 1967 Fairlane half-chassis car, by finishing off the dash top, upper door panels and package shelf with flat black paint. The interior floor was painted Testors Gull Gray. The dash face, interior side panels and rear bulk head were finished-off with aluminum. He painted the roll cage assembly flat black and added vinyl tubing to represent the padding. He finished the chassis in Testors Gull Gray, highlighting the suspension and driveline parts with shades of metallic and black paints for contrast. The final paint colors for the body shell were obtained from Model Car World finishes.

Decals by Slixx and Fred Cady design were used for this Mario Andretti Fairlane. The tires and wheels are period-correct resin pieces available from the Modelhaus.

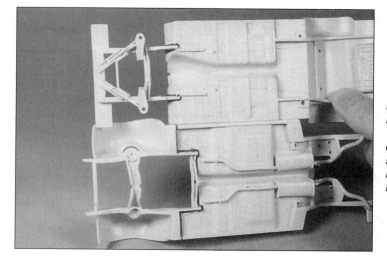

The major components to replicate an accurate 1966-67 Ford half-chassis race car are pictured here. At the top is an Ertl/AMT Fairlane chassis. On the bottom is an Ertl/AMT 1965 Ford Galaxie chassis. Note the heavy black lines indicating where to make your cut. Start by removing the front sub-frame, including the engine and transmission cross members, from the Ertl/AMT 1965 Galaxie chassis. Then remove the front sub-frame from the 1966 Fairlane chassis.

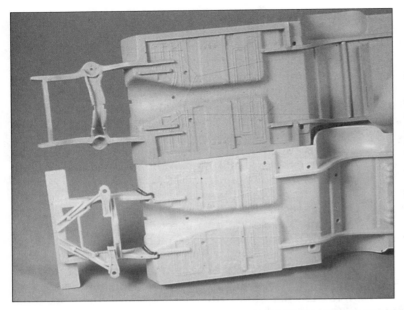

Attach the 1965 Galaxie sub-frame to the front of the 1966 unibody platform as shown. Next add two L-shaped frame rails to each side of the Fairlane platform. Make these pieces from 1/16-inch x 1/8-inch strips of Evergreen plastic bar stock. This effectively ties the front and rear sub-frame together similar to the stock chassis from a production 1965-1966 Ford Galaxie. Also, make a new transmission mount from 1/16-inch diameter plastic rod. Primer the new assembly to help identify any areas needing attention with filler or sanding.

All the major components to build a replica of the typical half-chassis race car. Derr added MCW paint and Slixx and Fred Cady decals to replicate an historically significant NASCAR stock car.

The completed engine compartment shows off the front snout and includes the correct dual front shocks, the fully detailed 427 cid engine which includes all lubricant and electrical lines and the smooth firewall with the master cylinder shown on the left side of the car.

This close-up shot of the rear portion of the Fairlane chassis shows clearly the leaf spring suspension with dual shocks, the rear end cooler including the pump driven off the rear of the drive shaft and the requisite fuel cell.

This close-up of the front end shows more clearly the complete front suspension and the lower surfaces of the big block Ford engine.

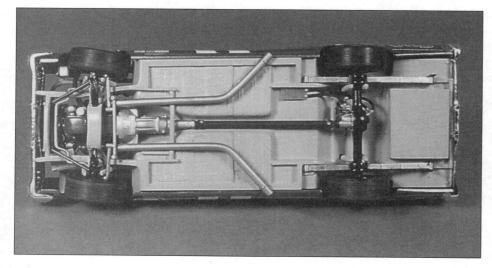

The finished Fairlane chassis shows the results of a great attention to accurate details such as a rear-end cooling system at the rear and the fully functional poseable steering transplanted from the 1965 Ford kit.

The finished 1967 Ford Fairlane. The only things missing from this '67 Fairlane is the smell of tire smoke, racing fuel and the race winner, Mario Andretti!

Attention to minute details like rear bumper end fairings, rear window safety straps, visible exhaust dump hangers and careful decal application result in a contest-quality model.

Radiused front wheel openings allow poseable front wheels to be affectively displayed in this view.

Lindberg's Historic Mopar

A closer look at the Lindberg 1964 Petty Plymouth

Model built by Daryl Huhtala

The History: Richard Petty began his legendary racing career in 1958 at the age of 21. His father Lee wanted it that way. Lee Petty didn't consider this to be a handicap for oldest son Richard as Lee didn't start racing in NASCAR until he was 35. He still won three NASCAR championships in his career! Richard Petty was selected as Rookie-of-the-year in 1959, only his second racing season. He won his first NASCAR race in 1960 and finished second in the seasons' points championship three of the next four years. In 1963, the familiar blue No. 43 Plymouth crossed the finish line first in 14 of the 54 Grand National events that year.

Richard Petty had proven he had all the hereditary skills to drive a race car and win. But by the early 1960s, NASCAR racing was becoming more and more a horsepower race on big fast ovals. The other automakers were providing their teams with large displacement engines. What young Petty needed most was more horsepower.

Chrysler was really getting tired of getting the proverbial "sand kicked in its corporate face." Petty Enterprises was doing all it could with what they had to work with. Until 1964, NASCAR Grand National racing was the exclusive hunting ground of Ford, Pontiac and Chevrolet. What Chrysler had up its sleeve for the first event of 1964, no one was really prepared for, especially the competition. There were eight factory-supported race cars, four Dodges and four Plymouths, fitted with the company's second-generation hemispherical-design, big-block V-8 engine. The dual-rocker arm, domed cylinder head design was fitted to the race-proven 426 cid big block and delivered what could only be described as AWESOME amounts of horse power. The Dodges and Plymouths qualified at speeds nearly 10 mph faster than the hottest Ford products. Drivers of factory-backed Fords and Mercurys could only try to draft the fleet Mopars for 500 miles to have any hope for a victory.

Richard Petty led the parade of Dodges and Plymouths under the checkered flag with a 1-2-3 sweep and the Chrysler Hemi powered five race cars into the top 10 at the finish. Some have described the 1964 Daytona 500 as one of the most lopsided events in the 2.5 mile ovals history. I guess if you had been taking it on the chin up to that point like Chrysler had, you might have a decidedly different view of history. The 1964 Daytona 500 marked Richard Petty's first super-speedway victory and the first big track win for Plymouth since Johnny Mantz drove to victory at Darlington in 1950. Petty went on to win nine races in 1964 and captured his first of seven NASCAR national championships. Certainly the Chrysler Hemi launched

Petty well on his way to becoming the king of the sport of stock car racing.

The Model Kit: It was with a great deal of trepidation that Petty fans, Mopar enthusiasts and dedicated vintage stock car model builders learned that Lindberg Models would release its first purpose-built stock car model, Richard Petty's 1964 Belvedere. Everyone was delighted that this was brand new tooling. Now understand, this Lindberg 1964 Plymouth is not completely flawless. For a first outing, Lindberg produced an excellent stock car kit. The Lindberg kit is a nearly complete and accurate version of the car Petty drove to his first Daytona 500 victory and the car that really established him as a racing super star.

The kit is molded in white and includes clear and chrome-plated parts, as well as four tires and a multi-color water-slide decal sheet. Body proportions are very good. The only flaw on the exterior, from my perspective, is a minor kink in the belt-line along the top of the rear fenders where the C-pillar attaches. I was able to fix the problem to my satisfaction with a jeweler's file and emery board. You just need to flatten out this line around the base of the pillar. When you're finished, the top edge of the fender line should be an unbroken flat arc from the front to the rear of the body shell. From here on, the Lindberg Petty racer suffers just minor deficiencies and omissions. There is no provision for front or rear hood pins or windshield retainer clips on the kit body.

Under the hood is an excellent 1960s-era Chrysler racing Hemi V-8. Included is a very nice racing air cleaner with cowl induction duct work attached. The valve covers are a bit uninspired, though there is a nice complement of three breather caps on the left cover. Daryl Huhtala replaced the kit pieces with Jo-Han single-plug Hemi valve covers from his spare parts box. Daryl removed a 7/16-inch x 5/8-inch section of the right and left inner fender panels. Construct a pair of shock absorbers (matching the kit stock rear shocks) for both sides of the front suspension to complete the list of proper racing equipment.

The interior is well appointed with a realistic roll cage, instrument cluster, a single bucket seat with separately molded belts and harnesses, suspended foot pedals and reversible interior door panels (stock and racing). You can add a resin rear-end cooling fan from the Modelhaus, as one was not included in this Lindberg kit.

The kit chassis is well appointed, except for the omission of a few absolutely necessary items. Huhtala added two more shock absorbers for the rear suspension by simply duplicating the single kit pieces from plastic tubing and rod. Next, he added a rear-end cooler and driveshaft-driven pump. The cooling reservoir again is available from the Model-haus and the pump was constructed from sheet stock and plastic rod.

The Lindberg kit wheels and tires appear to be a bit too small in diameter. They're well turned out pieces, just too small to provide the right look for a race car of the mid-1960s. The kit pieces were replaced with resin wheels and tires from the Modelhaus. Using the larger diameter resin wheel/tire combination defi-nitely gives this Plymouth a more aggressive stance. The plain sidewalls on the resin tires allows for the easy use of Shabo dry transfer lettering or Fred Cady water slide lettering for the Goodyear trademark sig-natures. You have the choice of Firestone or Goodyear markings as many of the Hemi-cars in the 1964 Day-tona 500 practiced on one brand and raced on the other.

Building the Kit: The version Huhtala decided to build from this Lindberg kit was the second place fin-isher from the 1964 Daytona 500. Fortunately after-market decal maker Fred Cady offers an excellent water-slide sheet of markings for the number 25 Ply-mouth driven by Paul Goldsmith.

Huhtala added the omitted details, such as dual shock absorbers front and rear, modifying the inner front fender panels in the engine compartment and substituting larger, more accurate resin wheels and tires from the Modelhaus. The interior and wheels were painted flat black, while the body and chassis were treated to a generous coating of Testors Guards Red. BareMetal Chrome foil was applied to all the kit's bright work. The Detailer was used as a wash to high-light recessed details like the front grill work. Func-tioning photo-etch hood pins were fitted to both the hood and rear deck lid. Detail Master cooling hoses, spark plug wiring and photo-etch items, such as bat-tery terminals, were used to finish-off the engine details.

Final Comments: With the substitution of Fred Cady decals this Lindberg 1964 Plymouth can be built as the Goldsmith No. 25 and No. 54 Plymouth driven by Jimmy Pardue. Whatever version of this kit you decide on, it builds into an excellent replica with some minor exceptions. This is Lindberg's first and only release of a dedicated racing stock car. Let's hope it will not be the last.

References: Sources of reference for this model include: *Richard Petty, The Cars of the King*, Saga-more Publishing; *Motor Trend*, May 1964; *Automobile Quarterly*, Vol. 22, No. 2; and *Racing Pictorial*, 1964 Color Annual.

Daryl Huhtala used the Lindberg Petty Plymouth to build the second place fin-ishing car in the 1964 Daytona 500 driven by Paul Goldsmith. Note the functional hood pins and the stock chrome side trim still in place on the race car.

This bird's eye rear view of the finished Lindberg model shows the rear window safety straps. Note that production door handles were still required to be in place on the race car.

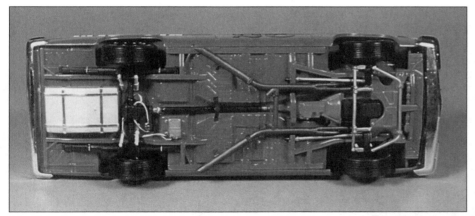

This underside view shows the excellent contrast of suspension and driveline components finished in flat black and metallics contrasted against the solid red chassis. Note the plumbing on the rear end cooling system.

Many model builders of vintage NASCAR stock cars gladly welcomed Lindberg's recent release of the 1/25th scale Richard Petty's 1964 Belevedere Plymouth stock car.

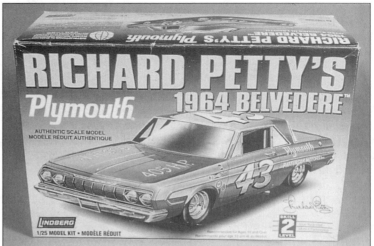

The finished engine compartment looks quite realistic. Note the full compliment of electrical and fluid line detailing, along with a clear view of the front suspension racing suspension features.

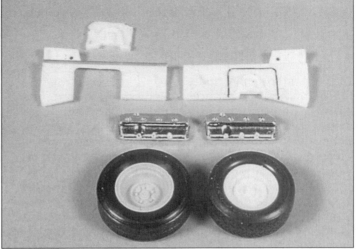

Pictured here are three of the items Daryl addressed in his build of the Lindberg Plymouth. At the top is pictured both right and left inner front fender panels and the required alterations; in the center is pictured a pair of Jo-Han Hemi valve covers and at the bottom is the kit wheel and tire on the right compared to the Modelhaus resin parts on the left.

Chapter 6

Stock Car Model Kits in 1/24th Scale

Revell-Monogram Strikes Pay-Dirt

If you believe that lightening doesn't strike twice in the same spot, then you need to re-examine the Revell-Monogram (R-M) NASCAR model kit line. The first time it was MPC in 1/25th scale. In 1983, time stood still for the stock car model builder for only the second time in history. Monogram Models, always known for high-quality products, introduced four new 1/24th-scale NASCAR stockers that became the foundation for the most successful plastic model kit series in the history of the hobby. There had never been any plastic stock car model kits in this unusual international scale of 1/24th. But that notion wouldn't last long.

The first releases included two Fords and two Buicks; the Bill Elliott Melling and Dale Earnhardt Wrangler T-birds, as well as Darrell Waltrip Mountain Dew and Buddy Baker's Uno card game Regal. The Fords rode on an unbelievably accurate and detailed Banjo Matthew's rear-steer chassis, while the two Buicks featured a front steer platform scaled down from a Mike Laughlin chassis. These four kits set off a virtual "feeding frenzy" that has not subsided for the last 15 years.

Since 1983, R-M has released dozens of kits in this series, including four different T-birds, two different Buicks and Oldsmobiles, along with three different Pontiacs and Chevrolets. Virtually every name driver has been represented in this series, including many Daytona 500 winners and NASCAR yearly championship race cars.

Recently, R-M saw fit to go "retro" with a few of their double kit releases that have seen revised tooling created for the 1981-82 "square bird" Thunderbirds and the venerable 1987-88 aero-style Thunderbirds. Many other vintage NASCAR Fords, Chevys, Pontiacs, Buicks and Oldsmobiles have been replicated in this series that today has sold in the millions of units.

A Bit of History

This phenomenally successful kit line was truly the miracle cure at the right time. Remember in 1979, the United States suffered its second worst energy crisis when OPEC (Organization of Petroleum Exporting Countries) again ratcheted-up prices after having wrestled control of the oil production business away from major Western producers in 1973. The first time around sent shock waves throughout Western societies when oil supplies were drastically reduced and the gas price at the pump doubled for a gallon of gasoline in short order. Since polystyrene plastic is a derivative of petroleum distillation, the crisis even effected the price and availability of this basic model making material.

In Detroit, domestic auto makers got the message in 1973. After that first energy shortage, they began designing a new breed of passenger cars: lighter,

leaner and more fuel efficient. By the late 1970s, Ford and General Motors (the two primary combatants in stock car racing by then) began downsizing their respective production car lines.

The Thunderbird, at Ford, where it had carried its stock car racing banner for many years, shrunk from beached whale-proportions of the mid-1970s to a small boxy coupe by 1980. Ford was not finished with its flagship personal luxury car; in 1983 Ford reinvented the marque with a whole new styling theme. Where earlier T-Birds had flat surfaces with sharp edges, the new Thunderbird was round and sleek and looked like a bullet.

Likewise, at GM, the hand writing was on the wall. Cars like the Chevrolet Monte Carlo, Pontiac Grand Prix, Buick Regal and Oldsmobile Cutlass were all quite a bit smaller than their predecessors by 1980. All four featured "freshened" styling for 1981, though not nearly as dramatic as the new '83 Thunderbird proved to be.

In the meantime, NASCAR continued to sanction the use of the older and larger cars many of which had not seen production since 1977. By late 1980, NASCAR finally had little choice but to revise the rules since the public was driving all the new smaller cars while the series featured nothing but outdated race cars. The new rules for the 1981 Grand National season (now called Winston Cup) mandated a shorter overall length and reduced the wheelbase requirements for all race cars from 115 inches to 110 inches.

Over the time period since the last new stock car kit had been produced by MPC in 1975, the sport of stock car racing had grown in popularity at a rapid rate. Stock car model builders suffered through the longest drought to date without the introduction of new models resembling a current stock car kit. Then something really exciting happened when R-M Models released four new 1/24th scale stock car kits in 1983. The level of detail and authenticity in these brand new, purpose-built stock car kits was nothing short of sensational. It was something never seen before in this type of scale model.

General Motors race cars. Of those first four releases, the Buick Regals rode on a Hutchison-Pagen style "front steer" chassis while the T-Birds were nestled down over a Banjo Matthews-style "rear steer" platform. Other versions of the '83 Regal were followed closely by an '84 Monte Carlo SS and a '81-'84 Pontiac Grand Prix. The availability of these benchmark kits spawned a new industry of after-market accessories. Quickly, these cottage industries responded with detailing items and a whole new market was created for stock car decals. Fred Cady Design, JNJ Hobbies, Blue Ridge, DNL, BSR, Chimneyville, Slixx and others, began producing accurate water-slide decals for dozens of the NASCAR stock cars seen on television.

Ultimately, that original R-M Hutcherson-Pagan, front-steer chassis was the underpinnings for the following R-M stock cars kits: Buick—1981-85 Regal and 1988-91 Regal; Chevrolet—1983-85 Monte Carlo notchback and 1986-87 Monte Carlo SS aero-coupe; Oldsmobile—1987 Delta 88 and 1988-92 Cutlass; and Pontiac—1981-85 Grand Prix and 1988-95 Grand Prix.

When R-M introduced the three Chevy Lumina kits depicting race cars from the movie "Days of Thunder," a totally new kit tool, using nothing from the original GM kits, except the Goodyear tires, was created. There were three variants of the new Lumina kit, they included:

1. 1989 Days of Thunder Chevrolet Lumina kits, No. 2917, 2920 and 2921. The 1989-1992 Chevrolet Lumina kit features a deep horizontal crease located between the front bumper and front air dam and a pronounced license plate housing in the rear. The embossed word "Lumina" is located very near the bottom lip of the air

dam. There is also a pronounced air inlet centered below the front bumper.

2. 1993 DuPont Chevrolet Lumina kit No. 2441. The 1993 Chevrolet Lumina kit has a very slight horizontal crease between the front bumper and air dam. The bumper width is much narrower with the air dam protruding slightly with a raised lip at the bottom. The word "Lumina" is positioned near the vertical center of the air dam. There is also an air inlet at the top of the air dam center bellow the bumper.

3. 1994 Kellogg's Chevrolet Lumina kit No. 2974. The 1994 Chevrolet Lumina has a clean front air dam with no air inlet between the bumper and air dam. Both the 1993 and 1994 Lumina kits have a clean rear bumper with no license plate housing.

For the 1995 NASCAR season, Chevrolet resurrected the Monte Carlo nameplate. Its race cars carried new MC sheet metal. R-M followed suit with the introduction of a new '95 Monte Carlo which featured basically the same chassis, roll cage and driveline as the earlier Lumina kits.

In late 1996, R-M tooled up a brand new 1997 Pontiac Grand Prix which shared few, if any, components with the earlier Lumina kit and even saw the final passing of those old Goodyear Eagles from the original releases. From the same basic new GP tool, R-M fashioned a new kit of the revived Chevrolet Monte Carlo for 1995. This version also has seen slight tweaking as R-M has responded to the ever-changing details on NASCAR Winston Cup cars.

NASCAR Fords. The R-M 1/24th scale NASCAR T-Bird kit remained virtually unchanged from 1989-1993. Then the manufacturer applied a face lift to the T-Bird for new releases starting in late 1994, like the Tide kit No. 2449. The kit still rode on the earlier chassis, but received a new nose clip resembling the 1994 production car. R-M again updated the T-Bird kit and this time the body shell got another new nose piece along with a new hood for kit released in 1995, like the Family Channel kit No. 2465.

For 1996, R-M pulled out all the stops by commissioning a brand new Thunderbird tool. The chassis resembled closely the unit found under the Grand Prix and Monte Carlo (both front steer cars) and the body shell reflected the alterations to the nose and hood found on the full-size race car for 1996, like the Havoline kit No. 2471.

For the 1998 NASCAR season, Ford Motor Company and NASCAR came to a compromise. For the first time in decades, a four-door production car was approved for competition. It was quickly discovered that there was no way production Taurus sheet metal would fit the T-Bird rolling chassis. What was finally decided on somewhat resembled a production Taurus, with the emphasis on the word "somewhat."

R-M was quick to tool up a new Ford Taurus body shell that was adapted to ride on the existing front-steer Thunderbird chassis, like the Cartoon Network Wacky Racing kit No. 2563. R-M also released new kits during this period featuring older style T-Bird body shells. Again, the original Banjo Matthews-style rear-steer platform was used in both kits with only minor modifications. Of these retro-style T-Bird kits to date, R-M has offered:

1. Double kit of 1981 T-Birds, No. 6857

2. Double kit of 1987 T-Birds, No. 6392

R-M's stock car kits, in constant production since 1983, are the single most successful model kit series in history. Currently, the total kit sales number into the millions of units. Many of the earlier releases are currently in high demand and have escalated greatly in value.

The continuing demand by the model collector and builder for unique subjects prompted R-M to engage in the selective release of short run, limited produc-

tion stock car kits. The choice of current and vintage subjects continues to be "all over the map." There have been special limited releases done specifically for a sponsor or manufacturer or to commemorate special events or occasions such as the Legends Series done to mark NASCAR's 50th anniversary.

Testors Corporation recently released a series of diecast metal NASCAR stock car kits in 1/24th scale. In actuality these pre-painted and decorated items are simply put, unassembled Racing Champions diecast models of 1998 Ford Taurus and Chevrolet Monte Carlo race cars. Save for the time to assemble these well-done releases, there is little to separate the finished model from one that is put together at the factory. There is surely a market for these items that may well bridge the span between the collector and the novice stock car model builder.

1/24th-Scale Price Guide

Shown here are the eight Snaptite stock cars that comprise the first two releases from R-M as part of its Pro-Finish series.

Top: limited production piece (1 of 5000) of the Quality Care Thunderbird kit No. 1312; bottom: Smith and Wesson Chevrolet Monte Carlo kit No. 8888. The 5-W car was to have been driven by Ron Hornaday in the October 1995 Busch series race at Charlotte Motor Speedway. Qualifying was rained out and Hornaday did not make the race.

Buck Fever/Revell Collection

(molded/some packaged by Revell-Monogram)

Stock #	Car #	Sponsor/Car	Value
0025A	No. 17	97 Parts America, chrome (white body shell in kit)	$35.00
0025B	No. 17	97 Parts America, Budweiser colors	$30.00
0025C	No. 17	97 Parts America colors	$30.00
0025D	No. 17	97 Parts America, Gatorade colors	$30.00
0025E	No. 17	97 Parts America, Mountain Dew colors	$30.00
0025F	No. 17	97 Parts America, Pepsi Cola colors	$30.00
0025G	No. 17	97 Parts America, Tide colors	$30.00
1306	No. 6	97 Valvoline Ford Thunderbird	$16.00
1307	No. 99	97 Exide Ford Thunderbird (Texas winner)	$16.00
1310	No. 24	97 Chroma Premier Chevrolet Monte Carlo	$20.00
1311	No. 24	97 DuPont Chevrolet Monte Carlo (97 Daytona 500)	$20.00
1312	No. 88	96 Quality Care Ford Thunderbird (96 Daytona 500)	$25.00
1347	No. 24	97 Jurassic Park Chevrolet Monte Carlo (Winston Select)	$22.00
1348	No. 60	97 Winn Dixie Ford Thunderbird, Busch	$15.00
1353	No. 31	97 Lowe's Chevrolet Monte Carlo	$22.00
1354	No. 31	97 Wrangler Chevrolet Monte Carlo (Busch series)	$16.00

Pair of racing Chevrolets—top: Wheaties/Goodwrench Monte Carlo driven by Dale Earnhardt in the '97 Winston Select; bottom: Wrangler Monte Carlo kit No. 1354 driven by Dale Earnhardt Jr. in the Busch series.

Pair of racing Chevrolets commemorating Darrell Waltrip's 25th year in NASCAR—top: kit No. 4112, the chrome-plated Parts America Monte Carlo; bottom: Gatorade version of the Parts America MC kit No. 0025D.

Pair of Buck Fever releases (packaged and molded by R-M)—top: Hooter's Ford Thunderbird driven by the late-Alan Kulwicki to the 1992 NASCAR WC Championship kit No. 0762; bottom: Chroma Premier Chevrolet Monte Carlo that Jeff Gordon drove in the 1997 Winston Select kit No. 1310.

Top: Parts America kit No. 0025C; bottom: Budweiser version of the Parts America MC kit No. 0025B. Part of the commemorative Darrell Waltrip's series.

Top: Mountain Dew version of the Parts America Monte Carlo kit No. 0025D; bottom: Pepsi Challenger version of the Parts America MC kit No. 0025F. These kits are from the series commemorating Darrell Waltrip.

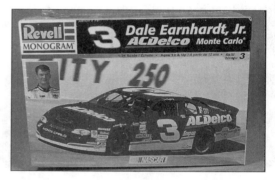

This R-M kit depicts the Busch Series Championship-winning Chevrolet Monte Carlo driven by Dale Earnhardt Jr. kit No. 1354.

Buck Fever

(molded/some packaged by Revell-Monogram)

Stock #	Car #	Sponsor/Car	Value
027	No. 87	97 Burger King Chevrolet Monte Carlo	$22.00
028	No. 75	97 Camouflage Remington Ford Thunderbird	$22.00
031	No. 6	97 Valvoline Ford Thunderbird	$22.00
032	No. 11	97 Lowe's gold 50th Anniversary Ford Thunderbird	$22.00
035	No. 3	97 AC-Delco Chevrolet Monte Carlo (Japan)	$22.00
036	No. 3	97 Goodwrench Plus Chevrolet Monte Carlo	$23.00
044	No. 24	98 Chroma Premier Chevrolet Monte Carlo	$35.00
0760	No. 7	91 AK Racing Ford Thunderbird	$30.00
0761	No. 7	86 Quincy's Ford Thunderbird	$30.00
0762	No. 7	92 Hooters Ford Thunderbird	$35.00
0793	No. 88	96 Welcome Back Ernie Ford Thunderbird	$30.00

Stock #	Car #	Sponsor/Car	Value
0663	No. 3	94 Goodwrench Chevy Lumina (for Sports Image Marketing)	$40.00
2472	No. 28	96 Red Carpet/Quality Care Ford Thunderbird	$12.00
2518	No. 75	97 Remington Ford Thunderbird (green)	$12.00
MOD028	No. 75	97 Remington Ford Thunderbird (camouflage)	$12.00
MOD037	No. 3	97 Goodwrench/Wheaties Chevrolet Monte Carlo	$35.00
8888	No. 16	95 Smith & Wesson Chevrolet Monte Carlo, Busch	$25.00

Two limited production kits (1 of 5000 pieces)—top: "camouflage" Remington Arms for Thunderbird kit; bottom: AC-Delco Chevrolet Monte Carlo driven by Dale Earnhardt in Japan kit No. 0035.

Two limited production kits (1 of 5000 pieces)—top: Burger King Chevrolet Monte Carlo kit; bottom: "green" Remington Arms Ford Thunderbird kit No. 2518.

Pair of Buck Fever releases (packaged and molded by R-M): AK Racing Ford Thunderbird kit No. 0760 and the Quincy's Thunderbird kit No. 0761 driven by the late-NASCAR champion Alan Kulwicki.

Top: Buck Fever (molded and packaged by Monogram) Welcome Back Ernie 1996 Ford Thunderbird kit No. 0793; bottom: Jurassic Park Chevrolet Monte Carlo kit No. 2525. The WBE T-Bird commemorates the return by Ervin to NASCAR racing after a near-fatal accident.

Built model of the Hooter's Ford Thunderbird by Mike Madlinger, driven to the 1992 NASCAR Championship by Alan Kulwicki and based on the R-M kit No. 0762.

Classic Hobby Distributors

(Monogram tooling)

Stock #	Car #	Sponsor/Car	Value
CHD9460	No. 60	94 Winn Dixie Ford Thunderbird	$45.00
CHD9571	No. 71	95 Olive Garden Chevrolet Monte Carlo	$35.00

Top: Olive Garden Chevrolet Monte Carlo driven by Dave Marcis, kit No. 9571(1 of 5000 pieces); bottom: Mark Martin's Winn Dixie Ford Thunderbird kit No. 9460 (1 of 10,000 pieces).

GMP (Georgia Marketing and Promotions)

Stock #	Car	Value
0664	Generic 83 Buick Regal (Monogram tooling)	$35.00

Top: Cheerwine Ford Thunderbird kit No. 0646; bottom: Georgia Marketing and Promotions generic 1983 Buick Regal (molded and packaged by R-M) kit No. 0664.

Model Empire

Stock #	Car	Value
6182	Generic 83-86 Ford Thunderbird (Monogram tooling)	$55.00

Revell-Monogram

Stock #	Car #	Sponsor/Car	Value
2204	No. 11	81-82 Mountain Dew Buick Regal	$80.00
2205	No. 1	83 UNO Buick Regal	$75.00
2206	No. 15	83 Wrangler Ford Thunderbird	$100.00
2207	No. 9	83 Melling Ford Thunderbird	$85.00
2244	No. 9	85 Coors Ford Thunderbird-SH	$75.00
2244	No. 9	85 Coors Ford Thunderbird-LH	$90.00
2244	No. 9	85 Coors Ford Thunderbird-Winston/84 T-Bird	$100.00
2245	Nos. 11/12	83 Budweiser Chevrolet Monte Carlo SS	$125.00
2298	No. 22	83 Miller Buick Regal-84 Buick GN	$40.00
2298	No. 22	83 Miller Buick Regal-84 Buick Speedway	$55.00
2299	No. 44	84 Piedmont Chevrolet Monte Carlo SS	$85.00
2428	No. 42	91 Mello Yello Pontiac Grand Prix	$20.00
2430	No. 28	91 Havoline Ford Thunderbird	$25.00
2431	No. 12	91 Raybestos Buick Regal	$17.00
2432	No. 75	91 Dinner Bell Oldsmobile Cutlass	$18.00
2440	No. 5	93 Tide Chevrolet Lumina (Ricky Rudd)	$22.00
2441	No. 24	93 DuPont Chevrolet Lumina	$25.00
2442	No. 27	93 McDonald's Ford Thunderbird-Hut Stricklin	$22.00
2442	No. 27	93 McDonald's Ford Thunderbird-Jimmy Spencer	$23.00
2447a	No. 3	95 Goodwrench Chevrolet Monte Carlo	$15.00
2447b	No. 3	97 Goodwrench Chevrolet Monte Carlo	$15.00
2447c	No. 3	98 Goodwrench Plus Chevrolet Monte Carlo	$12.00
2448	No. 4	95 Kodak Chevrolet Monte Carlo	$12.00
2449	No. 10	94 Tide Ford Thunderbird	$12.00
2450	No. 7	94 Exide Ford Thunderbird (Hoosier tires)	$12.00
2451	No. 15	94 Quality Care Ford Thunderbird (Lake Speed)	$12.00
2465	No. 16	95 Family Channel Ford Thunderbird	$12.00
2466	No. 75	95 Factory Store Ford Thunderbird	$12.00
2468	No. 87	95 Burger King Chevrolet Monte Carlo	$12.00
2469	No. 94	95 McDonald's Thunderbat Ford Thunderbird	$12.00

Stock #	Car #	Sponsor/Car	Value
2471	No. 28	96 Havoline Ford Thunderbird	$12.00
2472	No. 88	96 Quality Care Ford Thunderbird	$12.00
2476a	No. 24	96 DuPont Chevrolet Monte Carlo	$15.00
2476b	No. 24	97 DuPont Chevrolet Monte Carlo	$15.00
2476c	No. 24	98 DuPont Chevrolet Monte Carlo	$12.00
2477	No. 6	94 Valvoline Ford Thunderbird (1st Brickyard 400 paint)	$12.00
2477	No. 6	96 Valvoline Ford Taurus	$13.00
2478	No. 10	96 Tide Ford Thunderbird	$12.00
2479	No. 5	97 Kellogg's Chevrolet Monte Carlo	$12.00
2483	No. 3	96 Olympic Monte Carlo	$20.00
2484a	No. 29	96 Flintstones Chevrolet Monte Carlo (yellow)	$12.00
2484b	No. 29	97 Scooby Doo/Flintstones Chevrolet Monte Carlo (purple)	$12.00
2485	No. 29	95 World Championship Wrestling Chevrolet MC, Busch	$12.00
2486a	No. 94	94 McDonald's Ford Thunderbird	$12.00
2486b	No. 94	97 McDonald's Ford Thunderbird	$12.00
2486c	No. 94	98 McDonald's Ford Taurus	$12.00
2493	No. 43	97 STP Pontiac Grand Prix	$12.00
2518	No. 75	97 Remington Arms Ford Thunderbird (green)	$12.00
2523	No. 31	97 Lowe's Home Imp. Chevrolet Monte Carlo	$12.00
2524	No. 44	97 Hot Wheels Pontiac Grand Prix	$12.00
2525	No. 24	97 Jurassic Park Chevrolet Monte Carlo	$15.00
2550	No. 1	98 Coca-Cola parade car Chevrolet Monte Carlo	$12.00
2553	No. 26	98 Cheerios Ford Taurus	$12.00
2556	No. 99	98 Exide Ford Taurus	$12.00
2563	No. 9	98 Cartoon Network Ford Taurus	$12.00
2587	No. 3	98 AC Delco Chevrolet MC (Earnhardt Jr., Busch Champ)	$12.00
2706	No. 33	84 Skoal Bandit Chevrolet Monte Carlo SS	$95.00
2707	No. 47	84 Valvoline Buick Regal	$85.00
2722	No. 43	85 STP Pontiac Grand Prix	$100.00
2723	No. 15	86 Motorcraft Ford Thunderbird	$60.00
2734	No. 25	87 Folgers Chevrolet Monte Carlo SS Aerocoupe	$28.00
2754	No. 29	87 Hardee's Oldsmobile Cutlass	$55.00
2755	No. 17	87 Tide Chevrolet Monte Carlo SS Aerocoupe	$95.00
2779	No. 83	87 K-Mart Oldsmobile Cutlass	$20.00
2786	No. 26	89 Quaker State Buick Regal	$27.00
2787	No. 75	89 Valvoline Pontiac Grand Prix	$65.00
2900	No. 3	88 Goodwrench Chevrolet Monte Carlo SS Aerocoupe	$50.00
2900	No. 3	88 Goodwrench Chevrolet Monte Carlo SS Aerocoupe, reissue	$20.00
2906	No. 42	89 Peak Pontiac Grand Prix	$40.00
2908	No. 7	89 Zerex Ford Thunderbird Plus (driver, pit accessories)	$80.00
2914	No. 57	90 Heinz Pontiac Grand Prix Plus (driver, pit accessories)	$20.00
2915	Nos. 8/12/84	89 Miller Buick Regal Plus (driver, pit accessories)	$65.00
2916	No. 28	89 Havoline Ford Thunderbird Plus (driver, pit accessories)	$95.00
2917	No. 46	90 City Chevy Chevrolet Lumina (Days of Thunder)	$27.00
2920	No. 18	90 Hardee's Chevrolet Lumina (Days of Thunder)	$27.00
2921	No. 51	90 Mello Yello Chevrolet Lumina (Days of Thunder)	$27.00
2927	No. 3	90-91 Goodwrench Chevrolet Lumina (2 boxes, driver, pit acc.)	$32.00
2928	No. 6	90-91 Folgers Ford Thunderbird Plus (2 boxes, driver, pit acc.)	$20.00
2930	No. 66	90 Trop Artic Pontiac Grand Prix	$18.00
2932	No. 30	90 Country Time/Kool Aid Pontiac Grand Prix , Busch	$20.00
2939	No. 30	91 Pennzoil Pontiac Grand Prix	$18.00
2940	No. 8	90-91 Snickers Buick Regal	$16.00
2941	No. 10	91 Purolator Chevrolet Lumina	$18.00
2942	No. 22	91 Maxwell House Ford Thunderbird	$15.00
2949	No. 17	91 Western Auto Chevrolet Lumina (2 boxes, driver, pit acc.)	$25.00
2959	No. 6	92 Valvoline Ford Thunderbird	$18.00
2960	No. 2	92 Pontiac Excitement (R. Wallace) Pontiac Grand Prix	$18.00

1998 Exide Ford Taurus kit No. 2556 was the first release of the new Taurus tooling from R-M.

1995 Goodwrench Chevrolet Monte Carlo kit No. 2447 by R-M.

The new-for-1998 R-M Exide Taurus kit No. 2556 continues to feature the latest stock car technology under that sleek body shell.

1995 Kodak Chevrolet Monte Carlo kit No. 2448 by R-M.

1995 Burger King Chevrolet Monte Carlo kit No. 2468 by R-M.

1998 Exide Ford Taurus kit No. 2556 continues to offer the builder an excellent small-block push-rod V-8 Roush Racing engine.

1996 DuPont Chevrolet Monte Carlo kit No. 2476 by R-M.

Monogram 1/24th Wrangler Thunderbird driven by Dale Earnhardt for Bud Moore engineering in 1983. The Banjo Matthews-designed chassis shown in the foreground was a major breakthrough in 1983 as this kind of detail had never before been seen in a 1/24th scale plastic stock car kit.

1996 Valvoline Ford Thunderbird kit No. 2477 by R-M.

1995 McDonald's Thunderbat Ford Thunderbird kit No. 2495 by R-M.

The 1998 Cheerios Ford Taurus glue kit No. 2553 from R-M.

1996 Tide Ford Thunderbird kit No. 2478 by R-M.

Top: R-M Limited Edition Coca-Cola 600 Commemorative Chevrolet Monte kit No. 2550 (1 of 5,000 pieces); bottom: Woody Wood Pecker Chevrolet Monte Carlo kit No. 4132 (1 of 10,000 pieces) driven by Wally Dallenbach Jr. in Suzuka, Japan, November 1997.

The first four releases in 1983 from R-M in its then-new NASCAR stock car series: UNO and Mountain Dew Buicks and the Wrangler and Melling Thunderbirds.

One of the four versions of R-M kit No. 2244. This one features a different photo of Bill Elliott in the lower right corner of the box lid.

There are four versions of the 1984 Coors Ford Thunderbird that share the same kit No. 2244. Shown here are three of them. The slight changes were made in preparation for additional production runs of this popular kit. The differences between the various kits are on the box lid. There are four different pictures of driver Bill Elliott on each box, and two of the boxes read "Grand National Race Car" while the other two read "Superspeedway Stock Car."

This R-M kit features the special Olympic paint scheme used by the Richard Childress team at Charlotte Motor Speedway for the Winston Select in 1996.

Top: Cartoon Network "Scooby Doo" Monte Carlo kit No. 2484; bottom: WCW Chevrolet Monte Carlo kit No. 2485.

Built model of Petty/STP Pontiac Grand Prix kit No. 2722 is by Tom Dill.

Built model of the Goodwrench '90 Chevrolet Lumina kit No. 2927 is by Mike Madlinger.

Pair of NASCAR Goodwrench Chevrolets, at the top the Lumina Plus kit No. 2927 and at the bottom the Monte Carlo kit No. 2900 both from Monogram.

Pair of Petty/STP Pontiacs: 1985 Grand Prix kit No. 2722 and 1997 GP kit No. 2524 by R-M.

The John Deere Pontiac Grand Prix, kit No. 2492.

Top: Monogram's Dirt Devil Pontiac Grand Prix kit No. 2973; bottom: kit No. 2900 the "Pontiac Grand Prix" PGP (PC for Miller Genuine Draft), also from Monogram.

Pair of Ford Thunderbird kits by R-M: Quality Care T-B kit No. 2451 and Exide T-B kit No. 2450.

The 1991 Pennzoil Pontiac by Monogram kit No. 2939.

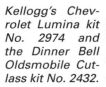

Kellogg's Chevrolet Lumina kit No. 2974 and the Dinner Bell Oldsmobile Cutlass kit No. 2432.

Built model of the '83 Wrangler Thunderbird kit No. 2206, by the author.

Two Fords: '83 Wrangler Thunderbird kit No. 2206 and the '89 Texaco/Havoline Thunderbird kit No. 2916.

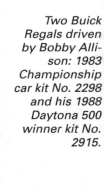

Two Buick Regals driven by Bobby Allison: 1983 Championship car kit No. 2298 and his 1988 Daytona 500 winner kit No. 2915.

Two Fords: 1989 Havoline Thunderbird Plus kit No. 2916 and 1989 Zerex Thunderbird Plus kit No. 2908.

Built model by the author of Bobby Allison's '83 Buick Regal kit No. 2298.

Top: 1989 Quaker State Buick kit No. 2786; bottom: Days of Thunder Chevrolet Lumina (the first release) kit No. 2917.

Built model of the '89 Quaker State Buick kit No. 2786, by Mike Madlinger.

Two NASCAR Chevrolets: 1993 Tide Lumina kit No. 2440 and the 1997 Kellogg's Monte Carlo kit No. 2479.

Built model of the '97 Hot Wheels Pontiac Grand Prix kit No. 2524, by Mike Madlinger.

Pair of Pontiac Grand Prix kits: 1989 Valvoline kit No. 2787 and the '97 Hot Wheels No. 2524.

Two Buick Regals: 1984 Valvoline kit No. 2707 and the 1991 Raybestos No. 2431.

Two Chevrolets driven by Steve Grissom: 1995 Busch Series WCW kit No. 2485 and Cartoon Network (Flintstones) kit No. 2484.

Two Goodwrench Chevrolets: 1995 Monte Carlo kit No. 2447 and the 1990-91 Lumina kit No. 2927.

1995 Burger King Monte Chevrolet Carlo kit No. 2468 and the 1995 Kodak Chevrolet Monte Carlo kit No. 2448.

Built model of the '95 Kodak Chevrolet Monte Carlo kit No. 2448, by Mike Madlinger.

6-45. Pair of McDonald's Ford Thunderbirds with the same kit No. 2486—top: 1997 version and at bottom is the 1996 kit.

Built model of the '95 Family Channel Ford Thunderbird kit No. 2465, by Tom Anderson. (photo by Pat Covert)

Two DuPont NASCAR Chevrolets: 1997 Jurassic Park Monte Carlo kit No. 2525 and the 1996 Monte Carlo kit No. 2476.

Two Ford Thunderbirds: 1995 Family Channel kit No. 2465 and the 1993 McDonald's kit No. 2442.

Pair of Tide Thunderbirds: 1996 version kit No. 2478 and the 1994 version kit No. 2449.

Two NASCAR Fords: Cartoon Network Taurus kit No. 2563 and the McDonald's Thunderbat kit No. 2469.

Two 1996 NASCAR Ford Thunderbirds: Quality Care/Red Carpet Leasing (driven by Dale Jarrett to win the '96 Daytona 500) kit No. 2472 and the 1997 Remington Arms kit No. 2518.

Two new-for-1998 Ford NASCAR Taurus kits: Exide kit No. 2556 and the Cheerios kit No. 2553.

Revell-Monogram ProFinish Snap Tite Series

Stock #	Car #	Sponsor/Car	Value
1310	No. 24	98 DuPont Chevrolet Monte Carlo	$12.00
1311	No. 3	98 Goodwrench Chevrolet Monte Carlo	$12.00
1312	No. 6	98 Valvoline Ford Taurus	$12.00
1313	No. 94	98 McDonald's Ford Taurus	$12.00
1314	No. 99	98 Exide Ford Taurus	$12.00
1315	No. 9	98 Cartoon Network Ford Taurus	$12.00
1316	No. 26	98 Cheerios Ford Taurus	$12.00
1317	No. 5	98 Kellogg's Chevrolet Monte Carlo	$12.00

Pair of R-M Snaptite 1/24th scale stock cars: kit No. 1310, DuPont Chevrolet Monte Carlo and kit No. 1312, Valvoline Ford Taurus.

Two R-M Snaptite stock cars: kit No. 1311, the Goodwrench Chevrolet Monte Carlo and the McDonald's Ford Taurus, kit No. 1313.

Revell-Monogram

(Special series for corporate sponsors, etc.)

Stock #	Car #	Sponsor/Car	Value
0663	No. 3	94 Goodwrench Chevrolet Lumina (for Sports Image Marketing)	$40.00
0763	No. 3	97 Silver Anniversary Chevrolet Monte Carlo	$55.00
0780	Nos. 3/24	Goodwrench/DuPont Chevrolet MC (Brickyard Winner's set)	$40.00
2721	No. 60	94 Winn Dixie Ford Thunderbird	$25.00
4124	No. 94	97 McDonald's Mac Tonight Ford Thunderbird	$15.00
4127	No. 5	97 Spooky Fruit Loops/Univ. Studios Monsters Frank, Chevrolet MC	$18.00
4128	No. 29	97 Cartoon Network Tom and Jerry Chevrolet MC (white)	$16.00
4129	No. 35	98 Tobasco Pontiac Grand Prix	$16.00
4130	No. 50	98 NASCAR 50th Anniversary Chevrolet Monte Carlo (gold plated)	$30.00
4131	No. 3	98 Goodwrench Chevrolet Monte Carlo (clear body)	$23.00
4132	No. 46	97 Woody Woodpecker Chevrolet Monte Carlo	$19.00
4133	No. 9	98 Cartoon Network "Birthday" Ford Taurus	$18.00
4134	No. 3	98 Bass Pro Shops Chevrolet Monte Carlo (Winston Select)	$18.00
4136	No. 44	98 Hot Wheels/Blues Bros. 2000 Grand Prix Pontiac	$18.00
4137	No. 3	98 Goodwrench Plus Chevrolet Monte Carlo (Collector's Tin)	$30.00
4138	No. 24	98 DuPont Chevrolet Monte Carlo (Collector's Tin)	$30.00
4139	No. 5	98 Kellogg's Chevrolet Monte Carlo (Collector's Tin)	$30.00
4140	No. 6	98 Valvoline Ford Taurus (Collector's Tin)	$30.00
4141	No. 98	98 Crayola Chevrolet Monte Carlo	$15.00
2961	No. 21	92 Citgo Ford Thunderbird	$24.00
2973	No. 40	94 Dirt Devil Pontiac Grand Prix	$12.00
2974	No. 5	94 Kellogg's Chevrolet Lumina	$12.00

Pair of Richard Childress Chevrolet Monte Carlos—top: Bass Pro Shop kit No. 4134 (1 of 19,500); bottom: Olympic version kit No. 2483 as run in the 1996 Winston Select at Charlotte.

Pair of Ford Thunderbirds—top: McDonald's Mac Tonite kit No. 4124 (run in five night races in 1997) and at the bottom is the Citgo Dalmatian kit No. 4113 (both 1 of 10,000 pieces) as driven by Michael Waltrip in the 1997 Winston Select.

Fictional Crayola 1998 Chevrolet Monte Carlo kit No. 4141 from R-M.

Four of the limited-production Collector's Tin stock car kits by R-M for 1998: Kellogg's MC kit No. 4139, DuPont MC Kit No. 4138, Valvoline Taurus kit No. 4140 and Goodwrench MC kit No. 4137.

Pair of Chevrolets—top: '94 Goodwrench Monte Carlo (produced for Sports Image Marketing) kit No. 0663; bottom: Silver Anniversary Monte Carlo driven by Dale Earnhardt in the '95 Winston Select at Charlotte Motor Speedway, kit No. 0763.

Combo Kits (Monogram & Revell-Monogram)

Stock #	Car #	Sponsor/Car	Value
6298	No. 3	Wrangler 81 Pontiac GP/86 Chevrolet Monte Carlo	$70.00
6367	No. 4	Kodak 90 Olds Cutlass/86 Oldsmobile Delta 88	$30.00
6368	No. 7	Quincy's/No. 90 Red Baron Ford Thunderbird	$30.00
6389	No. 42	82 STP Pontiac/81 43 STP Buick	$25.00
6391	No. 11	81-82 Mountain Dew Buick/83 Pepsi Chevrolet	$30.00
6392	No. 7	87 Zerex/No. 90 87 Red Baron Ford Thunderbird	$30.00
6857	Nos. 15/21	81-82 Ford Thunderbird No. 15 Melling/No. 21 Hodgdon	$30.00

The Petty Combo featuring an '81 Buick driven by Kyle Petty and an '82 Pontiac Grand Prix driven by Richard Petty. This is R-M kit No. 6389.

R-M produced a number of historic kits each containing the parts to build two finished models. This one, kit No. 6368, was released as the Rookie of the Year Combo Thunderbirds commemorating that title won by both the late Alan Kulwicki and Ken Schrader.

Built model of the 1986 Quincy's Ford Thunderbird kit No. 6368, by the author.

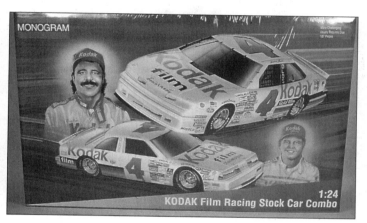

The Racing Petty Combo kit No. 6389 contains a 1981 Buick Regal driven by Kyle Petty and a 1982 Pontiac Grand Prix driven by Richard Petty.

This Kodak Films Racing Combo kit No. 6367 contains a late-1980s Oldsmobile Delta 88 and an early-1990s Oldsmobile Cutlass.

Built model of the 1986 Wrangler Chevrolet Monte Carlo kit No. 6298, by Mike Madlinger.

This early double kit No. 6298 was a high-volume success. The No. 3 Wrangler Combo contained two complete kits of a 1981 Pontiac Grand Prix and a 1986 Chevrolet Monte Carlo.

Built model by Fred Bradley based on the Petty Combo kit No. 6389 of the 7-Eleven Pontiac using after-market decals.

Built model based on kit No. 6392, the Thunderbird Combo, of the Bullseye car, by Wayne Doebling using Slixx decals.

Darrell Waltrip combo kit No. 6391 contains a 1981-1982 Buick Regal (driven to the Championship title both years by DW) and a 1983 Chevrolet Monte Carlo SS.

Built model of the '83 Pepsi Challenger Chevrolet Monte Carlo kit No. 6391, built and photographed by Drew Hierwarter.

Shown here is another R-M double-feature kit No. 6392, the 1987 Thunderbird combo kit. This kit was available during 1997, but is currently out of production.

Thunderbird Legends kit No. 6857 contains two identical 1981-82 T-Birds with different decals sets.

Revell-Monogram Limited Edition Series

Stock #	Car #	Sponsor/Car	Value
4112	No. 17	97 Waltrip Chevrolet Monte Carlo (chrome plated)	$25.00
4113	No. 21	97 Top Dog (Citgo) Dalmatians Ford Thunderbird	$15.00
4114	No. 5	97 Tony the Tiger (Kellogg's) Chevrolet Monte Carlo	$15.00
4117	No. 44	98 Hot Wheels Pontiac Grand Prix (Collector's Tin)	$25.00
4127	No. 5	98 Spooky Fruit Loops Chevrolet Monte Carlo	$15.00
4128	No. 29	98 Cartoon Network Tom and Jerry Chevrolet MC	$15.00
4129	No. 35	98 Tobasco Pontiac Grand Prix	$15.00
4130	No. 50	98 50th Anniversary Chevrolet MC (gold plated body)	$20.00
4132	No. 46	97 Woody Woodpecker Chevrolet MC (Japan/Dallenbach)	$13.00
4133	No. 9	98 Cartoon Network Birthday Ford Taurus	$25.00
4136	No. 44	98 Hot Wheels, Blues Brothers 200 Pontiac GP	$13.00
4141	No. 98	98 Crayola Chevrolet Monte Carlo	$12.00
4144	No. 18	98 Small Soldiers Pontiac Grand Prix	$13.00
4145	No. 94	98 McDonald's Gold Taurus (white/gold plated bodies included)	$22.00
4146	No. 9	98 Cartoon Network-Zombie Island Ford Taurus	$15.00

The 1998 Hot Wheels Pontiac Grand Prix was also available in this Collector's Tin, kit No. 4117.

R-M kit No. 4130 Chevrolet Monte Carlo featuring a gold-plated body shell to commemorate the 50th anniversary of NASCAR.

Top: Cartoon Network "Birthday" Ford Taurus (celebrating NASCAR's 50th anniversary) kit No. 4127; bottom: Cartoon Network "Wacky Racing" Chevrolet Monte Carlo kit No. 4133.

Two Chevrolet Monte Carlos from the Limited Edition Series (1 of 10,000 pieces)—top: Tony the Tiger version No. 4127 as run at Michigan, June 1997; bottom: Spooky Fruit Loops kit No. 4114 as run in the UAW-GM 500 at Charlotte, October 1997.

R-M kit No. 4112 of the Parts America Chevrolet Monte Carlo, molded with a chrome-plated body shell.

Top: Tobasco Pontiac Grand Prix kit No. 4129; bottom: Hot Wheels Pontiac Grand Prix "Blues Brothers 2000" kit No. 4136. Both kits are limited production (1 of 10,000 pieces)

Revell-Monogram Stock Car Legends

Stock #	Car #	Sponsor/Car	Value
3150	No. 15	81 Wrangler Ford Thunderbird	$18.00
3151	No. 43	84 STP Pontiac Grand Prix (200th victory)	$15.00
3152	No. 84	Piedmont Chevrolet Monte Carlo (championship car)	$12.00
3153	No. 28	84 Hardee's Chevrolet Monte Carlo	$15.00

Built model of the Hardee's 1984 Chevrolet Monte Carlo by the author.

Pair of items from R-M's Legends Series—top: '84 Hardee's Chevrolet Monte Carlo kit No. 3153; bottom: 1984 STP Pontiac kit No. 3151, driven by Richard Petty to his 200th career victory in the Firecracker 400 at Daytona International Speedway.

Two items from the Legends series—top: Wrangler Ford Thunderbird kit No. 3150; bottom: Piedmont Airlines Chevrolet Monte Carlo kit No. 3152, driven to the '94 NASCAR Championship by Terry Labonte.

R-M kit No. 3151 depicts the '84 STP Pontiac Grand Prix Richard Petty drove to his 200th victory at Daytona International Speedway.

Revell-Monogram NCTS (NASCAR Craftsman Truck Series)

Stock #	Car #	Sponsor/Car	Value
2458	No. 3	96 Goodwrench Chevrolet C-1500 race truck	$15.00
2473	No. 52	96 AC Delco Chevrolet C-1500 race truck	$12.00
2474	No. 1	96 Diehard Chevrolet C-1500 race truck	$12.00
2475	No. 6	96 Total Chevrolet C-1500 race truck	$12.00
2499	No. 97	24 Quaker State Chevrolet C-1500 race truck	$12.00
2519	No. 16	97 NAPA Chevrolet C-1500 race truck	$15.00
2529	No. 80	99 Exide Ford F-150 race truck	$12.00
2547	No. 2	98 ASE Ford F-150 race truck	$12.00

1996 Goodwrench Chevrolet C-1500 race truck driven by Mike Skinner to the NASCAR Craftsman Truck Series title. This is kit No. 2458 by R-M.

Diehard Chevrolet C-1500 race truck kit No. 2474.

Total Chevrolet C-1500 race truck kit No. 2475.

NAPA Chevrolet C-1500 race truck kit No. 2519.

AC Delco Chevrolet C-1500 race truck kit No. 2473.

Quaker State Chevrolet race truck C-1500 kit No. 2499.

Built model of the Goodwrench Chevy truck driven to the first series championship by Mike Skinner. Model by Mike Madlinger.

The under-hood detail of this truck right out of the box is on a par with the R-M stock car model kits. Model built by Mike Madlinger.

R-M spared no resources to replicate the rolling chassis for its line of NASCAR race trucks. Model built by Mike Madlinger.

Spectra Distributing

(molded by R-M, packaged by Spectra)

Stock #	Car #	Sponsor/Car	Value
DA1241993	No. 28	Mac Tools Ford Thunderbird	$80.00
DJ125	No. 32	95 Mac Tools Ford Thunderbird (D. Jarrett, Busch series)	$40.00
EI1241994	No. 28	Mac Tools Ford Thunderbird	$42.00
HG1241993	No. 7	Harry Gant/Mac Tools Chevrolet Lumina	$38.00
0646	No. 21	94 Cheerwine Ford Thunderbird	$27.00

Pair of Mac Tools-sponsored cars—top: Ford Thunderbird kit No. EI1241994; bottom: Chevrolet Lumina kit No. HG1241993.

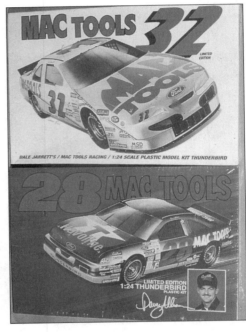

Two Mac Tools-sponsored Ford Thunderbirds—top: kit No. DJ124C (driven in 11 Busch Series races in 1995, DJ won the Milwaukee race, July 1995); bottom: kit No. DA1241993.

Testors Corporation

Stock #	Car #	Sponsor/Car	Value
* Value Pack	Nos. 3/30	No. 3 Goodwrench Chevrolet/No. 30 Pennzoil Pontiac	$25.00

* Sold with paint

Testor/Monogram value pack double kit which contains a R-M Goodwrench Lumina and a Pennzoil Pontiac plus paint and brushes, kit No. 3854.

Testors Corporation

(Diecast, pre-painted, pre-decorated metal stock car kits)

Stock #	Car #	Sponsor/Car	Value
7131	No. 94	1998 McDonald's Ford Taurus	$12.00
7132	No. 5	1998 Kellogg's Chevrolet Monte Carlo	$12.00
7133	No. 9	1998 Cartoon Network Ford Taurus	$12.00
7134	No. 10	1998 Tide Ford Taurus	$12.00
7135	No. 96	1998 CAT Chevrolet Monte Carlo	$12.00

Testors kit No. 7135 CAT 1998 Chevrolet Monte Carlo and 1998 Kellogg's MC kit No. 7132, pre-decorated metal kits.

Testors' new metal pre-decorated stock car kits No. 7133 and No. 7134.

Testors' new metal pre-decorated 1/24th stock car kits are, in actuality, unassembled Racing Champion diecast models. Paint and markings are well done.

Other 1/24th scale street-stock kits that could be modified into a race car include Monogram's 69 Dodge Coronet, 70 Plymouth GTX, 70 Plymouth Superbird and 70 Chevrolet Chevelle.

Ernie's' Rookie Ride

Building Revell-Monogram's Chevy Monte Carlo Aero Coupe

The History: After MPC's last 1/25th scale NASCAR release in the mid-1970s, things grew increasingly barren for the stock car modeler. From 1975 to 1983, a lot of changes took place in America's premiere stock car racing series. The 1977 Olds Cutlass and 1977 Chevrolet Monte Carlo became the most dominate body styles on the race tracks. Most GM teams used the aerodynamic Cutlass on the big super speedways while the boxy Monte Carlo was the weapon of choice for medium and short track competition.

Also, during that period, the United States suffered through two gasoline shortages. The major auto manufacturers began downsizing their car lines. NASCAR faced a bit of a dilemma since the new smaller street cars didn't come close to matching up with the well-established rule book. Finally, in 1981, the sanctioning body saw the handwriting on the wall. The new rules saw a reduction of overall length and the revised wheelbase dimensions reduced from 115 inches to 110 inches and maximum vehicle weight lowered from 3,800 lbs. to 3,500 lbs.

The track width was left alone since the new narrower production dimensions would have required major modifications to the race car chassis width or Goodyear would have had to design a new much narrower or more slender racing tire. Because of the increased width required by the new rules, 1980 marked the last year factory fender stampings were used. For the first time in 1981, hand-crafted side body panels that resulted in a bulging fender lines were permitted which effectively kept the tires inside the wheel arches.

Monogram Models, in late-1982, began to take a close look at the increasing interest in stock car racing, especially due to the rapidly increasing TV exposure. MMI considered the new venture as an attempt to expand its automotive kit line. The decision was made to move forward; for the first time, stock car models would be manufactured in 1/24th instead of the more widely accepted 1/25th scale.

By 1983, MMI released a four kit series, two Buicks Regals and two Ford Thunderbirds. The two Buicks both rode on Hutcherson-Pagen "front steer" chassis while the T-Birds were fitted with the more traditional Banjo Matthews' "rear-steer" unit. Front steer is derived from late-model Camaro front end geometry and has the steering mechanisms ahead of the center line of the front axles. Rear steer is derived from the '65 Ford Galaxie steering technology where the steering arms are behind the center line of the front axles.

These four releases marked the highest level of accuracy and detail to that point. The kits were an instant hit and were followed by other variations. On the H-P chassis, Monogram provided the stock car builder with two versions of Chevrolet's Monte Carlo, two versions of Pontiac's Grand Prix and an Oldsmobile Delta '88 and '89 Regal to join the original '83 Regal.

For nearly 20 years, we've been treated to many and varied additions to MMI's stock car line. To date, that original GM front steer tool has produced nearly 2.5 million kits!

Wherever your automotive allegiances lay, if you have not built one of these original Monogram Chevrolet Monte Carlos you are missing an enjoyable modeling experience. Though the kit parts show some signs of extensive usage, it remains one of the nicest of the early Monogram releases. Later tools have increased detailing and refinement. But this old kit, the running gear of which has been in continuous production since 1983, still remains one of the best examples of stock car model kit technology.

Ernie Ervan: Ervan has gone on to record very successful career statistics. Though he drove hard and bent the learning curve a few times during his rookie season, he was unable to grab the brass ring—the NASCAR Rookie-of-the-Year title. Ervan battled with eventual ROTY titlist right down to the bitter end, losing out by a mere three points to Ken Bouchard.

Don't forget to add the yellow rookie stripe to the rear bumper of similar models to Ervan's rookie model. This "caution sign" is still required to be displayed prominently by all drivers competing in the series for the first time or even for seasoned competitors participating at a race track for the first time.

Ernie won nearly $100,000 dollars during the 1988 season but the lack of major league experience and without front pack equipment, he finished far out of the top 25 in the final point standings.

Reference source: *The Official NASCAR '89 Yearbook and Press Guide*, pg. 62, Winston Cup Drivers, Ernie Ervan

The Project: One of my favorite models from that original Monogram tool is the 1983-1988 Chevrolet Monte Carlo. This car was released in two versions. The first mimics the 1983-1985 notchback body. The second version is the 1986-1988 aero coupe, featuring a sloping rear window glass. Other than a different profile, both Monogram kits are identical.

I started this project with the MC from Monogram's Wrangler Duo set, adding a set of JNJ decals with some of Testors new NASCAR paint to replicate the race car that Ervan drove during his rookie year in NASCAR Winston Cup racing. Follow along with me now as we tackle the building and detailing of a worthy subject.

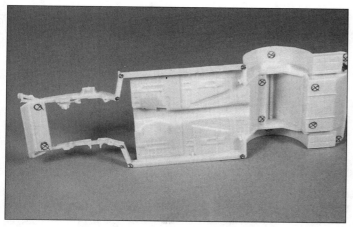

Start by cleaning up the flash, brand engraving and ejection pins marks on the kit chassis. The series of dark circles indicate the areas that need attention. Use a sanding stick, jeweler's file and something like the Nick Sander to remove imperfections.

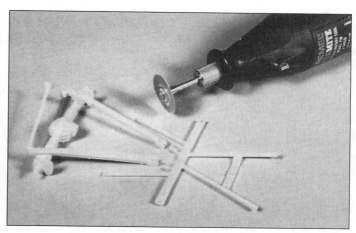

Carefully separate the rear suspension truck arms from their mounting bracket.

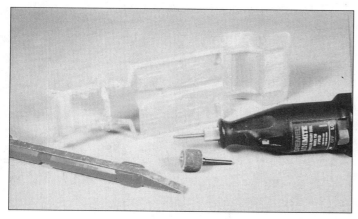

The blemishes have been addressed using both a sanding stick and very carefully working with the Dremel Mini-Mite with a sanding bit.

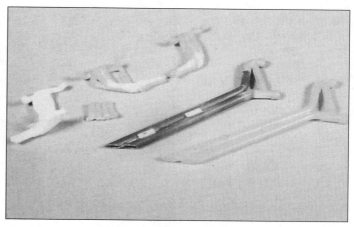

Remove the crossover header tubes on both exhaust manifolds. For additional detail, replace the kit dump pipes with plastic tubing.

Using a round grinding bit removes the molded-in dry break fuel filler.

Fuel Pump

The original GM small block racing engine lacks a fuel pump. I removed one from a scrap box engine and glued it into place on the engine block.

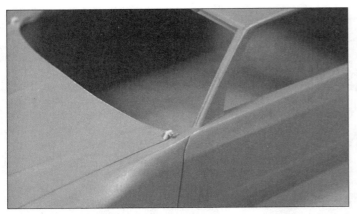

Exposed hood hinges were added to the MC using small wedges of sheet plastic and short lengths of aluminum wire.

Shown clockwise: wheel/tire no detail; detailed wheel & hand-lettered tire names; detailed wheel & dry transfer lettering and JAX hobby pad printed tire & detailed wheel.

You have a choice of ways to detail the sidewall lettering on the tires. You could apply water-slide markings. Once trimmed out with scissors, wet and apply to the smooth sidewalls. When dry, coat the entire sidewall with Polly S flat clear to seal the deal.

I chose Testors new line of NASCAR model paint colors for this project. I used flat gray primer from the standard Testors line as an under coat for the body. Number 6 white and Number X red matched up with my color reference photos quite well. Mask along the edges of raised surfaces to be painted. Once paint dries remove tape and presto; a clean shapr edge.

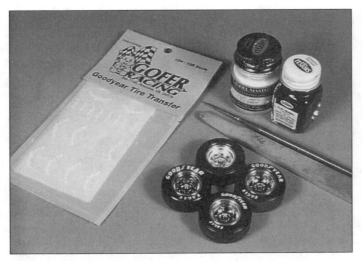

You can hand-paint the raised lettering with flat white bottle paint and a 3-0 brush. But, I decided to use Shabo dry transfer lettering. First, rub the appropriate signatures to the smooth sidewall. Coating with flat clear is optional.

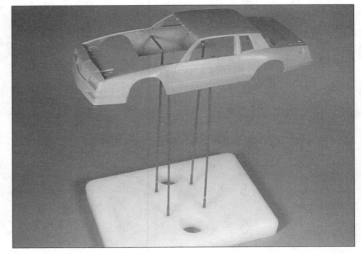

You can always bend up a old wire coat hanger into a suitable spray paint stand. If you'd like something a bit more sophisticated and more suitable for the task, this Shabo spray paint stand is an excellent choice.

Once the chassis and roll cage are assembled and painted, I began adding Scale Speedway vinyl roll cage padding tubing (shown here). Once each piece of tubing is cut to the proper length, carefully slit the tubing down the middle like a hot-dog bun and slip it into place on the roll cage.

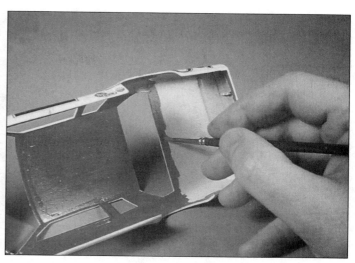

Either brush paint the inside of the Monte Carlo body shell after spraying on the gloss white to the exterior or mask it and spray the inside surfaces.

The last piece of vinyl tubing is attached to the cage.

You can rub out the white exterior with the LMG polishing kit and bring it to a high luster. Never apply any kind of wax to surfaces where decals are to be applied. Once these JNJ markings were carefully positioned and thoroughly dry, Pledge household wax was generously used on this Monte Carlo from bumper-to-bumper.

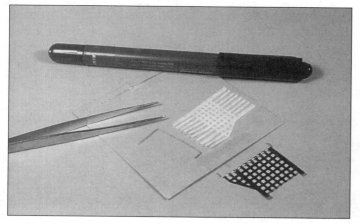

Scale Speedways NASCAR window safety net is easily assembled. When finished, it yields a very convincing piece.

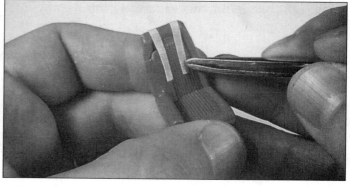

I often use 1/8-inch wide strips of masking tape to represent seat and shoulder harnesses.

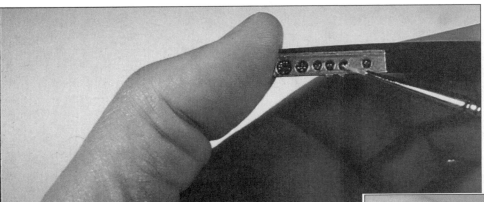

Detail the dash instruments first and then apply white glue in each recess. The glue will dry crystal clear, giving the instruments the look of being housed behind a clear lens.

From this view, note the location of the plug boots between the cylinder head exhaust ports. You can also see how the plug wire pass through the heat shields.

The small-block GM engine was painted using gunmetal, aluminum, steel and jet exhaust Testors bottle paints.

Spark plug wires, fuel lines, etc., are adding to the realism of this competition V-8 engine.

Firewall detail includes painting and plumbing the radiator overflow tank and the brake-system dual master cylinder.

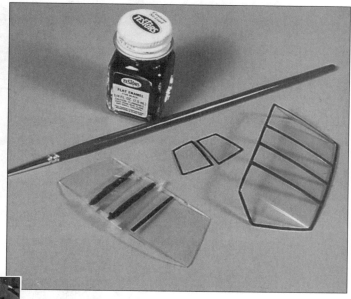

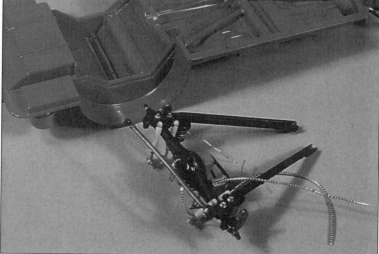

Don't forget to detail paint the masking around the front, side and rear window glass, as well as the safety straps on the windshield and bubble-shaped rear glass. Work carefully with a 3-0 brush and flat black bottle paint from the inside surfaces for this task. Mask along the edges of raised surfaces to be painted. Once paint dries, remove tape and presto, a clean sharp edge.

The rear axle and truck arm assembly is fully wired and plumbed with brake and cooling lines made from various sizes of foil craft braid found at craft stores.

I use Tamiya transparent red and blue to simulate the air-craft-style fitting on the oil cooling plumbing.

This front 3/4-view of the finished model illustrates how careful attention to detail can result in a very realistic appearing replica. I always apply Pledge household wax to remove all finger prints, etc., as a final step when all assembly and detailing is completed.

Detail of the finished engine compartment reveal that all the hard work and attention to detail has paid off. Note the radiator hose, engine wiring and plumbing that seems to be everywhere!

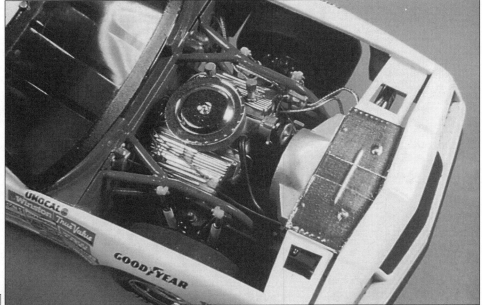

This rear 3/4-view of the finished model shows quite well the window net draped out and over the driver's side window sill. The Race Ready Replicas dry breaker gas filler and overflow tube can also be clearly viewed from this angle. Also note the yellow rookie stripe and its location on the rear bumper.

Chapter 7

Large-Scale Stock Car Model Kits

1/8th, 1/12 & 1/16th scale

The list of large-scale stock car kits is pretty short. The primary reason behind this situation is that the vast majority of stock car model builders work in 1/25th or 1/24th scale. The other reason is that this type of creative effort is determined by the availability of after-market products. There are virtually no large-scale resin parts for 1/16th or 1/12th scale and no decals to speak of. For many builders, this will stop a large-scale project in its preliminary tracks!

Those few subjects that have been replicated in large-scale kits are mostly decent examples of the engineering art. The high-water mark for large-scale stock car kits and arguably for all stock car kits is the MPC 1/16th scale 1973 Petty/STP Dodge Charger. Only released once in this form (the Petty kit and the K&K race car), many builders say that nothing since has topped this excellent kit.

The AMT Pontiac Grand Prix and Ford Thunderbird kits seem to lack the level of accuracy and refinement of the MPC kits. The Pontiacs are the best choice for a kit where things fit well and tend to represent the full-size race car. However, the finished model has a degree of stiffness with edges that are too sharp and many body surfaces that appear too flat.

The Thunderbird kits have serious problems with the way the body shell matches up with the chassis.

This is especially noticeable where the door sills meet (or don't meet) the roll cage side bars. Built according to the kit instructions, the top roll cage side bars extend noticeably above the door sills. This maybe why we don't see many of these journeyman kits built and on display at contests or model car shows.

AMT 1/16th-scale 1986 Hardee's Ford Thunderbird as driven by Cale Yarborough, kit No. 6717.

Large-Scale Price Guide

Ertl/AMT—1/16th

Stock #	Car #	Sponsor/Car	Value
6717	No. 28	85 Hardee's Thunderbird	$115.00
6718	No. 7	85 7-Eleven Thunderbird	$115.00
6741	No. 43	85 STP Pontiac Grand Prix (original issue)	$125.00
6746	No. 75	85 Nationwise Pontiac	$105.00
8249	No. 43	85 STP Pontiac Grand Prix (97 reissue)	$25.00

MPC—1/16th

Stock #	Car #	Sponsor/Car	Value
3053	No. 43	73 STP Dodge Charger	$250.00
3055	No. 71	73 K&K Dodge Charger	$175.00

Other large-scale kits that could be modified into a race car:

Monogram—1/8th

Stock #	Car	Value
2602	32 Ford Big Deuce roadster	$50.00

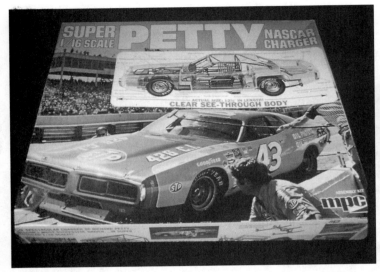

The MPC 1/16th-scale Petty/STP Dodge Charger kit No. 3053.

The MPC 1/16th scale Petty/STP Dodge Charger kit No. 3053 features an in-depth set of instructions and a large clear styrene body shell and hood.

Monogram—1/12th

Stock #	Car	Value
2800	57 Chevrolet Bel Air	$30.00
2802	69 Chevrolet Camaro	$35.00

Revell—1/16th

Stock #	Car	Value
1286	65 Ford Mustang 2+2	$35.00
7491	81 Chevrolet Camaro Berinetta	$30.00
7474	34 Ford Coupe	$42.00

Ertl/AMT—1/16th

Stock #	Car	Value
6722	65 Ford Mustang Coupe	$35.00
6719	55 Chevrolet Bel Air	$35.00

Big Time Jalopy

Bill Burtnett builds 1/8th-scale replica of his 1932 Ford stock car

Photos by Chip Maxwell

There are some people who don't do things in a small way. Bill Burtnett is a person who has lived large all his life whether in the real estate business, driving a stock car or building model cars.

Burtnett is a life-long model car builder with a preference for oval track stock cars. He always enjoyed driving race cars, as he says with a hardy laugh, "Just for fun!" His friends never quit encouraging him to build his own race car to compete at the old Jennerstown Speedway in Pennsylvania. About 1953, as Burtnett recalls, he found a complete and driveable 1932 Ford three-window coupe stored in the back of a neighborhood lawn mower repair shop. He bought the treasure and took it home for a mere $60.

At first, the old coupe just gathered dust in his garage for about a year. Finally, with the help of those same encouraging friends, Burtnett turned the hulk into a ragging short track stormer. With plenty of Corvette V-8 power, the little coupe gave Burtnett quite a ride. He ran the car in competition from 1954 until hanging up his helmet in 1962.

For many years after that, Burtnett dreamed he would build an exact scale replica of that great little car. The opportunity came in early 1991, at a time of real tragedy in his life. Over an eight-month period, while he was laid up recovering from the complications of prostrate cancer, he concentrated on building that one special model he had always dreamed about.

Burtnett knew from the start this was not to be just any model of his old race car—this was a big project. As usual, he was thinking really big. He started off by purchasing a 1/8th scale resin '32 Ford body shell from George Zurowski. His next purchase was the Revell-Monogram 1/8th scale Big Deuce 1932 Ford roadster kit from which he planned to take many of the primary parts for the project.

First, Burtnett cut a large opening in the top-center of the resin body. He then made a firewall from sheet plastic. He attached the new firewall in a near-stock location and added L-shaped tabs along the edges inside for added strength. The stock floor pan from the Big Deuce kit was added to the body placed in the stock location. Again, the same tab system was employed to attach the floor boards to the inside of the body as Burtnett's plan was to actually bolt it directly to the frame. This was done in case he ever needed to disassemble the model, and this system would make that possible.

Next, Burtnett moved on to the interior appointments. The roll cage was constructed from various diameters of Plastruct tubing and rod. As on the full-size race car, the cage was assembled from a series of

If any model car could deceive you into thinking you're looking at the genuine, full-size race car, this 1/8th scale '32 Ford jalopy by Bill Burtnett is the one. Built from a combination of resin parts, kit pieces and various items lifted from flea market finds, this big-scale replica has everything except the smell of high octane racing fuel.

metal elbow, couplings and straight lengths, and Burt-nett employed that system on the scale model. To determine the proper dimensions for height, width and length of the roll cage, Burtnett used trial and error after placing the body and floor pan onto the frame rails.

The race car's frame came directly out of the R-M Little Deuce kit. First, he reworked the front cross member by removing the molded-on spring bolts. New U-bolt style hangers were formed from paper clips. The rear cross member required drilling holes in the lip for its cross member.

The small-block Corvette V-8 engine came from an old Monogram kit number PE-62. Though this 1/8th scale kit is a collectors item, Burtnett was fortunate enough to find a built one on display in a local hobby shop and made the purchase for a measly $6. Burtnett carefully disassembled the big engine, stripping the paint and glue in the process. The rejuvenated power plant was mated to the three-speed manual transmission from the Big Deuce kit. This combination required an adapter plate between the bell housing and the tranny just like the full-size one did. After sawing the Corvette transmission from the bell housing, Burtnett stood the engine up vertically with the bell housing resting on a file card. Then he traced around the outside of the bell housing with a lead pencil mak-

ing a template to be used to cut an adapter plate from sheet plastic.

The radiator for Burtnett's jalopy racer was actually made from two Big Deuce radiators. Here he glued the two pieces face-to-face adding a filler tank to one side and relocating the outlet housing on the bottom of the new coupe radiator.

Next, he removed the stock louvered side panels from the Big Deuce butterfly-style hood since his race car ran only a partial hood. Then he placed the radiator, floor pan and body together in place on the frame rails. The partial hood was temporarily laid in place between the cowl and the radiator, allowing a bit of the core to be exposed in the front. The test-fit gave him an idea as to how the pieces fit together and lined up with the body shell. Not satisfied with just having the hood lay in place on the finished model, Burtnett was determined to build a hood that could be posed in the open position. This requirement would necessitate building a side hinge. First, he cut a length of small diameter tubing inside the passenger's side edge of the partial hood. Next, he placed the hood back into the closed position on the model to determine at what point the ends of the tubing lined up with both the back edge of the radiator and the upper tight corner of the firewall. Burtnett carefully drilled corresponding holes in these places and inserted

Posed with the partial hood in the open position, the large-scale '32 jalopy looks so real that you want to get in a drive it away.

short lengths of straight metal rod. The metal pins were inserted into the tubing during the final assembly to form the hinge.

Burtnett designed the engine mounts and frame cross members to allow him the option of removing the engine at some point. Here he modified the Big Deuce cross member and built the additional mounts needed. The final step was drilling appropriate holes required for the scale bolts in all pieces. Burtnett was careful not to glue any of the sub-assemblies into place which would have negated all his planning and hard work.

The front and rear suspension parts basically came from the Big Deuce kit. Burtnett modified each piece adding more detail where necessary. This was especially true for the buggy-style leaf spring as there was individual leaf detail on only one side. Burtnett used long narrow strips of thin sheet plastic insert into the open cavity on the back side to provide that bit of additional spring detail.

Stock kit radius rods were employed from the Big Deuce kit again and Burtnett added working tube-style shocks to the suspension system. He used the complete steering assembly from the Big Deuce kit while a hand-made column brace was required.

He then fashioned a dashboard from the top portion of the Big Deuce kit firewall, the part with the gauge cluster. To this Burtnett added a handmade starter button and kill switch. On the back side of the dash, corresponding to each gauge, Burtnett used short lengths of plastic tubing to represent the body of each dash instrument. From each gauge, he attached small-diameter coated wire to represent the electrical leads and brought them together into a bundle forming a wiring harness which ultimately connected to the distributor, generator and the engine.

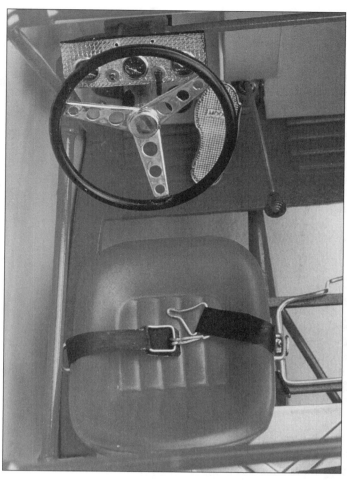

This shot of the interior through the opening in the coupe top is so realistic looking that you want to crank the Corvette engine and take it for a spin.

The small-block Corvette V-8 engine in Burtnett's '32 Ford jalopy has all the bells and whistles. Note the voltage regulator, fuel block, battery, generator (not an alternator) and the proper plumbing for the tri-carb fuel delivery system.

The tachometer mounted to the top-center of the dash board was originally a center wheel hub from a built Monogram 1/8th scale Jaguar E-type (one of Burtnett's flea market finds). The chrome bezel came from a model airplane kit, the instrument face is a decal and the gauge is actually clear epoxy.

The eight engine headers were each formed from equal lengths of small diameter soft tubing and epoxied to individual header flanges. The gas tank was handmade from sheet plastic, and strips of plastic were added as stiffeners. A small length of jeweler chain attaches the gas cap to the tank. The voltage regulator comes from the Big Deuce kit firewall. The driver's seat is from a built Monogram Big T kit with handmade seat belts and quick release hardware.

The radiator stone guard was made from aluminum tubing and fine screen door mesh, painted and then epoxied to the frame. Braces were mounted to the base of the radiator. To finish-off his jalopy, the parts were painted with Testors No. 3 red and bright yellow. This two-tone combination was topped off with a generous coat of two-art epoxy clear. The number and gumballs were hand-cut from Fred Cady white and black blank decal material. During the final assembly, Burtnett added all the finishing touches to the interior, the chassis and that gorgeous Corvette tri-power V-8 engine.

Don't look for this big-scale eye catcher at any model car contests or shows in your area any time soon. Burtnett says he built this jewel for himself and has never taken it out to an event of any kind and doesn't intend to in the future. He plans to keep this replica right where it's always been, at home under glass.

This head-on shot of the front of Burtnett's 1/8th scale '32 Ford jalopy reveals the attention he exercised, including the front suspension and braking system, as well as the fine mesh of the stone shield over the radiator.

Big Petty Dodge

Building MPC's 1/16th-scale 1973 Dodge Charger

If there is one kit of the over 900 individual model kits contained in this book that rises to the top like high quality cream, it's the MPC 1/16th scale 1973 Petty/STP Dodge Charger. First released in the mid-1970s, this highly detailed kit is without doubt the most technically accurate stock car model ever produced. It features a clear plastic body shell (possibly its one weak point). Just browsing through the in-depth instruction booklet will help you to better understand how full-size Mopar race cars were built at the time.

The next iteration of this venerable tooling was the first version of the Street Charger kit No. 3057 and the

second reissue was kit No. 3075. In both cases the NASCAR stocker with some modifications was turned into a street-driven car. This kit, with minor changes, was also released under the Ertl/MPC banner using the kit No. 6420.

With the interest in "The Dukes of Hazard" TV show, the big Dodge Charger tooling was eventually modified to produce a new kit which featured a 1969 Dodge Charger 500 body shell. All these kits are currently out-of-production.

Fred Bradley—budding race car driver, Dodge dealership parts specialist, stock car kit collector and model builder—stepped up to the challenge of building the premier stock car model kit. Working from a built model purchased at a swap meet for $50, Bradley carefully disassembled and stripped the model, ultimately replacing missing and broken parts on his way to completing this eye-catching replica.

Bradley also picked up partially built kits of the Street Charger from which many of the small detail parts (including suspension pieces) were replaced. He points out that many of the dedicated race car accessories from the Petty version of the tooling are not included in the later releases.

The model was painted with Testors Racing Colors model enamels including Racing Flat Gray Primer No. 52967, Petty Racing Blue No. 52955, Racing Flat White No. 52966 and Petty Racing Red No. 52970. The reproduction decals are by Slixx No. 1079.

The MPC 1/16th scale Petty/STP Dodge Charger is a fascinating and complex kit. The large scale demands the utmost in basic building skills and more than a casual knowledge of the inner workings of this vintage stock car. Bradley scores high on all these points, and the finished model attests to that fact.

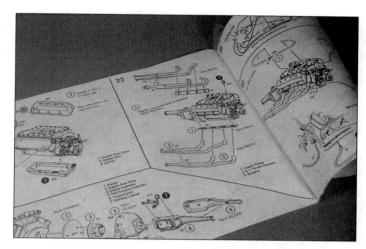

The instruction booklet for the large Petty Dodge is an education in itself featuring page after page of very detailed exploded views and precise diagrams.

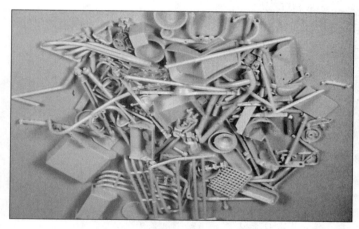

Avoid removing all the parts from any model kit until you are ready for assembly and painting. These same color parts are a virtual jigsaw puzzle once separated from the kit parts trees.

If you are starting with a pre-assembled model as Fred Bradley did, you don't have the option of leaving the parts on the kit trees. Once the model is disassembled, you can store them in a series of clear zip-lock bags until they are needed.

The primary reason for keeping track of all the parts for a project like this one is simple. The assembled engine shown here is surrounded by the multitude of parts it contains. The loss of one small piece could be crucial to finishing the model.

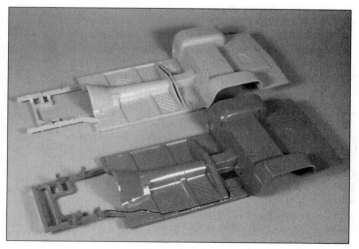

Petty race cars until the early 1990s were painted Petty Blue inside and out with the exception of the requisite florescent STP Red on the exterior of the body shell. Here the reconditioned chassis has been primered and painted in comparison to the original piece in the background.

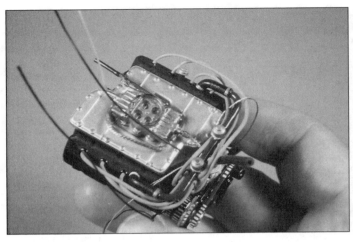

The massive hemi V-8 racing engine in this 1/16th scale kit just begs for additional detailing. Note the double-pumper four-barrel carb with machined fittings, the crossover breather and oil filler tube and the various wires and tubes for the electrical, spark plug and fuel system.

The unassembled kit pieces are displayed around the Dana differential and rear axle. Note the brake-line plumbing beginning to take shape along the top of the rear axle housing and the intricate detailing on the huge Bendix brake drums and shoes.

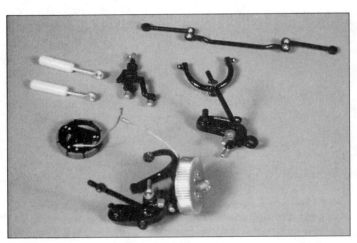

The front suspension components, front brakes and dual shocks are painted and detailed ready for assembly. Note the attention to hardware details and the brake line plumbing in place.

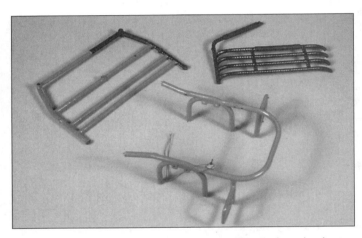

Parts of the roll cage and front hoop. Note that the larger diameter padding is finished in flat black while the smaller diameter roll cage sections is done in semi-gloss black to represent the correct wrapping of electrical tape on the full-size race car.

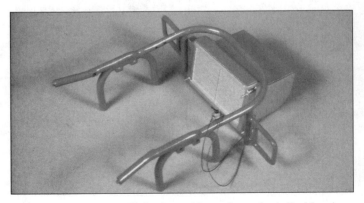

Here the radiator and air shroud have been installed in place at the front of the front hoop. Note the ignition coil attached to the right side of the hoop with wiring and the locator pins on the radiator for the top and bottom radiator hoses to be installed later.

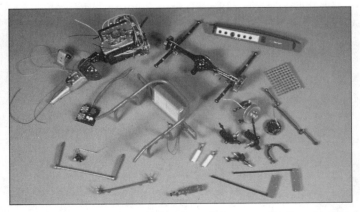

The photo gives you a little idea of the complexity of building the large-scale kit. Again thought should be given to keeping track of assembled, painted and detailed subassemblies until the time comes for their attachment into a final location.

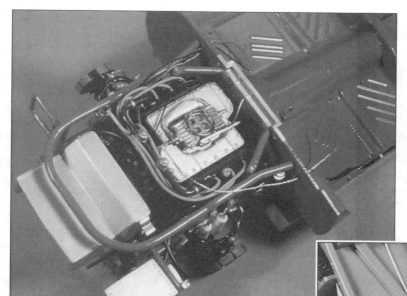

The engine and transmission have been test-fitted into the engine bay inside the front hoop. Note the location of the coil wiring, the oil filler tube, the ignition and electrical wiring running from various engine accessories to locations through the firewall and the air box for the dry sump oil cooler on the left front corner of the engine.

The engine is installed in its final location along with the wheel hubs, brake drums, upper and lower control arms, tie rod ends and steering arm and the front sway bar. Note the holes drilled to reduce the weight in each side bracket of the sway bar.

The rear suspension has been glued into its final location. Note the rear spring shackles (which allow for the adjustment of the rear ride height), rear end cooling plumbing and the fine-mesh screen inserted into the floor pan to replicate the underside of the cooling fan located behind the driver's seat in the cockpit.

This shot of the nearly-completed front clip allow us to see the exposed, vented Bendix brake shoes, location of the battery, brake master cylinder, radiator overflow tank and the cowl-induction air cleaner housing atop the carb.

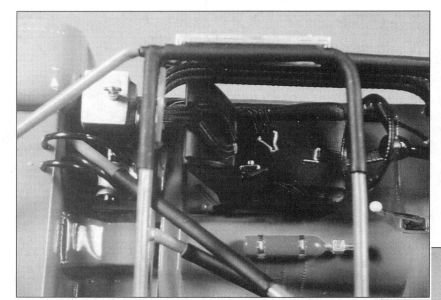

This view of the finished interior reveals the braided material Bradley found at a fabric shop used to replicate the seat belt straps, the dry sump reservoir behind the seat and the squirrel-cage rear end cooling pump and fan.

The finished Dodge Charger chassis. Note the location of the gasoline filler tube, window safety net, fire extinguisher and the used appearance of the tire tread accomplished by carefully sanding around the circumference of each tire.

This top view of the completed rolling chassis allow you to see the location of all the many essential components and in particular the dual solid state ignition boxes, located on the floor below the right corner of the dash board.

Another view of the finished Dodge Charger chassis.

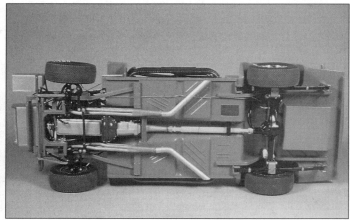

This view of the completed chassis shows the location of the brake line which runs from the master cylinder along the bottom of the floor pan back to the rear axle. Bradley cautions that properly attaching the exhaust headers to the engine will affect the placement of each exhaust dump to the floor pan.

This clear shot of the entire engine compartment reveals the degree of added details to the race-ready Dodge 426 Hemi engine.

A three-quarter view of the finished MPC 1/16th scale Petty/STP Dodge Charger. Attention to detail like the BareMetal chrome foil use around the window frames, the hand-painted white raised lettering on the Goodyear treaded racing tires and the careful application of the Slixx reproduction decals makes for a contest-quality replica.

Another view of the Petty/STP Dodge Charger.

The underside of this finished replica has received as much attention to detail as any other part of the model. Note the carefully sanded tire tread emulating wear.

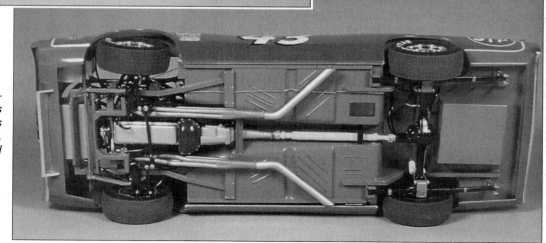

The After-Market

Building "Outside the Box"

For many of us, the mere thought of a model building world with no race car paint colors, no after-market decal sheets, no resin parts or kits, no purpose-designed plastic stock car kits and all the other things we've become accustomed to in the last couple of decades sends a profound chill through our collective bones.

Today's stock car modeler has a virtual potpourri of building mediums, materials, tools and supplies to choose from. I'd like to think we are unbelievably fortunate rather than hopelessly pampered. Today, as consumers and modelers, we are constantly challenged, not by the limits of our choices of building and detailing materials, but by the multitude of projects currently available with after-market products.

A little more than 20 years ago, the execution of a production-based race car model was most definitely the sole effort of a single individual. Brush painting or the use of a very limited range of basic spray paints was the accepted method of applying colors. Any added details were the singular hand-made work of each individual modeler. Hand painted body graphics like sponsor decals, numbers, lettering and so on, required a mighty steady touch with a brush. The fleeting vision of specific race car paints in spray cans, accurate and professionally produced kit or after-market decals, period-correct racing tires and wheels, seat belts, etc., was

nothing but a fantasy…even for the most enlightened and visionary stock car model builders.

Building such models was not an endeavor for the faint of heart. Novice or even modelers of moderate skills often shied away in droves from such projects. This was uncharted territory; the work was difficult and treacherous. Admittedly, some early annual kits from the late-1950s and early-1960s did contain an occasional roll bar, open stamped wheels and big water-slide numerals, but these things (though appreciated) fell far short of being much help in building an accurate replica.

The primary after-market product lines that many credit with forever altering the way we build stock car models are:

- Resin
- Decals
- Photo-etch
- Detailing materials
- Authentic racing paint colors
- Polishing kit

We'll look at these categories and some of the after-market companies that produce them.

The Resin Revolution

The molding material

Resin is a urethane material whose chemical components come from petroleum-based derivatives. It is a two-part mixture, a resin-carrier and a catalyst, which, after thorough mixing, is then poured into a hard rubber mold. The professional resin casters use industrial RTV rubber to make their two-part molds. The RTV mold is made in two-parts because one part of the mold captures the exterior contours while the second part forms the interior surfaces of the subject master.

Though urethane-type resin is classified as a hazardous material and is flammable in its semi-liquid

state, it presents little, if any, dangers to the modeler. This is more of a safety issue for the manufacturer and the resin caster than to the hobbyist, since once the resin material is cured (and having been placed in a vacuum chamber to force all stray air bubbles from the casting), the resin is inert. Always use the same safety precautions with resin as you would with any other hobby materials.

Unlike injection molding, in which steel dies are engraved by precision machinery, resin casting a requires a master be created (an original). This master can be anything from simply reproducing the parts for a long out-of-production kit or something created by scratch-building that never existed in model form before. But polyurethane resin is only half this story.

The Rubber Mold

RTV (Room Temperature Vulcanizing rubber—silicone) is the other key ingredient to the resin casting process. It was originally developed by a college professor who, try as he might, could not find a use for the silicone in its purest form. Eventually uses were discovered for RTV-1 which included industrial, automotive and household caulks and sealants.

RTV-2 was developed in the early-1970s. It differs greatly from RTV-1 in that it requires a two-part chemical reaction for the material to cure thoroughly. Quickly, RTV-2 became a mold-making medium utilized by the military, automotive, electronics and even the furniture industry where it was a perfect choice to cast finely detailed decorative and ornamental parts. Luck, which some say is when preparedness runs head-on into opportunity, brought polyurethane resin and RTV-2 rubber together and the stage was set for the hobbyist to enter a new golden age of model building.

Working with Resin

Cast resin pieces works very much like polystyrene, being pliable and responding to fillers and all types of glue and bonding agents intended for regular kit plastics. Resin can be filed, sanded and cut using the very same tools used for styrene plastics. A distinct advantage of resin is its compatibility with automotive surfacers, fillers, primers and acrylic enamels and lacquers. Polystyrene plastic always requires a primer-barrier coat as automotive finishes will attack unprotected plastic surfaces. As you can quickly see, this process opens up the possibilities to a whole new world for the model builder, as well as the collector who simply wants to resort some valuable piece from their stock-car kit collection.

After-market companies, such as The Modelhaus, Early Racing Classics, All-American Models and Ron Cash Models, specialize in producing individual parts (competition wheels and tires, engines, body shells and driveline accessory items) and complete resin kits of various stock cars and street-stock makes that can be easily modified to race car application.

With the continued interest in NASCAR Winston Cup stock cars and the availability of the very fine 1/24th scale Monogram Models line of stock car kits since 1983, resin casters have definitely answered the call. You can buy conversion pieces to turn a standard 1981-84 Pontiac Grand Prix into the limited-production 1986 Grand Prix 2+2 race car; or you can buy the entire body shell cast in resin which drops right over the Monogram race car chassis. The same goes for many other stock car bodies never offered in the Revell-Monogram line.

In recent years, stock car modelers have benefited from the availability of Holman-Moody, Weld and Basset wheels, along with a wide range of resin racing tires to fit virtually any era of stock car.

Some manufacturers produce specialized race car body shells, chassis plates and stripped interior tubs from great old kits, allowing the stock car modeler to tackle a wide range of projects without spending hundreds of dollars for an expensive collectible kit.

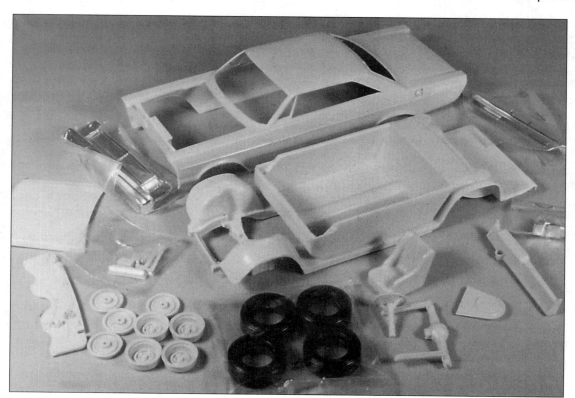

This Modelhaus resin kit of a 1965 NASCAR Ford Galaxie is a typical after-market product available to today's stock car model builder.

Resin Resources

The Modelhaus: Don Holthaus and a buddy attended the Hillside, Chicago, swap meet in 1984, discovering a gold mine of old original unbuilt kits...that they couldn't afford! But Don did find he could afford built models, especially the ones with broken or missing parts. He had read a story on resin casting in a magazine, bought a Kast-Pro starter kit and replicated the missing and broken parts he needed. As they say, the rest is history.

Don and Carol Holthaus have been molding resin parts since May 1986. Their products are mostly sold at swap meets or by mail order. There are currently two distributors for Modelhaus products, and the firm has customers worldwide. The Modelhaus product line includes many street-stock kits and body shells that can or have been converted into stock car racers by builders. Some of the most unique kits done this way include the 1957 Mercury, 1958 Ford and 1958

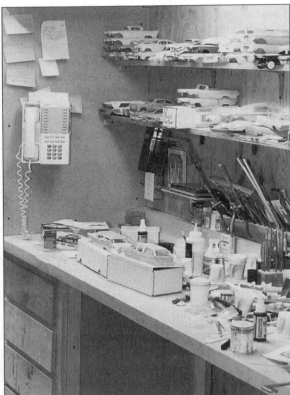

A typical resin pouring table at the Modelhaus with trays, mixing tools, bulk resin and the catalyst. Note the numerous molds on the upper shelves. (Terry Jessee Photo)

Pictured here is the work station where masters are being created at the Modelhaus. Note the bodies and a wide variety of tools and body fillers along with numerous types of bonding agents. (Terry Jessee Photo)

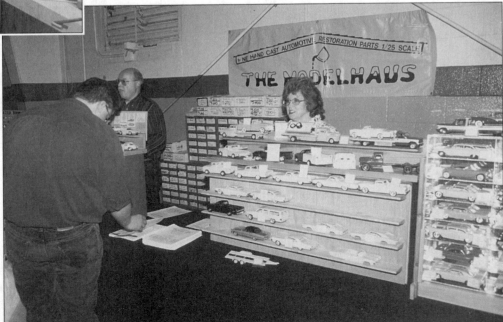

Here at a typical model car swap meet Don and Carol Holthaus have the Modelhaus "store" set up and open for business.

Pontiac. Modelhaus was one of the first after-market resin manufacturers to offer purpose-built stock car race car kits that include both the 1964 and 1965 Ford Galaxies. Don and Carol also offer a thorough line of period-correct stock car tires, wheels and a wide variety of accessory items, such as oil coolers, reservoirs and cooling fans.

Early Racing Classics (ERC): Karl Stark grew up in Connecticut, attending races at Danbury Fairgrounds in the early-1950s. Like many of us, he drew pictures of race cars and began building models as a kid. As an adult, Stark took up cabinet-making full-time, though his profound interest in racing and model stock cars only continued to grow with time. Self-described as "semi-retired," Stark moved to Charlottesville, Virginia, in 1980. With more time available he found he could tackle a lot of modeling projects he only dreamed about in earlier years. Sam Miller, a master of resin casting, lived near Stark and taught him the trade.

Content for years making resin parts and pieces for his personal use, Stark, like so many after-marketers, was lured into a retail business by the constant demands of fellow modelers increasingly willing to spend their disposable income on resin copies of vintage racing cars from Stark's vivid memories. He opened his retail business—Early Racing Classics—in late 1996, starting with a master from his own handywork of Ned Jarrett's '37 Ford coupe. That first item is what Stark refers to as "an experiment," just to see how the public would accept it. From that point on, he has found the public acceptance nearly overwhelming. The ERC line now includes countless body styles from the mid-1930s through the mid-1970s. ERC offers body shells, frames, engines, wheels, tires, quick change rear axles and delicate suspension assemblies.

As so many other after-market companies, ERC for Stark is a natural outgrowth of his long-standing hobby of building scale model stock cars. Many feel it's doubtful these vintage subjects, so fundamental to the current interest in stock car modeling, will be addressed by the manufacturers of injection-molded kits. ERC fills an important void in the race car modeling hobby.

Others: Other sources of resin parts and kits to build vintage stock cars include: All-American Models, Ron Cash Scale Models and Pro-Tech.

Karl Stark with his retail display for his Early Racing Classics at a model car show.

This 1934 Ford "Skeeter" is built from an Early Racing Classics 1/25th scale resin kit by Karl Stark (photo by Karl Stark).

Early Racing Classics resin kits of a 1937 Ford Modified built by Don Lajoie (photo by Karl Stark).

This 1936 Chevy modified is an Early Racing Classic 1/25th scale resin kit built by Karl Stark (photo by Karl Stark).

This 1936 Chevy modified is based on a ERC kit built by Karl Stark (photo by Karl Stark).

This Richie Evans modified Ford Pinto is based on an ERC 1/25th-scale resin kit built by Karl Stark.

This pair of 1/25th resin '37 Ford Sportsman stock cars are from an Early Racing Classics resin kit. The models were built by Karl Stark (Doug Whyte photo).

Karl Stark built this replica of the '37 Ford stock car Ned Jarrett won the 1957 NASCAR Sportsman title from an ERC resin kit (Doug Whyte photo).

Decals, Decals, Decals!

Professionally designed and printed water-slide decals are an invaluable element in the growth and longevity of the stock car modeling hobby. There have been leaders and pioneers in this market segment. Some of both categories are still with us; sadly, many are gone but certainly not forgotten.

The technology behind water-slide decals is not a great mystery. First, artwork is developed either on the drawing board by hand or with a desktop computer drawing program. Once all elements have been satisfied (size, proportion, fit, etc.), high resolution camera-ready versions of the particular decal set originals is output and sent to a printing house. Here the artwork is used to produce negatives and printing plate, an individual one for each separate color to be printed, and the end product is produced by offset or lithograph printing through a commercial printing press.

When decals are produced this way, great care is exercised to ensure that all the separate components are lined up correctly (registered), guaranteeing that every element is precisely positioned. Not all after-market companies produce their decals in this fashion. Slixx, JNJ, Blue Ridge, Yesterday's and Chimmneyville

do it this way. But Fred Cady, a pioneer in the after-market decal business, continues business in a time-honored way. Many seasoned stock car model builders had their imagination and creative appetites ratcheted-up many notches when first exposed to the Fred Cady Design product line of stock car racing decals.

Some examples of Fred Cady Design decals. These Petty items are out of production.

Fred Cady prepares black-and-white artwork on the drawing board. No computers here—just tedious work all done by hand.

Fred Cady uses out-sourced silk screens to print decals from his hand-made artwork. Here he points out that the silk screen is a synthetic, finely-woven mesh with a photographic image captured on the surface emulsion of his original artwork.

Fred Cady pulls a squeegee, drawing printing ink across the surface of the silk screen. This operation is necessary for each impression and for each separate color.

Fred Cady Design (FCD): Fred Cady is literally a one man show. Since he began making decals, Cady has done it all. He started making his own decals by creating each piece of artwork by hand on the drawing board in January 1980. He spent the first year designing artwork in his free time, when he wasn't at his regular job as a graphic designer and commercial artist.

He had dabbled with the silk screening of some sports car racing markings for his own use. As it is with so many other "modelers turned after-marketer," Cady began producing a few items for members of his local model club. Next, he ventured out to his first show in the Chicago area and met with success. He came away convinced that this was a valid business idea. He quickly made the decision to start Fred Cady Design. His first decal sheets for mail-order resale were markings for four 1965 NASCAR Ford Galaxies. They continue to be among his best selling products, even today.

Cady continues to work in the fashion that has worked for him for many years. The only part of the operation that he seeks assistance on is the creation of the individual silk screens. But once he has those framed silk screens in hand, he prints each color himself, by hand, for the number of sheets he plans for a run. There are up to as many as eight colors per sheet and as many as eight different decal sheet layouts on each screen. The most telling feature when looking at a Cady decal

Here each decal sheet is carefully stacked on a drying rack in preparation for final trimming and packaging. Drying time for the ink is about one hour.

JNJ Hobbies was responsible for hundreds of decals sheets (like these Petty markings) when the company was in business from the late-1980s to the mid-1990s.

sheet is the positioning of each color element. Fred's system does not allow for pre-registration of each color element. The builder is required to assemble each character or numeral set one layer at a time.

Since the start of FCD, Cady has created more than 300 individual sets of artwork for water-slide decals. As it has been since the beginning, FCD supplies wholesale distributors, hobby shops and a sizable mail-order business.

JNJ Decals: If Fred Cady was the first after-marketer to produce stock car racing decals commercially, then JNJ Decals must be credited with blowing the market wide open. John Cisco and Jack Higgins, friends and modelers, were motivated by the limited choices of stock car markings for the new Monogram kits. Jack and John responded by producing their own brand of water-slide decals, working with drivers, teams and sponsors to produce hundreds of stock car markings. Matched with the enthusiastic acceptance of the new Monogram kits, one is hard-pressed to decide which product line is most responsible for the rapid growth of this hobby segment.

By contrast to the way things are done at Cady Design, neither Cisco or Higgins were responsible for the bulk of JNJ's artwork. A series of professional commercial artists was employed to develop this key step in the process. Once the artwork was approved, commercial offset printing companies produced the tightly registered, multi-color water-slide decal sheets in quantity. JNJ must be noted as one of the very few decal makers to have produced foil markings, a difficult and expensive proposition.

Located in Knoxville, Tennessee, JNJ was a major player in the after-market decal business from 1985 to 1995. This was at a time when licensing bloodhounds were taking increased notice of the substantial growth of stock car model building nationwide. Though JNJ had always played by the rules, those rules quickly changed...and probably forever.

Increasingly, all participants needed for licensing approval wanted to be compensated handsomely. The era of perpetual licens-

Slixx decals set a new high-water mark for the stock car modeling hobby. Here are few examples of the Petty decals produced by the California company.

ing agreements ended. Each succeeding year's negotiations saw the ante upped to the point where a small run of 500 decal sheets could not be done profitably. Increased operating costs resulted in higher retail prices, accompanied by painful decisions not to produce items especially when there was no guarantee they would sell well. The handwriting was on the wall. As business slowly ground to a halt, health problems combined with financial needs saw the partnership dissolved and JNJ ceased business in 1995.

For the foreseeable future, hundreds of desirable JNJ decal sheets remain in the distribution and retail pipeline. But that supply won't last forever.

Slixx Decals: Slixx brought the after-market decal business to a new plateau. Whether it's a one-man operation or highly commercial, the basic elements remain the same. Accurate artwork, ink, decal paper and some type of printing process.

Slixx Decals began business in 1992 as a partnership of three friends Bill Robinson, Gene Sisemore and Jim White. All three were stock car racing fans and avid modelers. The trio wanted to expand the choice of after-market water-slide stock car decals and produce and distribute the No. 1 licensed decal line available. Today, Slixx is a family-run business by Gene and Becky Sisemore.

The first decal sheet produced was that of 1992 Winston Cup Champion Alan Kulwicki's Hooters Ford Thunderbird. Due to Alan's untimely and unfortunate death in April 1993, this sheet was soon discontinued.

From that rocky beginning the company moved forward establishing licensing agreements with such notable teams and drivers as Richard Petty, Bobby Allison and many others. Slixx continues to improve its product line; because of this, the company has had a major influence on not only the after-market, but the way major model kit manufacturers do things.

Each Slixx decal is usually produced not in the hundreds, but in production runs of thousands of sheets at a time. Creating artwork on computer software is now the norm rather than the exception. Micro Scale, one of this country's premier decal printers, finishes the whole process for Slixx. Each individually packaged Slixx sheet contains an intricate and highly detailed location illustration as part of the package.

To date, Slixx has produced nearly 400 stock car racing decal sheets. Licensing red tape and legal obstacles will continue to make the task increasingly more difficult to maintain those kind of numbers.

Others: Other brands of after-market decals: Yesterday's Decals, Chimmneyville Decals, David Romero Decals.

Photo-Etch

Today, the use of photo-etch (PE) hardware on all types of scale model cars is pretty much taken for granted. When constructing a stock car model, it may range from a minute item like a single piece of carburetor linkage or ignition hardware, or it could be as complex as a pair of working hood hinges. If photo-etch is an unfamiliar term to you, it's time to clear up that matter up once and for all.

The beginning step in the PE process is the creation of a camera-ready piece of black-and-white artwork. This original art is commonly drawn proportionally larger than the required finished size, usually two- or

four-times the final size. Such artwork can be hand-drawn; more likely today, it is computer-generated using a standard drawing program.

The next step can go one of two ways. The original art can be reduced to final size photographically, creating a high-contrast transparent negative (a reversal of the original artwork). In the second approach, once the final design has been created on the computer, the electronic image, on disk, is sent to a photo lab or service bureau where a photographic film negative is made.

Thin sheets of brass, nickel silver, stainless steel or copper (between .003 inch to .010 inch thick) are thoroughly cleaned and then coated with a photo sensitive emulsion (referred to as photo-resist). Next, the negative is placed directly onto the emulsion-treated thin sheet (a "plate") where it is treated to a timed exposure of very bright light. Then the exposed plate is developed with dark room chemicals. This process removes all the emulsion on the plate protected from exposure to the light source by the opaque images on the negative.

The final step requires putting the exposed and developed plate through a mild acid bath. The acid emulsifies all of the unprotected metal plate, while the material under the original emulsion is unaffected. The final PE metal parts which are left are an exact duplicate of the original artwork, reduced to 1-to-1.

Photo-etch parts come in many shapes and sizes for a multitude of applications. These small delicate parts are attached into place on the model using super glue, epoxy or clear enamel bottle paint. Some types of PE parts are attached to a tree like injection molded plastic parts and require being carefully cut free. In a simple application of hood pins for example, a minute drop of white glue is deposited at the precise spot where the PE part is to be attached. Then one at a time, the photo-etch hood pin scuff plates are carefully lifted from the backing material with an X-Acto knife and placed over the glue and into their proper position.

Replicas and Miniatures Company of Maryland (RMCM): RMCM is operated by Norm and Mary Veber. The company began in early-1980 as an architectural model building service. By the mid-1980s, Norm was also importing foreign model kits for mail order sales. He began using photo-etch in his architectural building services business. Being a model car builder, it wasn't long before he began to see the natural application of PE to the automotive hobby segment.

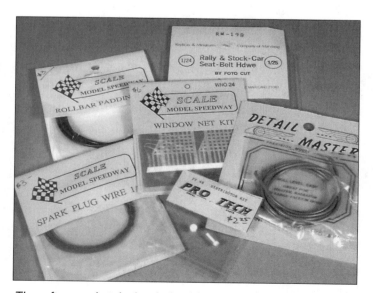

The after-market is loaded with manufacturers of a wide range of detailing items, as shown here from Scale Speedway, Replicas and Miniatures Company of Maryland, Pro-Tech and Detail Master.

Today, RMCM has more than 450 items in its product catalog. The Vebers have also added a considerable range of resin parts along with the photo-etch products. It's a full-time business for them since the mid-1980s.

Bob Korunow likes to get his product ideas directly from his customers. Here he has his packaged items on display at a swap meet.

The Model Car Garage (TMCG): It was a time when Bob Korunow found himself in a dead-end job. He'd worked in the auto body repair trade for nearly 20 years. Breathing in the chemical fumes, paint over-spray and constant dust particles were motivating him to strongly consider a new occupation. In the late-1980s, he had a renewed interest in building models. He began entering contests and attending some of the larger model shows and was amazed at the current building and detailing levels.

At one of his first events in Miami, Korunow struck up a friendship with some of the area's premier builders. After discussing with them what they were looking for in the way of detailing products that were not on the market, he went out and bought a small lathe. He began first making parts for his own use, occasionally selling extras. The Model Car Garage was born and was successful enough to allow Korunow to begin working his regular job part-time. He devoted the extra time to manufacturing, packaging and distribution, starting with his local hobby shops. The success of those first hand-machined aluminum parts allowed him to make the big leap to an expanded line of photo-etch.

Korunow attended the Great Salt Lake Model Car Contest in 1993. His purpose was to get public exposure of his considerable building talents and his parts line. He brought along some of his products and sold every item he brought on the trip (plus he won a first place award for his model entry!). Korunow discussed the prospects of a full-time after-market business with many of the vendors at the Salt Lake show. When he returned to Florida, he took the plunge. He quit his regular job and went into full-time operation of The Model Car Garage.

TMCG offers a plethora of stuff to satisfy the most picky stock car model builder on the planet. Disk brake rotors, detail wiring accessories, instrument gauge sets, grill inserts for all three current NASCAR body styles, drive belt pulley sets, racing engine air cleaners and nut and bolt head sets are just a few examples.

The Model Car Garage ships product all over the world. You can also visit the web site at: *www.modelcargarage.com* to view the compete catalog and many other assorted goodies.

Others: Other after-market sources for photo-etch parts: Detail Master, Pro-Tech.

Detailing Items

There was a time when adding spark plug wires to your stock car model was a big deal. At first, the use of sewing thread was the state-of-the-art material for this task. The really advanced builders would run each length of thread through bees' wax before use, grooming the errant thread fibers and giving the scale plug wires a more realistic appearance. The availability of more advanced after-market detailing items, such as actual coated wire for spark plugs and braided wire for radiator hoses and cooling lines, etc., has provided builders of moderate skills the opportunity to execute more authentic looking stock car models.

It may be difficult to understand today how important these innovations were to the hobby. Remember that sewing thread does not bend to shape like wire. And if you've never tried to heat and bend a plastic or metal rod into cooling lines and radiator hoses, you haven't really lived. After-market entrepreneurs like Dirk Johnson saw the possibilities of packaging coated electrical and printed circuit board wire into manageable quantities and market it to hobby retailers for sale to eager modelers.

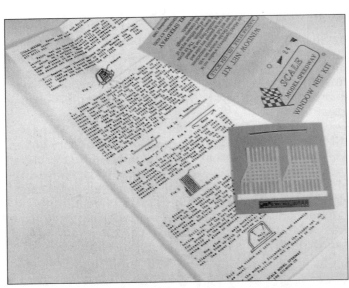

The Scale Speedway offers a great line of products aimed squarely at the stock car modeler, such as this coated wire for spark plug detailing and a fine window net kit.

The Scale Window net kit is one of the most convincing detailing items when assembled and installed on your model.

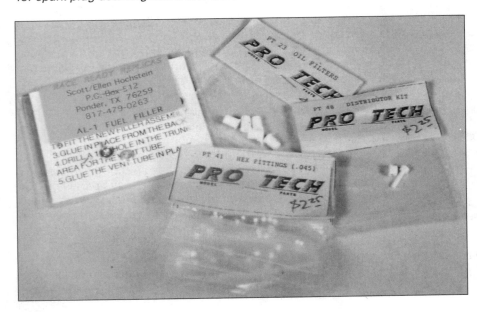

Race Ready Replicas sells a machined aluminum dry brake fuel filler (left), while Pro-Tech manufactures a variety of small stock car detailing items like hex fittings, distributor kits and oil filters in resin.

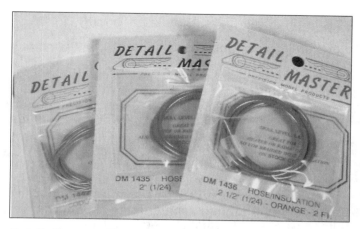

Detail Master offers a series of graduated diameters of coated wire to represent oil cooling lines.

Some examples of the finest photo-etch products available today to the stock modeler include RMCM's seat belt hardware, Pro-Tech's hood pins and Detail Master's ignition coil set.

Detail Master: Detail Master was the brain child of Dirk Johnson while he was living in Texas in 1985. Johnson's first products were packaged braided cooling lines and flocked paper. Dirk attended the Great Salt Lake Model Car Contest in 1986 and got a great insight into what the serious model car builders were looking for in the way of more refined detailing and building materials. Upon his return home, he began steadily developing a line of photo-etch materials: carburetor linkages, hose clamps, bolt and nut hardware, drive belt pulley sets, electrical and ignition hardware, disk brake, driveline and suspension hardware and a full line of spark plug wiring kits, including pre-wired distributors.

In a little over a decade, Detail Master grew into a mail-order company doing business worldwide. In 1998, Johnson sold his company to long-time employees, Sue Haenel and Schiryl Adams. The new owners are no strangers to this business, having worked for Johnson for nearly five years before the buyout. The product line has continued to expand and now includes a full complement of resin, photo-etch and pre-packaged detailing accessories.

Others: Other after-market companies that produce detailing items for stock car modelers include: Scale Model Speedways, Track Side, Parts by Parks.

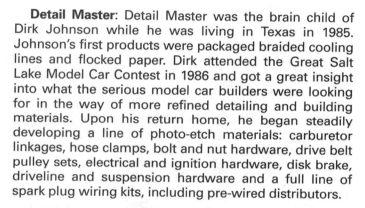

Stock car tire lettering detail can be applied with these dry transfer products from Gofer and Shabo.

Blue Ribbon Products specializes in ready-to-use products for stock car modelers. Here is a set of Goodyear slicks that are ready to be applied to the wheel rims of your latest R-M-based stock car project.

Authentic Stock Car Racing Paints

Model Car World: Model builder Dave Dodge was content working for a NAPA parts store in outside sales to body shops until January 1990. One day a customer asked for some touch-up paint for his '54 Chevy. He discovered the store still had mixing codes on micro-fishe for many of those old colors. Suddenly, it occurred to him how nice it would be to paint his models with authentic factory colors.

At first, Dodge would buy a full gallon of specialized custom-mixed factory colors. From this point, he would properly reduce the full-strength mixture and repackage it into 1 oz. and 3 oz. glass bottles for resale. The big break for Dodge came a couple of years later when he purchased all the paint mixing equipment, paint chip catalogs, paint formulas on micro-fish for lacquer and enamels from a local parts store that was closing its doors. Now he was equipped to do his own mixing in whatever quantity desired. Since relocating from the Midwest to North Carolina in 1992, Dodge has made the custom mixing and resale of a virtually unlimited listing of automotive paints in manageable quantities in both bottles (for air brush) and aerosol spray cans.

Almost any racing color used over the past 50 years is available from MCW paints. Dodge points out that he mixes paint for stock cars of all eras (and virtually any other motorsports series). Dodge said he doesn't use copyrighted or trade names to identify his paints, but they are exactly what is used by the big boys.

Model Car World paints are a regular feature at many swap meets. Here MCW proprietor Dave Dodge talks with customer in Toledo, Ohio.

BSR produces a line of stock car model paint in spray cans under the Metro label.

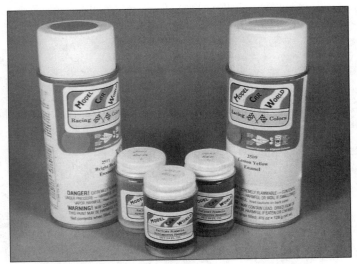

Model Car World automotive paints are available in either enamel in spray cans or lacquer in bottles, as shown here.

BSR Finishes: BSR was one of the first after-market companies to package automotive paints for model stock car builders. Originally, the Metro line included both bottles and spray cans. The bottles were eventually dropped from the line, mainly due to their short shelf life. BSR owner, William Brigman, began packaging racing colors like Petty blue in spray cans for his own model building use in 1991. Later that year, he took some of his packaged paints to a model car show and gave them away. Modelers who used the spray paint encouraged Brigman to sell it to the public.

The BSR line of stock car colors is packaged by the Metro company and is actually DuPont Centari acrylic enamel. There is also a possibility the bottle variety will be reintroduced soon, as the shelf-life problem has been corrected.

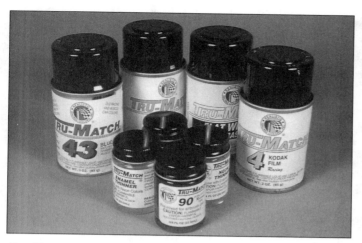

Tru-Match was one of the first manufacturers to produce stock car model paints specifically for model builders. The automotive enamels are available in spray cans or bottles.

Tru-Match (by Realistic Racing Colors): Curtis Rice is part owner in a heavy construction company in Richmond, Virginia. As a stock model builder and NASCAR fan, he had taken note that many modelers had difficulty securing the proper paints to finish off their projects. He pondered the possibility of starting a mail-order business packaging many of the actual team's racing colors in bottles and spray cans. Realistic Racing Colors was born with the release of its line of Tru-Match paints.

Curtis works closely with many of the top NASCAR teams to ensure that each bottle and spray can of paint matches exactly the color used on the race cars. There is no mystery about the composition of Tru-Match paint, as it is simply automotive acrylic enamel packaged in manageable quantities for hobbyists.

The Polishing Kit

LMG Enterprises: Tom Gaffney was a household name for a lengthy period in the early days of the model car hobby. He was first known for his monthly columns in *Car Model* magazine and later provided the same insights and valuable information to builders of all skill levels with a column and frequent features in the pages of *Scale Auto Enthusiast* magazine. In the fall of 1980, Gaffney happened across some miniature hardware in his work as a mechanical engineer and immediately saw a ready application to his model building projects. What a great revelation to be able to use .0003 in. and .0004 in. machine screws and nuts for detailing the chassis and suspension on his next model. He shared his find with other skilled modelers whose exhilaration was predictable. They all worked to convince him to market these items which led to the establishment of LMG Enterprises six months later.

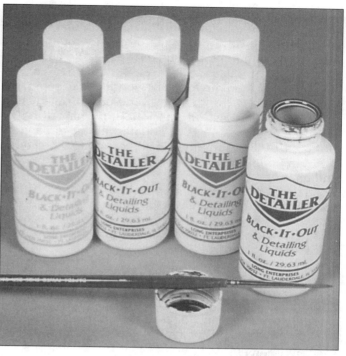

The Detailer is a color detailing liquid applied with a paint brush. There are multiple colors that are handy for tinting or highlighting recessed features like grill work detail.

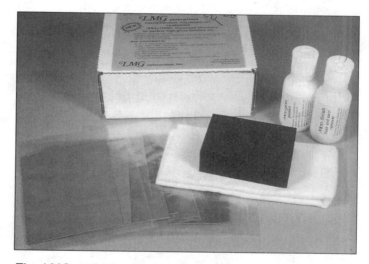

The LMG polishing kit has changed the attitude of many stock car modelers by salvaging mediocre paint jobs.

LMG recently introduced a sanding pad set which applies the graduated sand paper grits to thin sheet foam.

LMG was among the first after-market companies to offer .020 in. coated wire for detailing engines and then came the Ultra-Color line of powered paints that yield some of the most distinctive pearl and candy finishes found on scale model cars. But the one item that really put LMG on the map and continues to represent the greatest volume for this home-based business is the LMG Enterprises Professional Polishing Kit. The kit contains a system of graduated abrasive sanding cloths, a rubber sanding block, soft cotton polishing cloth and one bottle each of Micro-Mesh liquid polish and haze and swirl remover.

Again, Gaffney discovered this product in the course of his work. This polishing system was originally developed by a company specializing in reconditioning helicopter and jet aircraft canopies. The wear and tear on the exposed surfaces at high speeds fogs the transparency of the clear canopy surfaces. The Micro-Mesh polishing kit has saved countless poor or marginally painted scale model surfaces. Unlike virtually every other type of modeling, automobiles (particularly stock cars) have glossy paint jobs. The LMG product continues to improve with the introduction recently of the sanding pad kit. Here the same graduated abrasive cloths have been applied to thin sheets of commercial foam. Either way, for many model stock car builders, they'd rather give up the hobby than give up their polishing kits.

LMG is named for Gaffney's wife Linda, and she oversees the day-to-day operations. As so many after-market businesses LMG ships product around the globe.

One-Stop Shopping

Obviously, you can engage in an exhaustive search through classified and display advertisements to find the virtual cornucopia of after-market stock car modeling accessories. Another option is a sort of one-stop shopping center as it were for such things. Two establishments that I have dealt with and can recommend are:

The Fayetteville Model Shop (BSR's retail location): Not only is BSR a source for authentic stock car paint colors, you will also find its retail store front, The Fayetteville Hobby Shop, in Fayetteville, Georgia, 30 minutes southeast of Atlanta. BSR is also a mail-order source for just about anything the stock car modeler could imagine. BSR was started in 1989 by William Brigman, and he conducted mail-order business from his garage. Brigman's father was an avid stock car model builder and William's interest grew from that early exposure.

Entrance to The Fayetteville Model Shop/BSR.

The Fayetteville Model Shop/BSR offers stock car model builders and collectors a wide variety of products for every project. It may be hard to believe but this little shop near Atlanta is one of the top retailers of Revell-Monogram stock car model kits in the world.

Stock car model kits, paints, decals and more from The Fayetteville Model Shop/BSR.

Brigman moved the business to its present retail location in 1994. And, of course, BSR is still quite busily engaged in the mail-order business shipping to customers in this country, as well as China, Poland, Russia, Japan, Australia and Africa.

Paint, resin, photo-etch, decals and detailing items of just about every description can be found on premises or on BSR's web site. Since going on line in December 1996, Brigman boasts of over six million hits so far and an average of 450,000 hits per month currently. Looking up *http://wwwbsrrep.com* on the Internet will get you in touch with all the latest racing and model industry news, BSR's extensive catalog, a listing and race car reference pictures of all the latest stock car decals, and a lively rumor mill department.

BSR also has its own line of vintage stock car decals offered under the Yesterday's name. The line was first introduced in 1995 and currently features more than two-dozen separate sheets for old stock cars as diverse as the No. 99 '71 STP Plymouth, No. 6 '62 Cotton Owen Pontiac and the No. 22 '64 Ford Galaxie.

Southern Motorsports Hobbies: Owner Ronnie Setzer is an enthusiastic NASCAR fan and modeler. He has also taken his turn behind the wheel of a full-size stock car and is currently part-owner in a late model. He is fortunate to pursue his hobbies and leisure time interests as a full-time business. Setzer had operated from his home earlier on, hitting the occasionally model show and doing some mail order. The situation changed as more and more people began showing up at his door in the evenings. Mrs. Setzer finally told her husband it was time to "do this thing right" and open up a retail shop. In early-1991, Setzer opened his retail operation in Lenoir, North Carolina, and expanded his mail order services and attended more model car shows.

This dedicated stock car modeler found it quite easy identifying which product to stock his store with. He sought out those things he would want to use on a typical building project. The store has a heavy emphasis on stock car modeling, of course. Like BSR, if an item is available, SMH probably has it. If he doesn't, he'll get it or try to find it.

Front entrance to Southern Motorsports Hobbies which started out in Ronnie Setzer's garage in Lenoir, N.C.

Southern Motorsports Hobbies carries a wide range of stock car paint colors.

This small facility in North Carolina, Southern Motorsports Hobbies contains a real stock pile of vintage stock car kits and the latest new releases.

Southern Motorsports Hobbies is a central source for one of the largest ranges of resin stock car bodies as shown here.

Among the unique products offered by SMH are a distinctive line of 1/25-1/24th scale resin stock car bodies that are decidedly not something you'll find anywhere else. The list of such items includes: 1996 Lincoln Mk 8, early-1990s Mercury Cougar, 1980 Chevrolet Malibu, 1960 Plymouth Belvedere, mid-1990s Dodge Intrepid, 1977 Chevrolet Monte Carlo, 1977 Oldsmobile Cutlass S, mid-1970s Pontiac Ventura or Chevy Nova (Busch series), 1965 Plymouth Belvedere, 1962 Ford Starlite coupe.

Like so many of the after-market manufacturers and other specialty resellers, Southern Motorsports Hobbies ships to many far flung parts of the globe...including a strong contingent of stock car model builders in...New Zealand? Visit SMH in person or reach them on the Internet at *http://www.smhracing.com* for all the latest building and detailing items.

1999 Model Car Buyer's Guide: And finally, the ultimate one-stop-shopping publication may be the *1999 Model Car Buyer's Guide* by Scale Sports. This 48 page booklet lists over 800 suppliers of nearly every type of product information that might be of interest to the stock car model builder. Pick up a copy at your local hobby shop or reach Scale Sports on the net at *www.modelcarhub.com* and get in on-line.

Building After-Market Kits

Assembling a roll cage, driver figure and driver's safety net

The Roll Cage: We are truly in the golden age of stock car model building. When all the vast array of after-market building and detailing parts available today are considered, it's a very hard claim to disagree with: decals, resin parts, photo-etch parts, special authentic stock car paints and a virtual cornucopia of just about any part, piece or accessory that the stock car builder could envision.

Most of the after-market items we're covering in this guide require little or no assembly. But there are a few exceptions, and the amount of work required is minimal. Some of the most essential items to an accurate and believable replica include a thorough, accurate and correct roll cage. This is particularly true when you're building a race car from a street-stock model kit. There's no question that one can be constructed from plastic or metal rod and tubing. But the Plastic Performance Product Part No. RC is an excellent beginning point since the basic three dimensions—length, width and height—are nearly perfect for 99% of such applications.

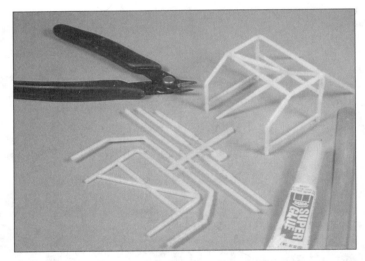

The kit's nine pieces can be easily trimmed from the runners with a sprue cutters. Once simple clean up is accomplished with an emery board, assembly using super glue is quick and clean.

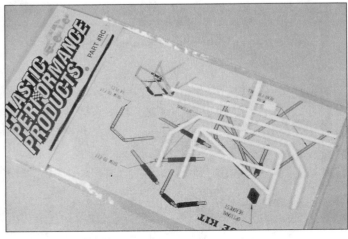

The PPP 1/25th scale roll cage kit comes nicely packaged with clear building instructions.

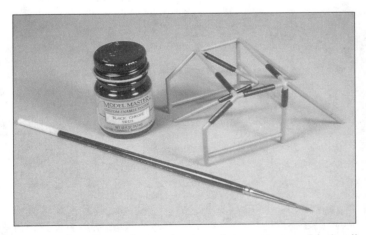

Choose the appropriate color to paint your assembled roll cage and detail the padding with a fine brush and flat black bottle paint.

The PPP roll cage kit is composed of nine injection molded parts, cast in polystyrene plastic. Assembly is straight-forward, but there's nothing that says you can't modify or embellish it to your liking. You only need the most basic of tools and supplies to complete this task. Once the individual parts have been removed from the runners with a sprue cutter, clean up with an emery board is quick and efficient. I used super glue for the assembly, again working on a hard flat surface. This is another situation when building a structure and keeping it straight and square are essential.

With the use of the appropriate diameters of tubing and rod, adjustments are easily made in the three basic dimensions. I decided to increase the overall width of the roll cage to better fit the interior dimensions of my project model. Once I determined how much that increase amounted to, I added a short length of tubing to the front header bar. I also determined from my research that, in the late-1950s and early-1960s, a single horizontal side bar was required. By using Plastruct tubing, I added this feature to both sides of the roll cage.

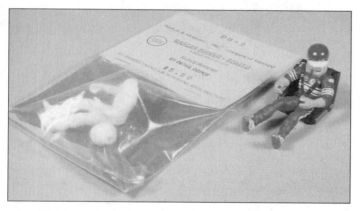

The 1/25th scale resin seated driver figure kit from RMM. Assembled and accurately detail-painted, the driver is ready to take his place in your next stock car model project.

The assembled roll cage was primed and painted to suit my project stock car's final paint scheme. The PPP kit also features padding molded into all of the proper places on the individual bars. I used flat black bottle paint and a 1-0 brush to detail paint these features.

The Driver: One of the most important elements of any race car is the person operating the controls...the driver. The inclusion of a driver figure in your next stock car model will add dimension, character and reality to what is an otherwise pretty sterile and stationary object.

Replicas and Miniatures of Maryland (RMM) offers a variety of resin and photo-etch to meet the multitude of needs and wants of the most discriminating stock car model builder. One of my favorite RMM products is the 1/25th scale seated driver figure. The resin kit can be had with either an open or closed-face helmet. Most of today's stock car pilots opt for the closed-face model. Some diehards like Dale Earnhardt still prefer the open front helmet. A few years ago virtually the only drivers using the closed variety were open-wheel competitors. The correct choice for the driver of a vintage stock car from the 1940s to the mid-1980s would be the open-face helmet.

Assembly of this resin kit is simple, containing just two pieces. Once the head-enclosed helmet is attached to the upper torso by inserting a pin into the neck hole, preparation and painting of the driver figure follows along the same route as any other painting and detailing modeling project. I recommend soaking or scrubbing all resin parts in household detergent before painting. Once this is done, primer and paint can be applied without fear of not sticking to the surfaces.

Refer to pictures in books and magazines to get a feel for the driver's uniform paint scheme. Today most uniforms correspond to the sponsor's colors and general graphic designs. Vintage driver's uniforms would have been a flat off-white; depending on how authentic you want to get, they would have shown the signs of use, such as oil, grease and dirt. In other words, it would not have been a pure lily-white color.

Remember, flesh and fabric finishes are flat, not glossy. The driver's helmet is the one exception to this rule. Strips of 1/8th wide masking tape can be used to replicate the required safety belts and harnesses on the front of the driver figure. RMM photo-etch buckle hardware can be added where required. Also remember that some adjustment to the driver's seat in the race car maybe be required. This can be usually achieved by removing a small portion of material form the seat cushion until the driver sits comfortably in position.

The driver figure needs to be installed in place in the cockpit of the model before the body shell is put into place over the roll cage and chassis during final assembly.

The Window Net: The molded-in driver's side window safety net in many of the injection molded plastic stock car kits is okay as far as it goes. For one thing, rarely does the car sit stationary with the net snapped into place when the driver is not at the wheel. There is a simple and easily-accomplished method to address this problem.

One of the handiest and most attractive items from the after-market is the Scale Model Speedways window net kit. This item is available in either 1/25th or 1/24th scales. Following the directions will yield an excellent miniature representation of the full-size piece. It requires the use of the most basic tools: X-Acto knife, tweezers, small drill bit, white glue and a black Sharpie marker.

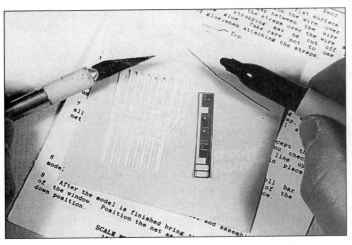

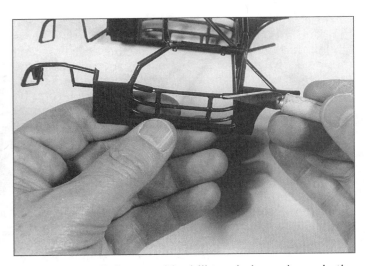

1. The Scale Model Speedways window net kit contains an instruction sheet, photo-etch hardware, unaltered window net and a short length of fine wire.

4. Using a small diameter bit, drill two hole as shown in the roll cage horizontal bar below the driver's side window to match the distance between the bent ends of the fine wire.

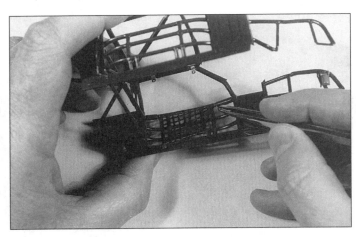

2. Determine the proper length the net and trim it. Choose the type of photo-etch hardware that is proper for your type and vintage of model. Cut the fine wire to length and bend both ends at right angles. Finally, use white glue to fasten the top and bottom of the net to the photo-etch hardware and bent wire. Use the marker to stain the soft window net material in your color or choice (black in this application).

5. Insert the bent fine wire attached to the bottom of the window net into the holes in the top driver's side roll cage bar. Use tweezers to bend the length of wire protruding through each hole to anchor the window net.

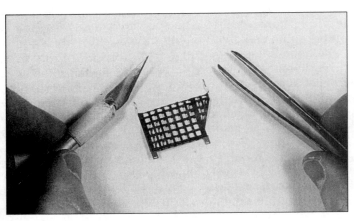

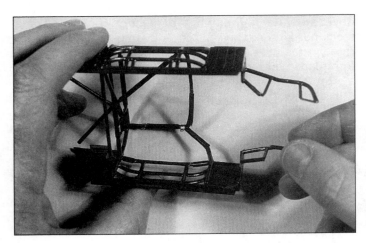

3. Attach corresponding photo-etch hardware to the back-side of the roll cage horizontal bar above the driver's side window as shown here.

6. If you've followed the directions and measured correctly, the finished and installed window net should line up in the opening in the roll cage and with the hardware as shown here.

1965 Ford Galaxie

Building a Resin Stock Car kit

The History: The '65 and '66 Ford Galaxie stock-based race cars represent the final chapter in large, full-size cars being used in American major league stock car racing. Though these behemoths bowed out of the limelight after the '66 season, their design and construction left an indelible mark on the technology of stock car racing that remains with us even today.

The technology developed for these cars throughout the engineering efforts of the craftsman at the Holman-Moody, Ford Motor Company's race car shop in Charlotte, North Carolina, during the 1960s, set the standard for NASCAR race car design and fabrication for decades.

The basic design of the roll cage, chassis and suspension system, as found on Ford and Mercury race cars during the mid to late-1960s, became the benchmark from which all future stock car construction sprang. Until the move to front steer geometry in the early 1980s, the rear steer design that originated with Ford race cars of the 1960s was the norm. The rear axle used in today's NASCAR stock cars is an exact copy of the venerable Ford 9-inch rear end in use from the late-1950s.

These parts and assemblies came into common use in stock car racing due to their proven durability and reliability. NASCAR quickly recognized a good thing and also in an attempt to contain the ever escalating cost of racing, adopted this technology for its rule books.

During the 1960s many prominent race teams labored for Ford Motor Company in pursuit of the glory and the gold. The Wood Brothers of Stuart, Virginia, rank among the most legendary and storied organizations building and campaigning factory-backed Ford stock cars. Some of the greatest names in motorsports visited victory lane at the wheel of a Wood Brothers race car.

One of the best known and most respected American race car drivers to ply his trade in a Wood Brothers race car was Dan Gurney. Gurney, born in New England, spent most of his formative years in California which has always been noted for spearheading the American car culture. He was quickly captivated by the auto craze and the allure of speed and racing competition. Gurney raced and won in Formula One, Indy Cars, sports cars and stockers, setting records that will never be challenged or equaled. At the wheel of his own creation, the Gurney Eagle, Gurney won races on the F-1 circuit. He was always competitive at Indianapolis and from 1963-1966, Gurney won a truly remarkable four Motor Trend 500s at Riverside Inter-

national Raceway. This feat is significant since he competed against the very best the sport had to offer in cars fielded by both the Wood Brothers and Holman-Moody. Gurney's total of five victories (including his win in 1968) will never be equaled, as RIR is gone forever, the victim of suburban sprawl.

Gurney ran a consistent pace in the early portion of the 1965 Motor Trend 500. He took the lead from Junior Johnson with 55 laps remaining and held him off to take the checkered flag. The victory was Gurney's third in a row at the legendary California racing plant. Photo reference can be found in the book, *Dirt Tracks to Glory*, p. 146.

The Project: The model presented here is a replica of the 1965 Ford Galaxie in which Dan Gurney dominated the Motor Trend 500 in January 1965. The 1/25th kit is an exclusive hand-cast resin piece from the Modelhaus. The decal sheet (No. 639) is produced by Fred Cady Design, and the paint (No. 2126 Metallic Red) was custom-mixed and is readily available from Model Car World. Such a project represents just how far the after-market has come in less than a generation.

The Modelhaus 1/25th scale 1965 Ford Galaxie stock car kit contains most of the pieces to complete an accurate replica of a mid-1960s NASCAR Grand National race car. You will need some scrap box items, as well as a few parts from an Ertl/AMT '65 Galaxie donor kit (the engine block, cylinder heads, transmission, exhaust manifolds and front suspension parts will be required). These kits are made from hand-cast resin.

Building a resin kit is similar to the assembly of a styrene piece, with some exceptions. Remember to wash all resin parts thoroughly before gluing, priming or painting. Removal of all mold-release agents is a necessity. Current types of resin are very flexible, much like commercial kit plastic, and respond well to all glues and epoxies commonly used with styrene. Resin will not craze or etch when used with automotive enamels and lacquers (like styrene does). In spite of this fact, I still recommend using a good brand of automotive primer over resin before applying paint.

The finished model seen here is a testament to how the after-market has changed the stock car model building hobby forever. Just 20 years ago, you could not replicate this '65 Riverside 500 winner in this fashion. There were no resin stock car kits, no after-market stock car decals and no source for getting 2 oz. of paint custom mixed for a modeling project. Sometimes progress is really sweet!

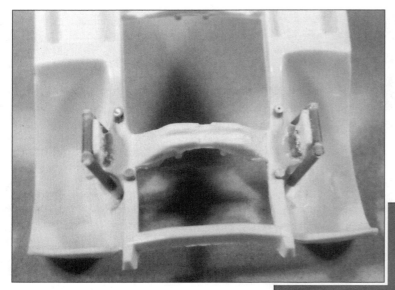

Note in this view the location of each shock absorber and the horizontal bracket used to attach each set in position against the lower control arms.

To remove the mold release present on most cast resin parts, I recommend using Westley's white sidewall tire cleaner. Place the parts to be treated and the cleaner into a container as shown and close the top. Allow the parts to soak for a couple of days. Follow this up by scrubbing each part with an old toothbrush in the cleaner to ensure the removal of every bit of the mold release. Then thoroughly rinse all parts under fresh tap water and dry them before proceeding.

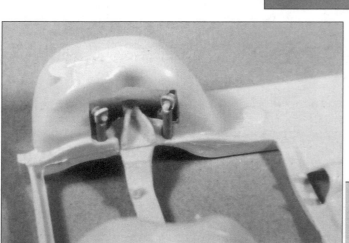

Construct two sets of front shock absorbers from .080 in. dia. tubing and .040 in. dia. plastic rod, like those in the photo. Cut two lengths of .060 in. dia. plastic rod (one set for each side of the front suspension) to form the shock towers as shown. Crimp one end of each length of rod. Then drill a corresponding hole through the top of each tower and attach the shock absorber into place as shown.

Cut a rectangular opening in each front inner fender panel approximately 3/8 in. x 3/4 in. This will allow the dual shock absorbers and shock towers to extend through the fender well and into the engine compartment.

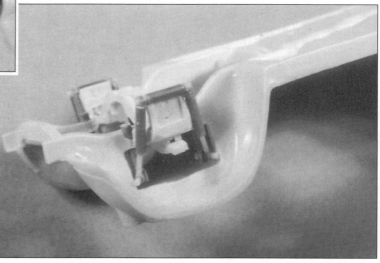

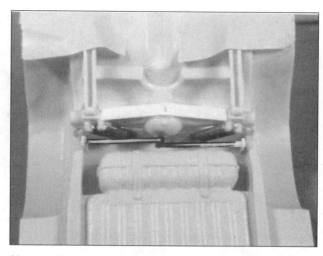

(On the left side of this photo) the rear axle and trailing arms to the rear of the chassis are positioned in place. Cut a strip of .020 in. to length and bend it in the middle. Attach the strip (axle stiffener) as shown to the rear axle. On the right, the front suspension assembly from an AMT '66 Ford Galaxie kit is test fitted into place at the front of the chassis.

Next, a Z-shaped Watts link is constructed from plastic rod and attached into place between the rear frame rails behind the rear axle. Two pairs of dual rear shocks constructed from .080 in. tubing and .040 in. dia. plastic rod are made and glued into place as shown.

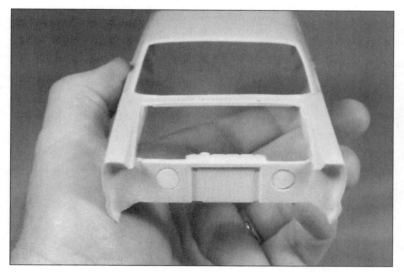

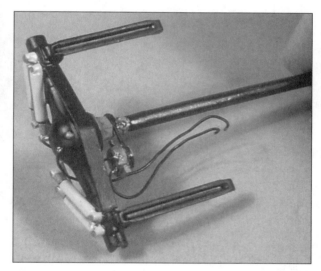

Most of the hard work has already been done on the Modelhaus Galaxie body shell. To build this road-racing variant, you will need to fill these openings in the core support with sheet plastic as shown. Also carefully remove the molded-in vent window frames attached to the right and left side pillars.

Here the rear axle assembly has been painted and the drive shaft and rear end cooler glued into place and plumbed with 0.22 dia. solid core solder wire.

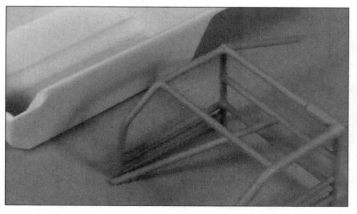

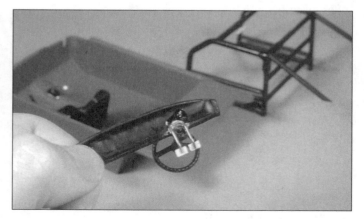

In this view, the resin kit interior is in the background with the assembled roll cage in the front. Use .125 in. dia. tubing and .090 in. dia. plastic rod to construct a roll cage. You could also begin with a Plastic Performance Products roll cage kit, adding the required side bars to complete the unit.

A suspended clutch and brake pedal were made from .030 in. sheet plastic and copper wire. This assembly was then glued into position below the steering column as shown here.

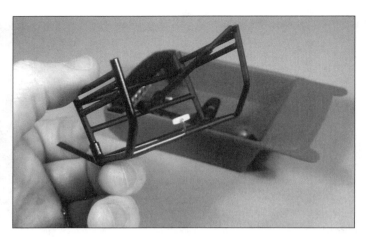

Next, the driver's seat was painted, detailed and glued into place on the left side of the interior bucket. Then the rear-end cooling fan was painted, plumbed and attached into place behind the driver's seat as shown.

Once the interior is painted and assembled, a rear view mirror was made form thin sheet plastic and copper wire. Once painted, attach the assembled mirror in place on the roll cage.

Here the assembled interior is shown. Note the instrument detail on the dash; the location of the gear shifter and the contrast of the semi-gloss black components to the Testors Gunship Gray interior panels.

Use a big block V-8 from an Ertl/AMT '65 or '66 Ford Galaxie kit. The Modelhaus resin kit contains a set of high-rise 427 valve covers that need to be painted chrome silver. Note here as the engine begins to take shape the location of the external oil filter and plumbing; the coil, distributor and the fuel line running through the mechanical fuel pump directly to the four-barrel carburetor. You can use a resin oil filter and coil by Pro-Tech if needed.

At this stage the engine continues to move toward completion. Note the addition of spark plug wires, fan, belts and pulley assembly, the alternator and a small water slide product decal to the oil filter.

This view of the nearly complete 427 engine shows clearly the plug wire location between the ports of the exhaust headers; the Autolite decal on the external oil filter and the oil cooler plumbing lines.

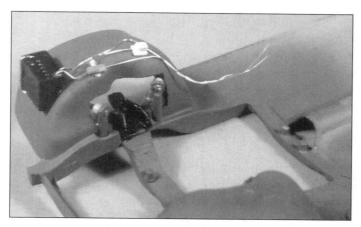

Here the battery has been installed to the right inner fender panel. A rudimentary ignition system is beginning to take shape with a solenoid and voltage regulator constructed from bar, rod and sheet plastic.

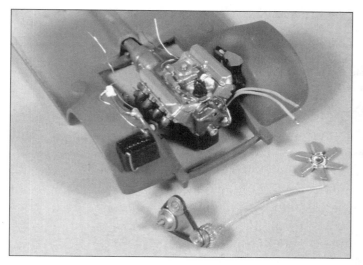

Remember to periodically test-fit sub-assemblies such as the power plant into the engine compartment as we've done here. Also note the ground wire on the left side of the battery.

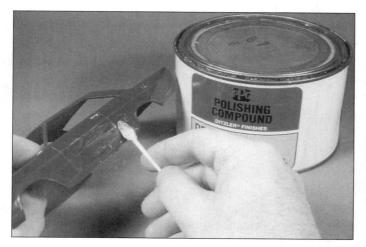

Once the body has been carefully wet sanded with a fine-grit 600 grade automotive sand paper, bring the luster back to the finish by applying polishing compound with a cotton swab to small areas at a time. complete the job with Micro Gloss polish and a soft cotton cloth for a mirror-like finish.

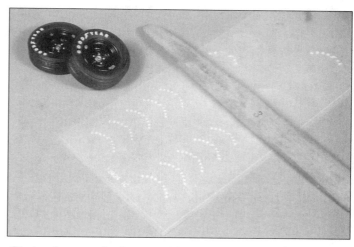

Shabo dry transfer letter was applied to the outside walls of the four racing tires with a small wooden clay modeling tool. Once the wheels are painted and detailed, adding wheel weights and valve stems and detail-painting the grease caps and five lug nuts with silver bottle paint and a small brush, they are ready for final assembly.

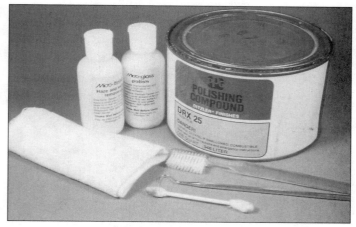

Just some of the items I used to rub out the lacquer paint job on this '65 Galaxie: automotive polishing (not rubbing) compound, Micro Gloss polish and haze and swirl remover, a soft piece of cotton cloth, an old toothbrush, a cotton swab and a scribing tool.

When applying decals to darker paint finishes, you may need to trim all excess clear film from the edges of the graphics. This photo shows clearly how the clear film appears against the dark red finish.

When multi-layered numerals are trimmed out close to the edge and applied properly, they should look like this when you're finished.

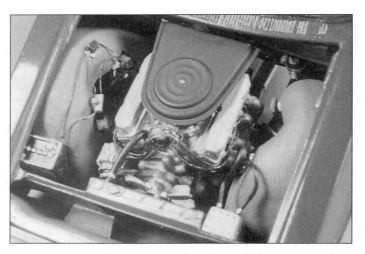

The finished engine compartment shows off the electrical wiring, including a rudimentary ignition system. Also note the battery, radiator, oil cooler and dual shocks on either side of the power plant.

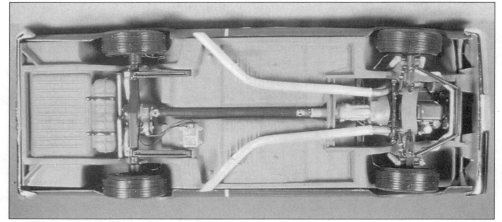

The finished chassis was painted with Testors Gun Ship Gray just like the interior bucket. Note the front and rear suspension components and requisite details, as well as the rear axle plumbing.

These 3/4 views of the finished model demonstrate how patience and basic building skills can result in a very realistic finished model. Note the Pro-Tech photo-etch hood pins with small loops of fine wire used to represent the pin lanyards. The Shabo dry transfer letter of period-correct Goodyear tire sidewall lettering is another touch of authenticity and realism.

Chapter 9

Stock Car Reference Materials

Early Publications

Accurate reference materials for stock car model building projects can be found from many sources today. There's an abundance of full-color magazines, books, posters, photos, post cards, videos and television programs on just about every current stock car subject you can imagine. If, however, you're into building models of vintage stock cars, the job of finding accurate reference materials can be a real challenge. Color references are essential, and that's where things can get tough.

Many of the mainline publications of the 1950s, 1960s and even the early-1970s (*Motor Trend, Hot Rod, Car Life, Speed Age* and many others) were mostly printed in black and white. There is a wealth of important information to be found in early issues, but the lack of color is a big drawback. I can't tell you how many stock car building projects I've had to abandon because I didn't know what the body colors were.

Decal manufactures like Fred Cady Design, JNJ and Slixx have done a great service for modelers interested in building vintage stock cars. But only knowing that a race car was red or white or blue isn't much help

There are thousands of color post cards distributed each year at shows, autograph signings and racing events. Sometimes, older items can be found at model car and flea markets.

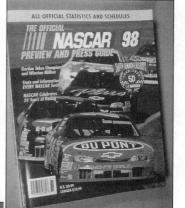

Each year, NASCAR publishes a "Preview and Press Guide" that contains pictures of every stock car in color that is expected to compete in that season's events.

For many years Motor Trend covered the growing sport of stock car racing. Again the covers printed in color are a great resource for model builders.

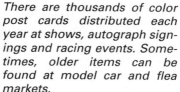

Even though this early issue of Hot Rod magazine is mostly printed in B/W, the detail shots are a great resource for showing how cars from this era were constructed.

if that color is as distinctive as Petty blue, STP red or Pennzoil yellow. That's not the decal makers' fault; they give us as much information as they can find.

This following reference source list is by no means complete; it's intended to give you a good idea of just how much reference material is out there and some of the many sources. I find the pursuit of reference material is a very enjoyable part of the stock car model building process.

Racing Pictorial: For those who prefer building model stock cars, there are many invaluable sources for color reference information for today's race cars. But for race cars from 20 to 40 years ago, there is but only one source: the magazine *Racing Pictorial (RP)*. *RP* was produced in Indianapolis from 1959 until the mid-1980s by Ray Mann and Company. It was a quarterly publication, sold by subscription or available at the race track. *RP* contains a veritable library of color

Luckily, many of the early issues of magazines like Stock Car Racing had full-color covers.

The front cover of the 1964 Color Edition of Racing Pictorial magazine.

It may take some real effort looking through classifieds or checking out products on sale at flea markets to find to valuable books like the ones shown here. Every stock car model builder will eventually tell you they never have enough reference materials.

This 1976 Fall Edition of Racing Pictorial features a color center spread showing many of the famous Petty race cars.

photos of nearly every famous NASCAR, USAC or ARCA stock car that competed during this period.

Today, about the only place to find *RP* is from memorabilia dealers and literature collectors. Expect to pay $25 to $50 for early issues and $15 to $20 for the later ones. Don't buy individual copies sight unseen, unless your intent is just collecting as many issues as you can find...or afford. From experience, some issues have a load of information and some are just nice to thumb through but don't have an abundance of color photos.

Racing Pictorial faded out of existence due to Mann's failing health and the growth of magazines which catered to and specialized in motorsports coverage from larger publishers. However, it took a good long time before any of these newer publications gave the model car builder the kind of color references needed to build an accurate replica like the pages of *RP*.

The following is a short list of *Racing Pictorial* highlighting some of the individual issues and their content:

1961-62 Annual: Ned Jarrett's championship '61 Bel Air is featured on the front cover in living color. There are many top NASCAR stock cars shown in individual color photos on the inside pages.

1963-64 Annual: All the top NASCAR and USAC stock cars that ran the Daytona 500 are shown in individual color pictures.

1964 Color Edition: This was the first half-and-half issue. This edition has two front covers. Depending on which front cover you open half the book is right side up and the other half is upside down. Richard Petty in his Plymouth is featured on one of the covers. Inside you'll find nearly all every front-running NASCAR stocker from the 1964 Grand National season.

1964-65 Annual: Another half-and-half issue, features Petty's No. 43 on the covers. Inside you'll find a color shot of Parnelli Jones' '64 Stroppe Mercury.

1967 Spring Edition: Excellent pictures of the starting field for the '67 Daytona 500.

1967 Summer Edition: Some great color shots of the new 1967 NASCAR Ford Fairlanes.

1968 Spring Edition: Excellent 8x10 size color pictures of Richard Petty's '68 Road Runner, the No. 71 K and K Insurance Dodge Charger and David Pearson's No. 17 Ford Torino from the '68 season.

1969-70 Annual: LeeRoy Yarborough in the No. 98 Ford Torino Talladega and the K and K Daytona in color on the front cover. Inside there are plenty more color pictures of famous Dodge Daytonas like Chargin' Charlie Glotzbach's No. 99 Dow Chemicals car out of the Ray Nichols' shops in Indiana, plus ARCA Champ Benny Parson's Ford Torino.

1971 Spring Edition: Inside is a full-color spread of NASCAR 1971 race cars from Daytona, including Plymouths, Dodges, Mercurys and Fords.

1974-75 Annual: This issue is a gold mine with contains 16 pages of mid-1970s NASCAR Winston Cup cars in full color.

1975-76 Annual: Richard Petty, 1975 NASCAR Winston champion, is featured in a full page color front cover. Inside are 14 pages of NASCAR stock cars in color.

1976-77 Annual: Newly crowned NASCAR Champ Cale Yarborough and the Holly Farms Chevy are featured in full-color. Inside you'll also find the Petty Dodge, Allison Matador, Baker Ford and Yarborough Chevy in spectacular two-page color spreads.

1978-79 Annual: Eight pages of late 1970s NASCAR Winston Cup cars in full color.

The 1969-70 Annual of Racing Pictorial contains some beautiful color shots of the legendary Dodge Charger Daytona "winged Warriors."

The front cover of the 1969-70 Annual of Racing Pictorial has a great shot of Lee Roy Yarborough's Ford Talladega.

Current publications

As mentioned, there is a wealth of reference materials dealing with current and the occasional historic stock car today. The following are recommended reading for stock car modelers:

Racer, "In Focus"

April 93:	#30 Pennzoil Pontiac
May 93:	#6 Valvoline Thunderbird
June 94:	#2 Miller Thunderbird
Aug. 94:	#4 Kodak Chevrolet
July 95:	#24 DuPont Chevrolet
Nov. 96:	#88 Quality Care Thunderbird
Sept. 97:	#44 Hot Wheels Pontiac
Nov. 97:	#6 Valvoline Thunderbird
Nov. 98:	#3 Goodwrench Chevy and #88 Quality Care Ford Taurus

This "In Focus" feature in Racer magazine depicts the 1997 Valvoline Ford Thunderbird driven by Mark Martin. The four-page spread leaves little to the imagination for correct colors, decal placements and finite detailing.

Each issue of Racer magazine contains a photo feature titled "In Focus" that should become a value part of every stock car modelers reference library.

Since the inception of Circle Track magazine, it has become a great resource for information for stock car builders.

Circle Track, "Circle Track Classic"

Oct. 83: "Tommy's Terror." This three-page article presents the Tommy Ellis '83 Pontiac LeMans NASCAR Sportsman race car. One page is color while the other two feature great tight shots of engineering details.

Nov. 83: "100% Ford: Marty Jones' '83 T-Bird Super Late Model is all Ford." Two-page photo feature with one page in color and the second page with excellent close-up detail shots of suspension and interior appointments.

March 85: "The Silver Fox: For David Pearson, winning is everything." Five of Pearson's race cars are shown in color in this five-page feature. As an added bonus, the "Circle Track Classic" is a two-page color spread of the legendary 1971 Purolator Mercury driven by Pearson for the Wood Brothers. The extra special bonus in this issue of *CT* is a two-page article with color photos of Cale Yarborough's 1985 Hardee's Ford Thunderbird titled "Figuring the Odds."

Sept. 86: "Bertha." This excellent four-page feature shows the gorgeous exterior and interior appointments of Darrell Waltrip's green-and-white Gatorade 1977 Chevrolet Monte Carlo.

Nov. 87: "Jumpin' Johnny Mackison's 1957 Ford 300 NASCAR Grand National Sedan." A rare factory-backed '57 300 two-door.

Dec. 88: Gober Sosebee's 1939 Ford coupe NASCAR Sportsman multiple winner on the beach at Daytona.

Dec. 89: Bobby Issac's '72 Sta-Powr Ford Torino. The first small-block Winston Cup race car.

July 89: "Richard's Return." Richard Petty's 1977 Oldsmobile Cutlass in which he won the 1979 Daytona 500 is shown in a two-page color spread.

Dec. 92: "The Power of Richard Petty: A Lifetime of Victory." This special Richard Petty issue offers more than 30-page feature with numerous color and B/W shots of many of Petty famous race cars.

June 94: Bobby Issac's '70 K and K Insurance Dodge Charger short track car driven to '70 championship.

July, Aug. and Sept. 94: "History of NASCAR Winston Cup," Parts 1, 2, 3. Legendary car builder and racing mechanic Smokey Yunick takes a retrospective look at the first 50 years of NASCAR racing. This three-part series contains excellent color photos of vintage stock cars.

Feb. 95: "Daytona Retrospective: Remembering Four Great Daytonas of the Past." Six-page feature presents race cars engaged in on-track action from 1960, 1965, 1969, 1970 and 1975.

Scale Auto Enthusiast, "Pit Pass"

Feb 92: #22 Maxwell house Thunderbird
Apr 92: #3 Goodwrench Chevrolet
Oct 93: #7 Hooters Thunderbird
Oct 92: #44 STP Pontiac
Dec 92: #17 Western Auto Chevrolet
Nov 94: #16 Family Channel Thunderbird
Dec 98: #3 Goodwrench Monte Carlo

Winston Cup Illustrated

Mar 96: Cartoon Network Monte Carlo (Fred Flintstone/yellow)
Jan 96: Kulwicki/Hooters '92 Thunderbird
Mar 97: Darel Dieringer #16 '64 Mercury
Apr 97: Richard Petty 1960 Plymouth
Dec 97: Terry Labonte #44 '77 Monte Carlo
Jul 98: Joe Nemecek #42 Bell South Monte Carlo
Nov 98: Richard Childress '76 Laguna
Jan 95: AMC Matador
Apr 95: Tim Flock '57 Mercury
Aug 95: R. Wallace '77 Monte Carlo and D. Earnhardt '77 Oldsmobile
Sep 97: Tim Richmond Folger '86 Monte Carlo and Ricky Craven '97 Monte Carlo

Scale Auto Enthusiast often features stock car models in color on the cover as shown in these two issues.

Today, Winston Cup Illustrated is one of the top resources for excellent color reference material for the modeler.

Scale Auto Enthusiast often includes in-depth information for stock car modelers. Drew Hierwarter writes a regular column on building and detailing race cars. The regular photo feature "Pit Pass" gives stock car builders two pages of detailing information in each issue, including a compete listing of the color of virtually every part of the race car.

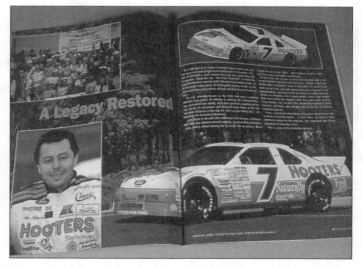

The color features on current and vintage subjects contained in Winston Cup Illustrated are easily worth the sale price. This feature on the restored championship race car of the late-Alan Kulwicki is a great example.

Other magazines that occasionally contain reference material or building and detailing information for stock cars: *On Track, Fine Scale Modeler, Motor Racing Models* and *Toy Cars & Vehicles*. In addition, racing programs available at the tracks are good references.

Occasionally, magazines like Popular Mechanix contain valuable feature articles on NASCAR stock car racing. This issue celebrated the series 50th year and highlighted the considerable contribution made by the Petty family.

Though Motor Racing Models has always been printed in B/W, it's a valuable resource for the serious stock car builder interested in in-depth details.

Racing programs from many of the nation's speedways will contain valuable pictures and information for stock car modelers.

Ertl/AMT publishes a newsletter called "The Blueprinter" that often contains building and detailing tips for stock car modelers.

Along with SAE, Fine Scale Modeler occasionally features how-to articles, providing readers tips and techniques to build more accurate replicas.

Library books

Stock car books found in my local county library:

Great Moments in Stock Car Racing by Irwin Stambler

Stock Car Racing USA by Lyle Kenyon Engel

The Road to Daytona by Curtis Crawfish Crider, as told to Don O'Reilly

Heroes of Stock Car Racing by Bill Libby

World of Racing, Stock Cars by Sylvia Wilkinson. The 50-page color book features many famous drivers and race cars from the 1978 and 1979 NASCAR season.

Great Stock Car Racing by Otto Penzler. This more than 30-page color book covers the 1974 NASCAR season.

If your model building or collecting interests concentrate on just a single driver, you will need to check with mail order and retail book sellers for the titles that might still be available, such as these books on Richard Petty.

I found these two books in a local library as part of the books that were being sold cheaply...what a find and what a bargain.

Other books

The following is a brief list of books that line the shelves of my reference library:

1957 Chevrolet Stock Car Competition Guide, author unknown. This 28-page B/W original factory publication came from Chevrolet division to car dealers telling them exactly what to do to modify a production '57 Chevy into a NASCAR legal race car.

Building and Detailing Scale Model Stock Cars by Bill Coulter. Traces the history of the sport with building features from many eras.

Chrysler, Plymouth and Dodge Stock Cars by Dr. John Craft. This 100-page color book chronicles Chrysler product race cars from the beginning of NASCAR in the late-1940s until the mid-1950s.

Legends of Stock Car Racing by Dr. John Craft. This 160-page book has comprehensive profiles of many of the greatest NASCAR drivers and their race cars. All B/W book.

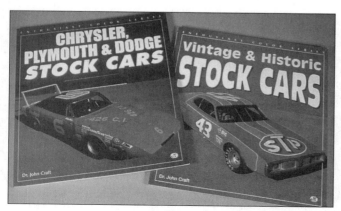

These two historic stock car books by Dr. John Craft will give the reader an excellent lesson in the construction of stock cars of the period.

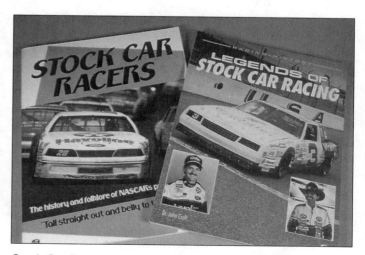

Stock Car Racers and Legends of Stock Car Racing are good reading and contain valuable information for serious builders.

Legends of the Dirt Tracks, author unknown. This 40-page booklet takes a nostalgic look at those halcyon days when stock cars were built from production-based automobiles and they mainly competed on dusty, pot-hole infested dirt bull rings. There are a few good color shots of restored cars from this era.

Race Fans Reference: Understanding Winston Cup Racing by William M. Burt. This is a thick, full-color treasure of information in visual form of virtually every nut and bolt that comprises the construction of a modern NASCAR stock race car. The only thing possibly missing from this excellent reference manual is tire smoke and the smell of racing fuel!

Richard Petty: The Cars of the King by Tim Bongard and Bill Coulter. The complete and definitive guide to all the cars driven by Richard Petty during his 33-year career.

Stock Car Racing by Allan Girdler. This book contains a wealth of in-depth information covering the first 50 years of NASCAR. The only serious drawback to this book is that it is entirely in B/W.

Vantage Point: A Modeling Guide by Dirk Johnson. This 12-page color booklet has more than 85 close-up shots of the components, assemblies and the inner workings of a '90s NASCAR stock car, designed expressly for the model builder.

Race Fans Reference is the most complete resource for modern stock car model builders available to date. The thick soft-bound book provides a close look at all aspects of the sport including the complete build-up of a typical stock car. Also shown is Vantage Point on the Left.

Vintage and Historic Stock Cars by Dr. John Craft. This 100-page color book highlights many famous NASCAR stock cars: Oldsmobiles, Hudsons, Dodges, Plymouths, Chryslers and various Chevrolets.

Video Tapes

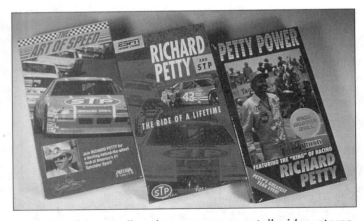

Available from mail order sources or retail video stores, there are many video tapes dealing with stock cars. Some are of a general nature and many are specific to a particular driver as these on Richard Petty.

Though maybe not as handy as a book or magazine, I have found many of the race cars I needed to see on old race films recorded on video tape from: Rare Sportsfilms, 1126 Tennyson Ln., Naperville, IL 60540. Titles include:

1958 Daytona Beach Race and 1958 Southern 500
1959 Daytona 500 and 1959 Southern 500
1960 Daytona 500 and 1960 Southern 500
1961 Southern 500
1963 Daytona 500
1964 Firecracker 400 and 1964 Darlington 500
1970 NASCAR Grand National Season Highlights
Thunder Highway, 1972 Early Season Highlights

Television

Many television programs on regular broadcast channels and cable can provide valuable references. They include:

Race Day/ESPN
RPM 2 Night/ESPN2
NASCAR Race Week/Fox Sports Network
On Track/Speedvision
Inside Winston Cup Racing/Speedvision

Victory Circle/Speedvision
Car and Track/Speedvision
Stock Car Classics/Speedvision
This Week in NASCAR/Speedvision
Inside NASCAR/TNN

Chapter 10

Stock Car Model Collections

Collecting unassembled and built model kits is a time-honored hobby. Accumulating plastic promotional cars, metal car banks or stock car model kits requires an investment not only of money but of time to achieve a predetermined objective.

Today, it's often very difficult to draw a distinct line between the stock car model kit collector and the builder for example. This isn't so much the case in other areas of the model car hobby since it is possible to collect diecast stock car models having never built a single plastic stock car kit. Today's stock car modeler probably has a little bit of everything in his (or her) collection. Generally, there's a treasure trove of varying proportions of unbuilt kits in that coveted stash. Of course, unbuilt kits were originally salted away (not initially as an investment) but as "something I'm gonna build someday."

For the kit collecting side of our modeling nature, first, there's the pride of ownership especially as tempered by the sheer volume. As a collection grows, next it's the satisfaction that you have a complete set of factory-sealed kits of a particular series, etc. Even-

tually, there's also the tracking of escalating kit prices. It is, after all, something you amassed through dedication, perseverance and sacrifice. An ever increasing value should at least be one positive benefit.

By contrast, building a model is a very personal experience. You have, after all, put something of yourself into each and every replica produced. Many of us longtime stock car modelers have established a collection of miniature replicas painted, assembled and detailed by our very own hands; each additional scale model becomes very special to us, and the overall collection continues to mean even that much more to us.

The main reason we value these built collections so highly is that individual subjects represents fantasy fulfillment and represents in miniature the cars piloted by our favorite drivers...past and present. Over time, the small or moderately-sized, hand-built collection becomes an impressive array of model race cars depicting any of a number of unique situations that often capture those "3D moments in time" from various driver's careers.

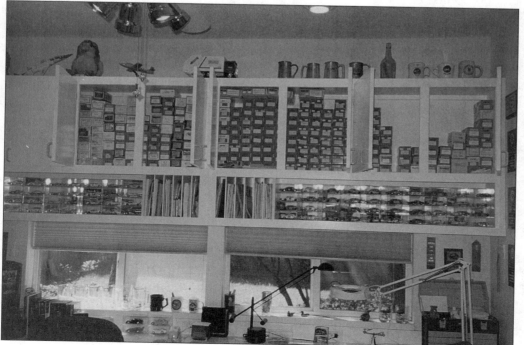

Builder in 1/43rd scale, Roy Vaughn has the best of all situations. Here, storage for his unbuilt kit collection is located right along with his display area which is directly above his work bench. (photo by Vaughn)

Salt Lake City's Rick Sailer has a Richard Petty passion. Though he builds other model subjects, his stock car model collection only consists of 1/25th-1/24th scale replicas of virtually every race car driven by RLP during his 33-year career.

Building one stock car model or purchasing one unbuilt kit does not a collection make. Usually it's not for some time that we collectors and builders begin to realize we have this burgeoning number of kits that at first begins only occupying a little space on a shelf. Even when those neatly stacked boxes have grown to the point that their girth begins fighting for space with your clothing in the closet and even then we may still not see the light.

When you realize that this accumulation of built models or unassembled kits is approaching the unmanageable state, it might be time to decide on a theme—thin out the old collection and begin narrowing your focus building and collecting at that point with a specific purpose in mind. Don't be discouraged when you wind up with a few excellent kits that now may not fit your new direction. You could have the makings for a stock pile of really great trading stock. Or you could advertise in a collectibles or model magazine and sell off the excess, then use the profits to pursue new items for your redefined collection theme.

Factory-built wood and glass lighted cases offer easy access to your models and keeps them virtually dust free.

Your model collection can be displayed on open front shelves as shown here. However, house keeping is an on going head ache. Dust is the constant curse of the model builder.

Both Ertl/AMT and Revell-Monogram offer excellent plastic cases that will hold most sizes of replicas up to and including 1/24th scale. They can also be stacked on top of each other when shelf space is at a premium. Once the case is closed over your model, dust will have a very difficult time getting in.

Displaying your built collection can vary from individual plastic cases to large factory-built lighted cases. Both Revell-Monogram and Ertl/AMT offer excellent two piece plastic cases with a solid opaque base and a clear top. The R-M cases feature various driving surface finishes on the base and they are a bit taller when closed than the Ertl/AMT item.

Private Kit Collections

The typical seeds of a stock car model kit collection. In 1995, Fred Bradley's closet collection had already crowded out the clothing.

Bradley's unbuilt stock car kit collection in recent times. Certainly there's room here for growth, and he'll need it!

It's a typical story. This guy, Fred Bradley, picks up a plastic kit here and there and the next thing you know...Presto! Chango! He's suddenly got a whole bunch of kits in his collection. Bradley started out nearly 20 years ago at a time when he really got interested in stock car racing. At first, it was just a couple dozen unbuilts in a spare closet. Today, the unbuilts number into the hundreds.

Bradley takes great pride in reviewing his extensive collection, now lined up against a wall in the base-ment of his new house. Fred not only knows he's the owner of a lot of kits, he is now a veritable reference book full of interesting facts about almost every kit. Bradley also can tell anyone who asks exactly which items he is still looking for that would make his current unbuilt collection complete. Bradley keeps a catalog that lists each kit and value range for each item. Not only is this handy stuff if the collection was damaged, destroyed or stolen, it would be invaluable for replacement purposes by his insurance carrier.

Built Model Collections

John Strick: John Strick as a race fan and modeler was always fascinated with stock car models. Though he was an experienced builder of a wide variety of scale models, he just never felt he was knowledgeable enough to tackle such a project... and then along came the Starter NASCAR stock car kits in 1/43rd scale!

He was intrigued enough to make that first purchase. After he built that first Starter 1/43rd scale stock car kit, he was hooked. Strick was quite pleased when he saw how the first kits built up into very attractive replicas. His large collection is his historical view of the sport of stock car racing from 1988 through 1996. Little did Strick realize when he started that the phenomenon would trail off to a mere trickle. Strick displays his collection in small individual plastic cases with pride and appreciates the small scale which allow him to show his whole collection of built models in a very confined space.

Wayne Moyer: Moyer is a lifelong modeler. This retired aerospace engineer builds 1/72nd planes,

1/1200th ships and 1/43rd race cars, but only in those three scales. His choice for stock car models has always been 1/43rd. Today, Moyer is considered by many to be the most knowledgeable builder, collector and writer on the subject of 1/43rd stock cars.

Though Moyer builds many different subjects in 1/43rd scale, his collection of built stock car models has a prominent place in a central location in his den. Wayne likes his collection to have a theme and he has favorite drivers with models of Davey Allison and Alan Kulwicki's cars high on his list.

Mike Madlinger: Madlinger has built other types of models in the past; since the mid-1980s, he is best known for his extensive collection of 1/24th hand-built, curbside-style NASCAR Winston Cup race cars. Unlike Fred Bradley, Madlinger doesn't horde hundreds of unbuilt kits. Collecting built models is his thing. He has a private collection of nearly 100 of his favorite 1/24th scale stockers built with his own two hands.

Madlinger is not known for extensive competition-style details; in fact, his models are an excellent example of museum-quality static display replicas. He has a knack for picking unusual subjects, finding the correct after-market decals and choosing off-the-shelf spray can paints that seem to glisten with that look of true team color-mixed formulas. He began early on displaying his models in individual plastic cases. By using the closed cases, he is able to display his work in open-front shelving and keep his collecting virtually dust-free.

Part of the Wayne Moyer stock car collection has a prominent location in his den. Here a lighted factory-built wood and glass case permits easy access to the models and provides a near dust-free environment.

John Strick's collection of 1/43rd scale stock car models. Strick only builds those kits of cars and drivers that have a special significance to him.

Shown here is a small part of Mike Madlinger's stock car model collection. The combination of clear plastic cases and open front shelving works well for effectively displaying models and keeping them clean.

Tom Dill: Like Fred Bradley, Tom Dill has a number of unbuilt kits stashed away for future use. But what most impresses visitors to his home is the extensive display of hand-built stock car models that dominate the scene.

Dill is retired and the extra time allows him even more of an opportunity to devote to his favorite leisure time activity. His specialty is vintage NASCAR stock cars...even the ones that ran on dirt short tracks or on the old Daytona Beach course. Since the 1950s, Dill has collected stock car kits, trading cards, books and magazines. He attends eight to 10 NASCAR races each year, a tradition for him dating back to his first major event in 1956, when he attended the Southern 500 at Darlington, South Carolina. Add to this extensive resume the fact that Dill actually worked on a real, genuine NASCAR Winston Cup team for a few years and you have possibly the consummate stock car race fan/collector/modeler.

Dill not only holds a sizable private stock car model collection but another unique distinction—his handywork is notably displayed at the North Carolina Motorsports Hall of Fame in Mooresville, North Carolina.

Publicly Displayed Collections and Museum Collections

Much like the sport of stock car racing, building models of such things is relatively new when compared to the long history of ship and aircraft modeling, for example. It has also taken a few years for the automotive segment of the model building hobby to gain its full measure of respectability. Stamp collecting, bird watching and photography are the top three hobbies or most popular leisure time activities today. It wasn't too long ago that modelers (and especially model car builders) were mildly scorned about their chosen pastime. Happily, most of that attitude is changing forever.

Stock car model kit collectors and builders have been at the forefront of the paradigm shift in public perception of this hobby. When even the most casual observers get a full eye's view of the caliber of building as seen between the covers of this book for example, the response is usually very positive. It would seem that even the uninformed recognize excellent work when they see it. Add to this what has happened to the ever escalating prices of vintage stock car model kits. In this world, it often seems that increased respectability and big money are hand-in-hand.

Major model car contests and exhibits around the country (literally from coast to coast and border to border) are moving the process along at a breakneck rate. Model car events in Toledo, Ohio, Parsippany, New Jersey, Birmingham, Alabama, Detroit, Chicago, St. Louis, Salt Lake City and many locations in California and elsewhere, have brought out not only the dedicated builders and collectors, but continually expose the general public in a positive way. The response continues to be positive.

A recent occurrence that indicates to me just how far the respectability of stock car model building has come is the number of prominent motorsports museums which now feature specific displays of stock car models as part of the museums' overall themes.

North Carolina Auto Racing Hall of Fame

This excellent facility has literally been bursting at the seams with race cars of all sizes and shapes since it first opened in the mid-1990s. The museum has more than 40 race cars from different eras on display.

Museum executive director Jerry Cashman takes great pride in making stock car models an integral part of the various theme exhibits throughout the facility. The models of Ohio's Tom Dill are on prominent display in this museum. Through out the facility there are a number of display cases each with an individual theme featuring hand-built models and supported by collectible items like photos, event programs and a wide variety of memorabilia.

The front entrance to the North Carolina Auto Racing Hall of Fame in Mooresville, N.C. (photo by Trevor Bladon)

The display of stock car models by Tom Dill found in the North Carolina Auto Racing Hall of Fame. (photo by Trevor Bladon)

A theme display at the North Carolina Auto Racing Hall of Fame featuring stock car memorabilia in support of hand-built scale stock car models. (photo by Trevor Bladon)

Another theme display, this one of Richard Petty. (photo by Trevor Bladon)

Joe Weathery Museum

This hallowed facility has long been recognized as the home to many of the most significant examples of historical stock cars in existence. The sizable display is housed in a separate building that is part of the complex known as the Darlington International Speedway.

Rabid stock car race fan and dedicated modeler Buford Wilburn and the members of the South Carolina Modelers Association spearheaded a project that is a key point of interest for the thousands of visitors to this historic facility each year. Wilburn enlisted the services of nearly 20 stock car model builders (some from outside the club and including Tom Dill) to replicate the various winning race cars starting with the inaugural Southern 500 in 1950. This on-going display was dedicated on March 1997.

The front entrance to the Stock Car Hall of Fame, Joe Weatherly Museum on the grounds of the Darlington International Raceway. (photo by Patrick Mulligan)

The first 28 winners of the Southern 500 on display in the Joe Weatherly Museum as part of the scale model collection "Legends of Darlington." (photo by Patrick Mulligan)

The most recent winners of the Southern 500 captured in miniature at the Darlington Joe Weatherly Museum, part of the Legends of Darlington stock car model collection. (photo by Patrick Mulligan)

The 1950 Plymouth driven by Johnny Mantz to win the first Southern 500. Model built by Scott Hochstein. (photo by Buford Wilburn)

The 1951 Hudson driven by Herb Thomas to win the second Southern 500. Model built by Scott Hochstein. (photo by Buford Wilburn)

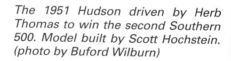

Fonty Flock won the 1952 Southern 500 in this Oldsmobile. (model and photo by Buford Wilburn)

Tom Dill built this replica of the Dodge Buck Baker drove to victory in the 1964 Southern 500. (photo by Buford Wilburn)

Ronnie Setzer built this replica of the '69 Mercury Cyclone driven by Bobby Allison to win the 1971 Southern 500. (photo by Buford Wilburn)

Petty Museum

The Petty Museum is located near Level Cross, N.C. as part of the Petty race car building operation. What is now a one-story display facility of approximately 4,000 square feet was at one time the garages where race cars were prepared for Kyle Petty's Hot Wheels Pontiacs.

Museum general manager Daris Gammons, says that the place was opened to the public in 1988. On display, visitors will find a Petty Plymouth Superbird, his '69 Ford Torino Talladega, his title winning '77 Oldsmobile, one of the famous '72 STP Dodge Chargers and a '92 Pontiac from Richard's Fan Appreciation Tour, the last year he competed as a driver in NASCAR.

There are dedicated displays of models fans have built and sent to Petty. There are more than 100 scale models on display at any given time. Daris says that

The front entrance to the Petty Museum that is part of the Petty Enterprises stock car building compound. (photo by Trevor Bladon)

this display is in honor of the fans and that the display is changed every 90 days. This rotation guarantees that everybody gets a show at the limelight.

Using stock car models as an integral part of the theme displays at premier motorsports museums in the United States appears to be a growing trend. You can find stock car models at the International Motorsport Hall of Fame Museum in Talladega, Alabama, and the Indianapolis Motor Speedway Museum in Speedway, Indiana, and that list continues to grow each year.

Whether yours is the vision of a small private collection or if you would like your best work considered for display at the nations' most respected motorsports museums, aspirations are unlimited. What you decide to set as a goal for your collection is an individual decision. Whatever you decide, enjoy the pursuit of that objective and see just how far it takes you.

More Petty model cars. (photo by Trevor Bladon)

Display of Petty model cars built and donated by fans to the Petty Museum. (photo by Trevor Bladon)

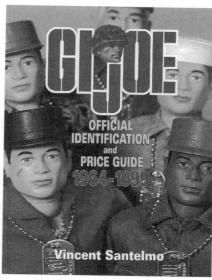

'TOY SHOP' MERGES WITH 'TOY TRADER'

ToyShop
The Toy Collector's Marketplace
July 16, 1999

G.I. JOE FIGHTS MIDDLE AGE
What's Next for America's Favorite Soldier?

BEST BETS IN ACTION FIGURES

FREE
Hot Wheels® Car
while supplies last

www.collectit.net

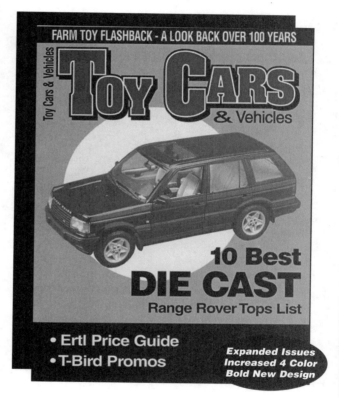

FARM TOY FLASHBACK - A LOOK BACK OVER 100 YEARS

Toy Cars & Vehicles

TOY CARS & Vehicles

10 Best DIE CAST
Range Rover Tops List

• Ertl Price Guide
• T-Bird Promos

Expanded Issues
Increased 4 Color
Bold New Design

Toy Shop Magazine

The complete marketplace for buyers and sellers of toys, models, figures and dolls. Thousands of easy-to-read, categorized classified ads, display ads and a complete editorial package.

*Order Today and have 26 bi-weekly issues of Toy Shop delivered to your door for only $33.98, plus you get a **FREE** limited edition Hot Wheels® 1963 Thunderbird!*

Toy Cars & Vehicles

Subscribe Today and receive a **FREE** limited edition Hot Wheels® 1970 Barracuda with your paid 1 year (12 issue) subscription *for only $19.98 while supplies last!*